Broken Prom

Broken Promise

Annie Allsebrook and Anthony Swift

eadway · Hodder&Stoughton

© 1989 Annie Allsebrook and Anthony Swift

First published in Great Britain in 1989

ISBN 0–340–50906–6

Phototypeset in Ehrhardt by Wearside Tradespools,
Fulwell, Sunderland
Printed in Great Britain for Hodder and Stoughton Ltd, Mill Road, Dunton
Green, Sevenoaks, Kent by Thomson Litho Ltd, East Kilbride

Contents

Acknowledgements

The authors would like to thank Ann Perry for making available the photographs on pages 1, 5, 42, 45, 61, 69–71, 77, 79, 80–83, 85, 87, 90, 102–104, 106–110, 113, 198, 204, 209, 233, 238, 239 and 241.

Note
The views expressed by the authors in this book are not necessarily those of the organisations and individuals mentioned.

About the Authors

Annie Allsebrook and Anthony Swift are freelance journalists with an interest in social and development issues. Annie Allsebrook mainly does radio work and has contributed regularly to the BBC World Service and Radio 4. Anthony Swift was a newspaper journalist in South Africa for a number of years. He now lives permanently in the UK and has contributed to various publications, including *The Guardian*, *The Scotsman* and the *New Internationalist*. The authors both worked for several years in the communication division of the development aid agency, Oxfam.

Introduction

This book is a response to a yearning we must surely share with others: to be in a world free of daily images, amid plenty, of violence, hunger and people dressed in rags.

By looking at what it is like to be the most powerless members of the human community – children with little or no adult protection – we hope to stir awareness that the fight against poverty and deprivation must be given a new priority. Through events like Band Aid and Comic Relief many people in the UK have already strongly expressed this view. But deprivation is not restricted to poor countries; it flourishes in the wealthiest of nations and it is not restricted to physical manifestations – emotional deprivation cripples children in the most comfortable of homes.

With 1989 the tenth anniversary of the Year of the Child and also the year in which the new Convention on Child Rights is due to be adopted by the UN, the time is auspicious for such a book.

Our intention was to produce a popular book that got as close to the experiences of children as possible. We have made little mention of statistics. Most statistics are unreliable, anyway; estimates of the number of street children, for instance, range from 30- to more than 100-million world-wide. It is enough that the children whose life experiences we describe represent at the very least a minority internationally of many millions.

We have set about our task not as experts in any particular field but as journalists with a broad interest in social and development issues. Our book represents a personal journey of discovery and an attempt to piece together a rounded view of a subject normally presented in a localised and fragmented way.

The importance of establishing such a view resides in the fact that, in an era of great specialisation and rivalry for control of information, it has become increasingly difficult to know what is going on. We are continually exposed to one-dimensional interpretations of events that deeply affect others. The daily reports on the nation's inflation rate or the rise and fall in share prices tell us nothing of what these events mean in human terms locally, let alone globally.

Nobody, least of all a child, asks to be impoverished. Nor is poverty usually created by the poor and almost never by the poor alone. It arises most often from the decisions of powerful people who either do not see or do not care about the consequences of their actions.

The same is true of an individual's arrival at a state of

psychological bankruptcy – children do not choose to grow up to be criminals or otherwise anti-social. They make a series of smaller choices often to defend themselves against more powerful people. Each choice may seem individually right to them but the combination brings them to a destination that is disastrous both for themselves and others.

Most of our information has come from children and people who work directly with them. We have also drawn from other writers.

The part of our work we like best is what we have gathered from listening to children. They continually surprised and encouraged us with the clarity of their observations, their ingenuity and the courage with which they face the most adverse circumstances. We also are both moved and impressed by many of the people who work with deprived children and who demonstrate values very different to those which leave children to fend for themselves in dangerous situations. *Broken Promise* refers to the promise of childhood as well as the promise of the guardianship of children by the adult world. What has kept our spirits up when this second promise is so often and so thoroughly broken is the frequency with which the resilience of children, the humanity of those who try to help them or the love of a struggling parent can do much to redeem the situation.

The information in our book was gathered directly in only ten countries. Though the experiences of children can be affected by cultural differences our findings are by no means peculiar to these countries. Indeed one of our purposes has been to show that, wherever adults are subject to great stress and insecurity and families lack support, children will find themselves at risk.

There are a number of gaps in our book; for instance we conducted no research in an Islamic or Eastern Bloc country. Our material has been gathered sporadically over a period of three years. Some of the situations we write about in the present tense have changed. Our stories from Nicaragua are written as though the war is still in progress, whereas now there is a clearer winding down in hostilities.

We wish to acknowledge all those who have contributed towards the making of this book, both those named in its pages and the many who are not. For their own protection, not all the children whose stories we tell are identified by their real names and for the same reason we have in one or two cases disguised the locations of our meetings.

A small part of the material published here has appeared in

different forms in articles in *The Guardian*, the *New Internationalist* and *Community Care* and in interviews on BBC Radio. The story of the Wright family first appeared with a different purpose in a booklet about homelessness published by the National Federation of Housing Associations.

Our special thanks must go to Dr Jocelyn Boyden, of the Oxford-based research organisation, Children In Development, for her encouragement and many suggestions, her generous sharing of resource materials and for her reading of our manuscript. Barbara Kahan, Chairperson of the National Children's Bureau, also kindly read parts of our manuscript. We owe a debt of gratitude to OXFAM, who have strongly supported our efforts. The Joseph Rowntree Charitable Trust, the Irish development agency, TROCAIRE, and the UK Committee for UNICEF made valuable contributions to research costs. The NSPCC was among several organisations that gave us help and advice. The views we express, it must be said, are ours and do not necessarily reflect those who have supported us.

The photographs were taken in the main by us or by Ann Perry, whose contributions are listed on page vi. Ann helped us considerably in thinking through the issues of the book. The work of other photographers is acknowledged on the pages on which it appears.

Grandmother and granddaughter in a remote village in West Orissa, India

Home sweet home

When you have a family of your own what will you hope to do for your children?

Jason   Help them to be happy.
Darren   Clothe, feed and protect them.
Jason   Give them some money of their own.
Paul   Pocket money.
Darren   Give them a bit of freedom.
Paul   Make them feel responsible.
Jason   Help them with their future.

If you were to lose your family . . . what would you miss most?

Darren Someone to talk to.
Paul   Someone to look after you, to be there, to be with you.
Darren Yeah, to be there if you had a problem.
Jason   The warmth of someone that knows they're caring for you.

Darren, **Paul** and **Jason** are friends in their mid-teens. They live in a settled working class community in the south of England, where they were born. So long as the local major employer, a car factory, remains in production, the foundation of their community is secure. For them, families are good places to be. So, generally, is the school they go to and the area they live in.

In their minds, family support merges into community support. They can't really imagine themselves getting into any kind of trouble they couldn't handle by themselves, or with the help of adults around them at home or at school.

They know there are homeless youngsters of their age living on the streets in London and much younger children living and working in the streets of places like India and Brazil. They can't imagine themselves getting in to such a situation. Were they to lose both parents, they feel certain they would be taken in by the families of friends, or by relatives, rather than be put in a children's home. 'We're lucky,' says Darren.

Their luck is to have parents who have given them the idea that concern and consideration for others is normal rather than rare. Their luck is to live in what is, at least for the moment, a stable and privileged niche in the world economy.

POWERFUL PARENTS?

'We grow our first and deepest roots within the family and home. Strong positive feelings about ourselves and firm emotional ties to others will anchor us in life, nourish our security, and permit us to weather the adversities of our existence.'

Dr Bruno Bettelheim[1]

[1] *A Good Enough Parent – The Guide to Bringing Up your Child* by Bruno Bettelheim, Thames and Hudson, London 1987.

'Our national rhetoric not withstanding, the actual pattern of life in America today is such that children and families come last'

Report to the President[2]

[2] As reported in *Two Worlds of Childhood: US and USSR* by Urie Bronfenbrenner, Pocket Books, New York 1973. Page xiii.

Christopher Wright won't remember the day his Dad snatched the food from his plate and ate it himself – he was very young at the time. But his father, Steve, will. 'It happened in a moment. I was thinking, "I'm the breadwinner. I've got to have a square meal in me."'

A nurturing parent before and since, Steve learned from the incident how anxiety and hunger can pitch even members of loving families into competition with each other and how, in such an event, the power of a parent over a child can so easily be misused.

The Wright family were not experiencing the extreme stress of unemployment in an inner city or Third World zone of poverty, where the scramble for survival most directly threatens human relationships. But Steve and his wife, Christine, were in a stressed situation. Four years earlier, they had left the economically depressed north of England to seek advancement in Steve's profession as a journalist, relying on the promise of greater long-term security in the wealthy south.

An accomplished feature writer, Steve had landed a job with an Oxford paper, with his sights on an eventual move to the nationals. In the interim, the family became caught in the classic housing trap awaiting northerners who try to move south to the new work centres of the eighties.

Their house in the north was slow to sell and, when it did, fetched little money. House prices in Oxford had rocketed so there was no question of buying. There was a three-and-a-half year waiting list for subsidised council housing. Take-home pay that had looked good by northern standards was halved by the rent they had to pay in Oxford. The family was left with less money to live on than they would have got on the dole had they stayed in the north and been buying a house on a mortgage.

In winter the rented house proved damp and cold. Christopher developed asthma. The family could not afford to heat the house properly, 'Ours was the only house in the street whose ground floor windows iced over during a freeze. We felt the neighbours must be talking,' said Steve. Without the support of friends, grandparents and other relatives they had left in the north, Christine could not think of taking a job. There was no-one she could safely leave Christopher with to get time to herself.

'Food was our only diversion,' said Steve. 'I was paid weekly and generally we ran out about Wednesday.' It was one breakfast-time that he snatched his son's food.

The couple tried to resolve their financial difficulties: Christine took Christopher to her family for the following winter to cut down on heating needs. They thought that if they could survive two winters in that way their problems might ease. But after some weeks apart they realised that was no way to carry on. Their attempt to invest in Steve's career as a basis for their future security was threatening their wish to provide a loving and healthy home for their child.

Despite uncertain work prospects, they decided to return to the depressed north and to the more traditional security of a supportive network of extended family and friends in a familiar community.

This decision to put their family relationships first was made possible by the provisions of a welfare state. 'I was fairly sure I would find work. But I knew that if it took a while I could, as a last resort, rely on the dole.'

The move paid off. Before long Steve found acceptable work. The family was able to buy a house and so be free of the whims of landlords. They again had a network of established friends and relatives at hand to ease the pressures of parenting and provide Christopher with a better environment to grow up in.

Childhood is widely perceived to be a time for the young to develop within the security of a loving family. It is from within this small world that children evolve a sense of themselves and other people and have their first taste of what life is like.

What children experience within families varies greatly from culture to culture and in different periods of history. In both wealthy and poor countries it has been deeply affected by major social, economic and political developments within the past 200 years – among them industrialisation, the growing influence of the consumer culture and the current radical emphasis on self-reliance and competitiveness.

Recent decades have been marked by dramatic changes in family structure and a greater complexity in family relationships.

The model family of the West – composed of working father, home-minding mother and two children – has yielded ground with the large increase in the numbers of working mothers, single-parent families and step-families, where one or both parents were married before and may have children from former unions. There are now more than a million single-parent families in Britain and the number of children born outside marriage is rising – they accounted for 23 per cent of births in 1987.[3] On the basis of current conditions it is projected that two in five new marriages will end in divorce.

[3] *Social Trends 1989*; HMSO.

In cases of divorce and of remarriage there is a danger that the interests of children will be submerged in those of the adults. Single-parent families may be severely economically disadvantaged, increasing the stress on parent and child alike. A study published in 1986 shows that one-parent families in the United States were disadvantaged by inadequate services for working mothers and these have since been subject to further cuts. They are also victims of a wage structure that 'locks

[4] Current Problems in Paediatrics, December 1986, *The American Family in Crisis: Implications for Children*; Year Book Medical Publishers, Inc. pages 714–715.

[5] *A Good Enough Parent – The Guide to Bringing Up your Child* by Bruno Bettelheim.

Father and sons working in a field near Calcutta

women into poverty' and there is a lack of social support for children made necessary by changes in the family.[4]

The extended family – a network of relatives within easy reach of each other in a stable and supportive community – is being rapidly dismantled in many Third World countries and is largely a thing of the past in Western capitalist countries.

In pre-industrial times the main problem for many people was staying alive. But Bruno Bettelheim, the eminent child psychotherapist, argues in his book, *A Good Enough Parent*,[5] that if the curse of a pre-industrialised humanity was a 'short, brutish life of back breaking labour', it was at least a life shared and mutually sustained by the people closest to you. People usually lived out their short lives in their place of birth so it paid them to invest in their relationships with kin and community.

With the exception of a small elite, children worked alongside their parents in the home, the fields or the workshop. They could observe and participate in the arduous labour of their parents, expended in their joint interest. Children would learn and appreciate their parents' skills. Girls acquired knowledge of mothering by helping their mothers. You still see this kind of parent–child relationship in remoter areas of the Third World that are still relatively untouched by the

industrialising process. In the absence of rapid social change, the skills learned in this way held their value and equipped children for life.

At the same time children were valued as active contributors to family subsistence and parents could expect those who survived to repay their early care by looking after them in their old age. The relationship allowed for the development of a mutual respect between child and parent and made reciprocity a key social value.

Guatamalan woman and children

If progress has brought longevity, it has also brought new forms of stress; perhaps above all that of loneliness and not belonging, of having no roots, of not being sure you will be supported in times of crisis. Many of the support functions of kin and community have been replaced by impersonal commercial and state services, subject to unpredictable changes in the economic and political climate. Isolation can be experienced by the family as a whole and by individuals at the heart of the family.

Progress has shifted the status of the child from contributor to a potential rival consumer of family income, more directly subjecting family relationships to the question of what parents can earn and the vagaries of the economy. In Britain, the cost

[6] National Foster Association.

of rearing a child from birth to 18, calculated in 1989, ranged from just under £1800 to just over £3500 a year, depending on the age.[6]

Family members rarely work together in industrialised countries. The parents go out to work and the children go to school. The modern child learns little about life skills directly from its parents, and may have scant sense of their work – the means by which his or her welfare is secured. In addition, during times of rapid change, the experience of one generation diminishes in value to the next, whether it be in the fields of education, skills or parenting, so there is less to share. Families unite around what Bettelheim refers to as 'less important' recreational activities. Often it will be around the television set. Watching TV is Britain's most popular leisure activity accounting on average for more than 25 hours a week.[7] Meals may be 'shared' by family members who are watching TV, instead of talking to each other. They may even be eating and watching separately, in different rooms or at different times.

[7] *Social Trends 19, 1989*; HMSO.

A milestone American *Report to the President* observes that 'the primary danger of the television screen lies not so much in the behaviour it produces as in the behaviour it prevents – the talks, the games, the family festivities and arguments through which much of the child's learning takes place and his character is formed.'[8]

[8] As reported in *Two Worlds of Childhood – US and USSR* by Urie Bronfenbrenner.

Dr Manuel Carballo, a child care expert with the World Health Organisation (WHO), says: 'I suspect there are certain transcendental values and needs with regard to child care, to family life ... one is for there to be sufficient time, free of stress in which parents can provide love and physical care for children and children can have meaningful contact with their parents.'

People come to parenting with less relevant preparation and are faced with greater complexity in the role than ever before. The parent–child relationship has changed in duration as well as quality. Adolescence, today the most problematical phase in the relationship, scarcely existed in an age where children started work before the age of twelve.

Parental uncertainty, argues Bettelheim, is reflected in the confusing avalanche of books advising people on how to bring up children. Insecurity increases the stresses of parenting and can detrimentally affect children's development.

In a highly competitive climate, where the penalties for failure and the rewards for success are intensified, there is pressure to put the demands of the employer or of the marketplace above those of personal or family considerations. It is these pressures that the Wrights resisted. In recent years there has been a call to families and individuals to 'get on their bikes', sacrificing community ties to the need to become more flexible (and more isolated) competitors for job opportunities. This expectation that families be ready to uproot themselves to seize economic advantage contributes to their isolation. As the Wrights' experience illustrates, such shifts can greatly increase the stress of parenting, threatening the ability of even the best intentioned of parents always to act as they would like to towards their children. A distinctive factor in child abuse within families is the isolation of the parents from a supportive social network, often combined with poverty.

A young girl in accommodation provided for homeless single-parent families near Chatham in the north of England
ADRIAN ROWLAND

Abrupt family moves disrupt a child's own attempts in a given environment to build a sense of the world and his or her own identity within it. Friendships with other children and adults outside the family are eclipsed even before they are fully formed. The intricate process of establishing acceptance in the community and school is cancelled and has to begin again.

Increased competition is also likely to increase pressure on parents to urge their children to ever greater levels of achievement. 'Many adults are extremely concerned about their kids getting a competitive edge from an early age,' says Howard Polsky, social science professor at Columbia University, New York. They put pressure on their children and 'think of them already as something to be moulded in their own image so that they can compete better with others.'

In extreme cases, children who fail parental expectations can find themselves being switched and swopped from school to school. Some children experience parental approval and love as being conditional upon their performance. Remorseless manipulation of children to meet parents' ambitions and anxieties rides roughshod over a child's quest for an individual identity and can cause severe psychological distress.

Children come under tremendous pressure to live up to what everybody else thinks they should be, says Mark Raskin, of the Day Top Programme, a US drug rehabilitation project. 'Job pressures, school pressures, the pressure of wanting to be loved, the pressure of drugs being so readily available.'

Yet what children need is the space to master 'each new stage of psychological and social development', writes Bettelheim. And this requires understanding and sensitive help from parents, if the children are not to 'bear the scars of psychological wounds' in later life. Parents must resist the desire to create the child they would like to have. Rather they should help their children develop 'in their own good time – to the fullest, into what they wish to be and can be, in line with their natural endowment and as a consequence of their individual life history'.

Confusion about family priorities is further intensified by the consumer culture's translation of important human emotions and values – happiness, pleasure, love, 'success' and 'failure' – into material terms. Possibly at no other time has there been so much pressure on individuals to identify themselves as consumers and to interpret life in consumer terms as there is currently in the West. The exploitation of children's consumer roles makes peer group acceptance partly dependent on the ability to identify with fashions and crazes, again putting pressure on parents to earn. When a television crew came to film an alternative-to-custody programme in London's East End, the teenagers all turned up dressed to the nines. 'You should have seen the kids, dressed up with gold,' says child counsellor Pat Roach, of the Arches project. She asked where the gear came from and was told it was borrowed. 'It's what you look like, what car you drive, what clothes you have that matters to them today – and to us adults I suppose.' Consumerism defines the loving parent not as the one who spends time with his or her children but who buys them what their peers have.

Inability of parents to keep up with commercialised peer group demands is one reason for children dropping out of school and running away from home. Police Officer Eugene Lewis, of New York City's Runaway Unit, says: 'They go to school as long as they can, as long as their pride will let them. They try to compete, not only in schoolwork but in dress – to have the material things the other kids have. It becomes very difficult for them to maintain grades in school and grades in social terms so they have a tendency to drop out.'

The extent to which the drug and alcohol culture has infiltrated the world of children is a symptom of their isolation from the care and protection of adults. In research for her book on child prostitution, journalist Gitta Sereny interviewed two 13-year-old English girls from middle class homes who were prostituting themselves. They did it, they said, to go to discos and buy the latest fashions and drugs.[9]

[9] *The Invisible Children* by Gitta Sereny, Pan Books London, 1986.

The *Report to the President* asserts that children are finding themselves increasingly isolated from the rest of society in a 'world devoid of adults and ruled by destructive impulses and compelling pressures both of the age-segregated peer group and the exploitative television screen. By setting our priorities elsewhere and putting children and families last, by claiming one set of values while pursuing another, we leave our children bereft of standards and support and our own lives impoverished and corrupted.'

Despite evidence that families are vulnerable to stress there is a strong expectation that they will continue to absorb social pressures and cope with change. It is largely left to parents to take care of their children and secure opportunites for them to grow and develop as best they may. 'Failure' to meet this responsibility, usually signalled by a child becoming a nuisance or of concern to others, can trigger strong public condemnation.

Crucial to popular expectations of the family is that it is a place of retreat and rest from the struggle for survival. The

Millions of homeless and jobless

suffer malnutrition epidemic

Doctors find starvation increasing in US survey

The Guardian
7th December 1987

family as refuge is explicit in the sentiment that 'A man's home is his castle'. The warrior of the British workplace can close the portcullis on the power-play for advantage over his fellows, abandon his armour and anxieties and rightfully enter a world where love, loyalty and compassion prevail, where his brow can be soothed, his gains protected and peacefully consumed and his children safely raised.

In popular mythology, the keeper of this emotional oasis has been the wife/mother/saint. Her place has been conceived of as being 'in the home', away from the tainting struggle for survival, and empowered by a special relationship she is said to have with her children. This notion is still actively promoted, along with more recent models. A UK television advertisement fuses images of a wife, magically restoring her ailing husband by administering a commercial potion, with a flash-back of his mother patching a wound to his knee as a young child and deftly wiping away a tear. This concept of the family has weathered assaults such as the high divorce rate and the wife and child battering exposés of the 1960s and 70s and it persists despite the advent of the employed mother and the entrepreneurial mother. It has also survived the exposure by feminists that such a concept is based not only on unrealistic and exploitative expectations of the woman but also of the man. It depends on his ability manfully to absorb the stresses of the work-place and not carry them over the threshold of the home. But in too many cases men omit to remove their armour on returning home and instead relieve their residual feelings of anxiety, humiliation and defeat on their wives and, it is increasingly realised, their children. Far from being crucibles of caring, families may directly reflect the broader social power relationships in which the stronger dominate the weaker. People batter their children, observes author Richard Gelles, because they can.[10]

[10] *Family Violence*; Richard J. Gelles, Sage Publications, London, page 17.

Revelations about the number of children who are sexually assaulted within their own homes have dealt the most recent and damaging blow to complacency about the family and to the assumption that children can always be safely left to the responsibility of their parents.

Perhaps the tenacity of the idea of families as sanctuaries of rest and recreation resides partly in our profound wish to have such an entity in the world we have created.

However, something different from the outside scramble can and fortunately often does happen within families. Many parents recognise the destructiveness of economic and social stresses and find creative ways to guard against them. A Birmingham study argues that the families of black minorities

[11] *The Empire Strikes Back, Race and Racism in '70s Britain*; Birmingham Centre for Cultural Studies, pages 212–235, Hutchinson, 1982.

in the UK and US operate as sites of resistance to, as well as refuge from, a commonly experienced oppression.[11] Some families have the resources to take a break when the going gets tough. There are some people who absorb stress themselves and do not transmit it to others. A considerable number of younger couples are renegotiating family roles and, for instance, sharing domestic and child rearing duties and career opportunities more equitably. Not all parents are so driven to seek success that they hardly see their children, despite the market pressures. For some there is a degree of manoeuvrability; at the risk of career prospects, the Wrights can defy the trend and go north again.

Many families manage to go some way to fulfilling the promise of childhood. They send children out into the world who know that, because they are loved, they are lovable; because their choices have been respected, they can make good choices; because they have experienced reliability and trustworthiness in the small world of their family, human beings in general may be trusted and relied upon. Families can, and many do, give children a 'hopeful inner core'. What is surprising perhaps is how many manage to achieve just that, even in the most adverse circumstances.

Psychiatrists, psychologists and others differ over the fine print of how it is done, by whom and in what period of time.

Schoolboys wait for a bus at Falford Estate, England
ADRIAN ROWLAND

But they do not doubt it is the best thing families can do for children. And it is probably what most parents would dearly like to do, if only they were able.

DISABLED FAMILIES

I remember, I remember
The place where I was born
The little window where the sun
Came peeping in at morn;
He never came a wink too soon
Nor brought too long a day;
But now I often wish the night had
Born my breath away.

Thomas Hood
(A favourite poem of Liz's
at the age of eight.)

In her early twenties, **Liz** could not remember whole areas of her childhood; it lay in her mind as a jumble of disconnected episodes. She reckons now she had blocked out the bits that confused and frightened her almost as soon as they happened.

By her account, her mother was a shadowy figure, dominated first by her own mother and then mother-in-law. 'Mother didn't have much to do with me. Father would come home from work and play with me and I'd eat some of his dinner. We were close.

'Once I was playing with a doll's pram and had it tilted on end. I was using it as a deck chair. He came out and tipped it up and raced me around the yard with me screaming with delight. My mother came out and said, "Don't be stupid, you silly man." And he just stopped, put me down and walked into the house and shut the door. He wasn't at all sure of himself.'

Liz's father was a farm labourer but when she was four the family went to live in the East End of London. They moved into a small flat occupied by his mother and sister. Liz slept with her parents in the only bedroom, as she had always done. Her aunt and grandmother – 'a kindly but domineering woman' – shared a sofabed in the living room.

Liz remembers herself as a young child as having a strong

personality, 'demanding, stubborn, feeling everyone should make way for me.

'On my first day at school I remember a lot of children crying. Not me; I went around telling them all off for being stupid babies. I was quite bright. When I was found to be disruptive, they put me up a class.'

After a year in the flat Liz's parents bought a house and the whole family moved in. Liz finally had a room to herself.

'It's the next three years I find hardest to puzzle out. The facts seem straightforward. Father worked as a labourer in various factories and mother stayed at home doing very little apart from knitting and reading. As in my first home, grandmother ruled the roost and mother just helped out.

'I don't think I was ever clear in my mind who mother was. She was an adult in the house, but I had no particular regard for her as a mother. I was a great one for reading, but she wouldn't be bothered to read to me, she'd push me away and tell me to go and play or something. So I had a strained relationship with her. As in the countryside it was my father who'd take me out for walks and to the library. Mother never came.' Most of the cooking and cleaning in the house was done by the grandmother.

Despite the additional space, the move added to the unease in the family relationship – increased stress for the bread-winner father, having to pay the bills, and increasing tension from the demotion of Liz's domineering mother-in-law to the status of guest in her house.

Sometimes in the mornings Liz's parents invited her into their bed. 'I think this is when it all started, when I was five. I was effectively being used as part of their sexual play. I don't think I particularly took an active part in it, though they did get me to fondle her breasts and they used to touch me.

'What happened wasn't what I'd call particularly harmful, there was nothing threatening about it, they just seemed to like my presence and I quite enjoyed it. I don't think I ever really understood what was going on except there was always a point when I was thrown out of the bed and told to go away. That was the harmful bit, the rejection, I didn't know what I'd done to deserve it.

'I don't recall my body actually being tampered with. But I had continual trouble with my bladder and bowels. My mother would frequently put me on a chamber pot of steaming water, presumably thinking the heat would open the bowels. She also gave me hot baths. I can remember her sitting in the bathroom with me crying because I was in so much pain. And she was crying and saying, "You've got to get yourself better because if

you don't I'm going to have to take you to the doctor and I
don't want to have to do that."'

At one time Liz's mother was confined to her room for
several weeks and she was neither allowed access to her, nor
told what was going on. 'I now suspect she'd had a miscarriage.
When I eventually did get taken in to see her, I maintained it
wasn't my mother. She'd changed beyond all comprehension.
She'd been quite a sharp tongue, and now she'd just faded into
nothingness and wouldn't say boo to a goose.

'I felt confused at the time because I was surrounded by
adults but was actually almost completely on my own because
they were all wrapped up in their own lives and I was just
battling on trying to be me.'

Liz sees her father as a clever man who was too insecure and
isolated in the world to allow himself to use his intelligence. He
had spent much of his childhood in care. As an adult he was
'basically a friendless person', never seeming to get to know the
people at work and, Liz apart, having 'nothing to do with
anybody at home. There was an awful lot of pressure on him
just to survive.'

The visits to her parents' bed stopped when she was seven or
eight and a new, far more sinister episode began.

'I had began to be very afraid of the dark. I seemed to get
very hung up about an awful lot of things and my real worry
was I'd go to bed, I'd go to sleep but then you could almost
guarantee I'd have this nightmare, that what I called the big
bear who lived in the park up the road would come into my
room, and I used to wake up.

'My mother knew about it because I'd been telling her,
saying, "There's something wrong with my hand," and she kept
saying, "What?" And I'd say, "Well, it's normal size and then it
feels as if it's getting larger and I can't control it and it feels all
sticky."'

Liz now conjectures that her father was coming into her
room and getting her to masturbate him. 'But I couldn't work it
out at the time because I was only half awake.

'To me it was my hand that was getting bigger and I used to
scream and cry and they used to tell me not to be so silly.
During that period, which went on for a couple of years, they
used to make me lie on a towel in the bed and I used to have
one on the pillow under my head to stop me making a mess of
the bedclothes because, they said, it was easier to wash towels
than sheets every day.

'Because I didn't like the dark I had a small bedside light. So
when he came into the room there was always this big shadow
cast on the wall. It was a lot bigger than him, and it was a

vaguer outline, so it was much easier for me to think that it was that shadow, that big bear, not him. I quite liked my father, I didn't like the bear and I was frightened of the bear, but I didn't put the two together.'

Liz noticed that these nightmare experiences didn't happen when a friend shared her room with her. Nor did they happen if she went to the friend's house. Her friend had no such dreams, nor did any of her other school friends.

'That made me feel something was wrong. I didn't tie it all up with my parents but I felt they knew something that I didn't and were shutting me out of it. Somewhere along the line I felt they were the cause of it, but I didn't know how.

'I felt very alone and became more and more isolated.' She was struck by differences between herself and other children. 'They were all born in the East End, I wasn't; they'd cried when they went to school, I hadn't; if things went wrong for them they ran home to their parents and told them and their parents sorted it out, I didn't, I sorted it out; while they were reading children's books I was getting adult books out of the library and reciting poetry. So at every level I was different.'

Isolated at the heart of her family, Liz experienced an elemental fear. "It can't be equated with the other sorts of fears that one tends to know as a child because for better or worse you rely on your parents as being the foundation of your life. You can go into other people's homes and families and you can see parents chatting to each other, children playing. You can even hear parents arguing or children crying but there's an inter-relationship, there is something there. And then you could walk into my home and my parents were there, and they weren't arguing, they weren't speaking. Nobody touched anybody else, no sort of cuddling or affection. It was just a void.

Liz (right) at the zoo

void. So then you got the feeling of well, *why?* And then the fear.

'Because so much of the antagonism around seemed to be directed at myself, the feeling then came that, "Well, I must be one of the causes of it." Then you start thinking, "There must be something odd about me to make everything around me so different", so you then actually increase your isolation.'

Liz suffered from a growing suspicion that she was the cause of everything going wrong around her. 'I felt guilty about the possibility of causing extra washing, having to have towels in the bed. That sort of thing made me feel inadequate. Adults had to be right and if they were right I must be wrong. It didn't occur to me to think of it as their fault.'

At the same time she suspected the only way she might be free of whatever it was that was upsetting her was to be rid of her parents. She even thought of killing them.

'By now I'd become rather contemptuous of my mother. She lost any control over me she'd ever had. If she went to smack me, I'd say, "Catch me first", and if she did I'd just stand there, I wouldn't cry or say anything. She'd get very frustrated. She would threaten to tell my father. But when he came in all he had to do was say very quietly, "I want to talk to you", and I'd burst into tears, totally go to pieces, and say, "I'm sorry, Daddy, I didn't mean it." That annoyed her even more.'

Unable to secure affection from her husband or give any to her daughter, Liz's mother became locked out of the growing intimacy between father and daughter. Unable to form close relationships with adults, Liz's father turned increasingly and then exclusively to his child.

Liz now believes there was always a quality of desperation about her mother which deepened as Liz's sense of power over her grew. 'I found I could reduce her to being frightened. I think that developed with my ability to get round my father. Instead of forcing herself between us and trying to distract him, she would stand back and act in an injured fashion in the hope that that would work. It didn't.'

Liz's father asserted authority in the home through the imposition of petty rules. 'He was the sort of person who'd only let us have the radio on for certain programmes; meals were eaten in total silence; he wouldn't have cushions around or rugs on the floor – it was all quite sparse and strict.'

When Liz was nine her mother changed tack, trying to be friendly and compete for her allegiance. 'She started running father down a lot, moaning about the way he wouldn't let us do things and encouraging me to listen to programmes he wouldn't let me listen to.' Then she became pregnant. 'I remember her telling me about the arguments they were having over this baby.

'When my sister was born my mother seemed to come into her own. She seemed to want that baby and looked after it well, though I got lumbered with taking care of her a lot. Father ignored the child totally. I was ten now and used to get terribly embarrassed about everything. Most of all I hated having to take my sister out, particularly if my father was with us, because I felt people would think she was my baby.'

As relationships within the family deteriorated further, Liz's mother confided in her a plan to be rid of the in-laws by 'making sure there was not enough room in the house for them' – which meant having another baby. This she did, with the desired effect. 'I think my mother was showing me the power of sex.'

Liz was aggravated by her mother's approaches and was exploring her own ability to wield power. The sexual relationship her father demanded of her 'had developed quite a lot, although I wasn't consciously aware of it, because I couldn't really live with that. But it gave me power over him which I could use, and use against her.'

The companionship her father enjoyed with her increased her hold over him. 'We had certain common interests, like books and walking down the street or going to the library. He could talk to me and be himself. He never really treated me as a child, it was always as an adult. And because he wanted to keep the relationship going and it was his only outlet I could almost call the tune.'

As Liz approached puberty, the relationship became much more overtly sexual. 'I became much more involved in it. It just built up gradually to full intercourse when I was eleven, and that continued, maybe a couple of times a month.

'I think that as I got older and the relationship progressed I actually began to enjoy sex. Basically there was no reason why I shouldn't and in a sense it was a way of scoring off my mother because she was always moaning that she didn't like it. I sort of felt, "Well, I can do better than you." But then to an extent it backfired because he became more demanding. Also, once my mother had the second baby and she was mistress of her own house, she changed again towards me; the friendliness went.'

Liz had a growing awareness of too many things 'going on over my head' and of not being able to cope. 'When mother let on that she was thinking of taking all three of us children and leaving I actually wanted her to do that. When she didn't I rounded on her.' Liz also had an ongoing terror that she would become pregnant. She tried to tell a neighbour 'that things were happening to me at home that shouldn't be happening'.

'The reaction was, "Don't be silly, you've got a very nice Mummy and Daddy, you should be grateful for what you've got and stop telling tales. All children fall out with their parents from time to time so don't be silly."' She also thought of going to the police but feared they would ridicule her.

She continued to do quite well at school and went on to grammar school. However she didn't do well at making close friendships. What friends she had were 'rather negative personalities and more my friends because I told them they were than by choice.'

By the age of 13 Liz was feeling very uncomfortable on all fronts. 'My form teacher tried to get me to talk to her. She said she'd noticed changes in my behaviour. She wanted to know if I had any problems at home, but again I was scared that she wouldn't believe me, so I didn't really tell her anything.

'Everything finally came to a head on my fourteenth birthday. Unusually, I got up early. My parents had bought me a record player and I was very pleased about that. My mother was on her own in the kitchen. I went in and she turned round and said, "Oh, you can get up this morning can you?" I sort of looked blankly at her and she said, "I'm surprised you can get up, in fact I'm surprised you've got the nerve to even show your face after the way you two were carrying on last night."

'There was a clock on the mantelpiece and I just sat staring at the hands. It was at half past seven, it's etched on my memory. My father had come into the room by now and she just let out a tirade at both of us, called me every name she could lay her tongue to. I was a slut and a whore and she didn't know why she kept me in the house. She'd had enough. She carried on and on and my father just picked up the paper and read it, totally blotted it all out.

'I can remember walking out of the house, going to school, trying to carry on.'

Liz's father didn't speak to her again until she was 17. He directed any communication through her mother – 'Would you ask Liz what so and so is?' or 'Tell Liz she can do this or she mustn't do that.' 'The sexual relationship had stopped dead but my mother continued to call me all the names under the sun and tell me nobody would ever want me, I was ruined for life.

'Shortly after the outburst, I had what probably was a grumbling appendix. I was examined by a locum who said if I was a bit older he'd have sworn I was pregnant. That didn't go down at all well. My mother threw him out of the house and when father came in she slated him up one side and down the other.' The relationship between Liz and her mother had become one of all out war, stoked by the mother's resentment and fear of exposure. 'She kept repeating that I had to do what she said. If I spoke to anyone and the police found out, my father would go to gaol and she and the two babies would be out on the streets. The disgrace would be such that none of us would ever be able to hold our heads up and that included me. The guilt was poured on.'

Liz's school work went rapidly downhill. Her mother feared questions being asked. 'She told me I'd got to do better. She knew I wanted to stay on at school and kept threatening that if I didn't improve she'd take me away and put me in the army. I wasn't at all sure whether she could do that or not.'

At the end of fifth form, a teacher, alarmed at Liz's poor performance, called the mother in to oppose any intention to take her out of school. 'He told her he wasn't going to say a lot, only that if I was made to leave and go out to work it would destroy me. I needed another two years to gain some protection against life and have a chance to sort myself out.

'She was so scared I might say something or that he might do something that she went along with it, and I went to school for the next two years.' A subsequent teachers' query triggered frightened interrogations by her mother – 'What the hell have you been saying we're doing?'

Verbal assaults from her mother continued after she had left school, accusing her of sexual relations with any boy she met and predicting that a 'slut' like her would get pregnant.

'Once my mother was ranting and raving at me because I was upset about falling out with a boyfriend. Father suddenly put down his paper – which he was always hiding behind – and said, "For heavens sake shut up and leave the girl alone, she's entitled to feel upset if she felt something." That marked the beginning of him talking to me again. He broke three years silence to spring to my defence against mother. But of course in this case he wasn't threatened. It was when she was threatening him as well as me that he always backed off and hid.'

At 19 Liz got engaged to someone at work but the engagement was broken off after a row. 'My mother went absolutely hysterical. She lay on the bed, crying and screaming. In the end my father said, "Look, she's not going to stop, she thought everything was going to work out all right, that you were going to leave, and now everything's been thwarted. I haven't said much to you over these last three years and I haven't given you many orders but now I'm telling you, ring him up." I would probably have come round to marrying Tom anyway, but my father did sort of order me to, which I did.'

This resolution of the parents that Liz was their main problem, one best solved by marrying her off, found more direct expression when several years later her mother finally left the father. Both parents blamed Liz for their breakup.

Child sexual abuse directly affronts expectations we have of the family as a place of love, refuge and security and provokes an extremely angry public response.

Liz's story conveys the desolation and emotional aggression children can suffer at the heart of their own families. But her parents emerge – in her own account – as neither monsters nor madly intent upon harming her. Rather they are confused, severely emotionally disabled people with a very limited capacity to recognise and respond to the needs of others, least of all their children. Much of the time they are trapped in their own isolation. They relate to Liz as an equal rather than as a child. The only island of affection, reciprocity and companionship she experiences in the family comes packaged with an insistence that she meet adult needs with consequences so scary that she turns them into a private nightmare and blots them from her memory. But, while there is no question that her father was seriously in the wrong in abusing her, he does not seem to have been strategically affectionate towards his daughter in order to have sex with her. Rather, unable to form relationships with adults, he inappropriately seeks his main relationship with Liz and brings his adult sexual needs along as well.

Looking back she says of her mother: 'It was very much a case of, "You can have it, if you do this, or you don't do that". All the affection I got from her was conditional. There was nothing spontaneous, whereas with my father there was much more spontaneity, although at the end of the day a lot of what I got from him was also conditional.

'Under the present sort of public exposure the general reaction would be that what hurt me was the actual sexual abuse, and that it ought to have been stopped,' says Liz. 'In fact that was the least damaging thing I went through.'

Ironically, it may well be that the companionship she enjoyed with her father, subverted though that was, together with the support she got from teachers equipped her to understand the destructiveness of the rest of her early experience.

Liz's adult life has been a concentrated exercise in damage limitation. Aided by good psychotherapy, her own intelligence and resolve and the instruction of two broken marriages, she has curbed her capacity to damage others by strictly limiting her involvements.

When she became a mother, she discovered that: 'In many ways I'd stopped developing emotionally at about the age of five and I had an awful lot of growing up to do. There was a vacuum and I couldn't relate to the children. I became quite determined that they had a right to be children. They were entitled to have the right sort of relationship with their parents and I hadn't a clue what my role was. All I was capable of being was either a child myself – silly and childish – or domineering, which is just as childish.'

To protect them from herself, Liz agreed to her first husband keeping custody of their three children. 'I spent three years crying myself to sleep and worrying but I knew he was capable of looking after them and I wasn't.' She has gone further and cut all intimate relationships out of her life.

Now she says: 'I often feel I'm living life in second gear, I rarely get into top. The way I cope is by taking life logically and reacting accordingly, remaining in control. Emotion is out.

'I've spent my life in a glass case. I can see everything outside but I can't get out and touch it.'

The good part of her relationship with her father has also left her more ready to understand him than her mother. 'I wouldn't have worried too much if you'd taken me away from my mother but I'd have been devastated if you'd taken me from father. By all accounts he was the one who was doing the abusing. But that was the only relationship I had and it was the most vital thing.'

Child sex abuse expert Lorraine Fox explains that mothers often take more than their share of victim resentment because of the powerful cultural expectations upon them.[12] Children's books and programmes, advertising and the popular media present the mother as the all wise, reliable fixer-up of children's (and husband's) problems. Even in cases of sexual abuse where the mother has no involvement children commonly assume they do and at the very least allowed it to happen. 'Of course, she knew. She's my mother, they say.' Real or imagined, a mother's failure to intervene may seem to the child the unkindest cut of all.

Liz now views her father as lonely and weak, the victim of circumstance and his own make-up, unable to assert himself in the outside world and turning to his family for 'whatever he needed'. 'I think he was almost more of a victim than I was. I think he's wasted his life.'

There are growing misgivings about the kind of media and professional responses to the sexual abuse of children and the amount of attention it receives compared with other forms of abuse. As was previously the case with child battering, the focus has been far more on the act of abuse and the need to punish the offending parent and rescue the child than on

[12] Lorraine Fox is a consultant and partner in the child care and social service agency, Professional Growth Facilitators, San Clemente, US.

The sight of a loving family relationship can deepen the despair of an abused child

BARNABY PICTURE
LIBRARY

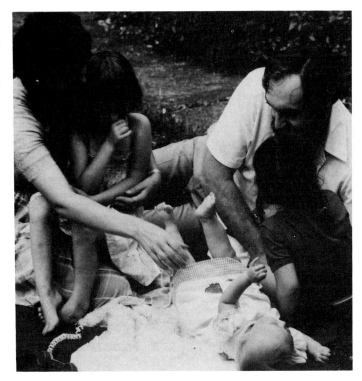

understanding either the motivation of the parent or the experience of the child.

Thus we have the paradox of 'concerned' society at times rushing in to 'rescue' children from allegedly abusive parents by removing them from their homes in ways and with consequences which in themselves are likely to be damaging. We have the parallel paradox of public sympathy expressed for the abused child turning to angry condemnation of those child victims who grow into damaging adults.

While child sexual abuse is currently grabbing the lion's share of interest in family trauma, it is not necessarily more damaging than other forms of abuse and in some cases may be less so. The sex, on which attention focuses, may not in itself be as damaging as the emotional and psychological context in which it takes place. Part of this context arises from fearful anticipation of society's reaction to the breaking of a powerful taboo.

Violent sexual abuse, battering and neglect directly threaten the lives and physical health of children as well as leaving them

Child sex abuse: How to break the vicious circle

The Observer
10th July 1988

Dedicated but lacking judgment

The Guardian
7th July 1988

Sense of urgency on child care led to overloading of system

The Guardian
7th July 1988

Children who told of their confusion

The Guardian
7th July 1988

The Guardian
7th July 1988

Social worker who was cast as conspirator

Stigmatised parents want doctors to be struck off

The Guardian
7th July 1988

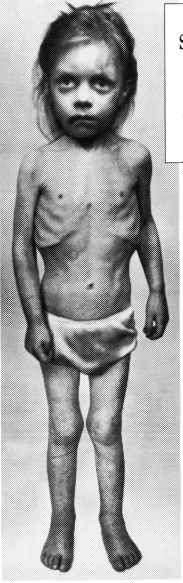

Four years old. Seriously underweight for her age. Scavenging for food where she can find it. And she's English.

With a stepfather who refused to ac-knowledge her existence and a mother too frightened to help her, this child was being slowly and deliberately starved.

She'd reached the point where she was feeding herself out of dustbins.

It didn't happen in the famine stricken third world, it happened in an English town, (like the one you live in).

The NSPCC's first, most urgent concern is for the child.

Above all the child has to be protected. But, where appropriate, we can also provide help for children and parents.

£20.66 can begin to protect a child from abuse. And that's the sum we're asking for now.

If you can't afford quite that much, all donations are gratefully received.

The NSPCC through its campaign called 'Forgotten Children' has drawn attention to the problem of child neglect

feeling they are worthless. Sustained emotional abuse can make children feel they have no bargaining chips at all in relating to others.

In 1988, records collated for the first time showed that 40,000 children and teenagers were registered by English local authorities as being at risk of sexual abuse, other physical abuse and neglect. But some social workers believe the incidence of abuse to be considerably higher than these figures indicate.

'Current estimates of sexual abuse vary literally from 5 to 25 per cent of girls and a much lower proportion of boys,' says Professor Larry Aber, assistant professor of clinical psychology at Columbia University, New York. 'The best estimates for physical abuse and neglect are three per cent of the population as a whole. If those of sexual abuse are accurate, our estimates of maltreatment as a whole are way out. And I believe that instances of child sexual abuse are tremendously underestimated.'

Launching the NSPCC's 'Forgotten Children' Campaign in Britain in 1986, Dr Alan Gilmour said the society dealt with more cases of neglect – the denial of food, warmth, shelter and love – than direct physical and sexual abuse put together. 'Thousands of children are suffering and only a small percentage of cases is brought to light because neglect is a silent problem.' A US Department of Health and Human Services Report shows that there is an annual incidence of child abuse and neglect of nearly 1.6 million cases (the majority of which receive no child protective services from public agencies).

Less explored than physical abuse and even neglect, but increasingly recognised both as an important component of such abuse and in its own right, is emotional abuse and neglect. Consistent verbal assaults upon or indifference towards a child by a parent leave no physical signs of damage but can destroy the sense of self-worth and ability to exercise concern and compassion for others every bit as successfully as physical violence. Emotional mistreatment can often have more serious developmental consequences than physical injuries, according to child abuse experts.[13] However, emotional abuse goes largely unmentioned in the media and is unrecorded because of the difficulty and complexity of specifying and documenting emotional harm.

Child abuse generally is still widely represented as the aberration of individuals and families, something to be dealt with by punishment or, more rarely, treatment depending on whether the aberration is regarded as a symptom of 'evil' or sickness. This view is rooted in the medical and ensuing psycho-pathological interpretations of child abuse. It was the observations of radiologists which, in the 1960s, first put child physical abuse on the map though it had long been a concern of social and welfare workers. Its 'discovery' in the West arose because radiologists began to acknowledge that not all multiple fractures were explicable in terms of accidents or bone disease.

'Medical models of explanation were put forward,' says Larry Aber. 'And medicine's close relationship to psychiatry meant

[13] *Developmental Considerations in the Definition of Child Maltreatment* by J. Lawrence Aber III and Edward Zigler, New Directions for Child Development, 1981.

that there was an early theory about parents being grossly
psycho-pathological. So that was the first school of thought –
that they were people who were crazy in various forms.'

Some people still want to restrict the explanation of child
abuse to individual and family history and pathology and this
view still strongly influences practice in the handling of child
abuse cases. However, early research into cases of child abuse
did not substantiate such a view. The climate of social concern
of the 1960s saw the emergence of a sociological view that
behaviour within families cannot be interpreted independently
of conditions and pressures imposed by society. Environmental
and economic stress was a major factor in determining whether
a parent became abusive or not.

Over the years a range of specific stress factors has been
identified as contributing to child abuse. This in turn has
produced a realisation that abuse is triggered by a complicated
interaction of psychological and social pressures and events.

Families are inherently vulnerable to stress and prone to
conflict. This is because of the intensity, closeness, duration
and interdependency of family relationships; the changing and
conflicting needs and interests of the members; the fact that
membership is involuntary and that the experiences of one
member directly affects others. These pressure points are likely
to be aggravated in an era that stresses individualism and
devalues community and community support.

Dr Eli Newberger, director of the Family Development
Study at the Children's Hospital in Boston, believes there is a
link between child abuse and recent changes in family structure
in the West as well as male unemployment.

'Most of the cases of sexual abuse that we now see involve
mothers' boyfriends and very often they have caregiving
responsibilities while the mothers are at work. In some
environments it's much easier for a woman to get work than for
a man and, such is the nature of the dissolution and
reformation of family bonds in our society right now, that very
frequently you find strange men taking care of kids. It's a
set-up for sexual or for that matter the physical exploitation of
children.'

Violence against women by their partners has for some time
been at least partly ascribed to power relationships in the
family. But the connection between this and child abuse is only
now being looked into seriously. Many of the abused children
seen at clinics run by the Family Development Study have
mothers who have been battered. 'When men are feeling
powerless they will very often make themselves feel powerful by
pushing around people who they can push around, and this can

[14] *Explaining Child Abuse and Neglect*; Richard Gelles and Jane Lancaster, Chapter 9 'Stepparents: Risk of Maltreatment', Margo Wilson and Martin Day.

take physical or sexual forms and involve women or children,' says Dr Newberger. Particularly vulnerable, a recent US study concludes, are children living with one natural parent and one step-parent. They are 'much likelier to be physically abused or killed than children living with two natural parents'.[14]

Child battering often takes place within a wide social acceptance of physical punishment. It is frequently explained by parents as punishment that went too far. Between 80 and 85 per cent of people in the US are estimated to have had some personal experience of corporal punishment in childhood.

According to history Professor Phillip Greven, of Rutgers University, punishment is strongly underpinned by protestant religious belief. Fundamentalists, in particular, follow bible readings about beating the child and saving the soul literally. Corporal punishment ranges along a continuum 'from mild to mortal'.

In Greven's view any form of corporal punishment should be considered to be child abuse. 'When an adult hits a child, that is a form of assault' and the violence done to a child will be transmitted in some way to others.

In his book *Family Violence*, Richard J. Gelles argues that widespread acceptance of violence in US society (as evidenced by support for the death penalty and corporal punishment) and of the use of physical punishment within the home, interact with the 'conflict prone' institution of the family to make it a training ground that will feed violence back into society. Children learn that it is OK to hit people you love; for powerful people to hit less powerful people; to use hitting to achieve some goal; to hit as an end in itself.[15]

[15] *Family Violence* by Richard J. Gelles, Sage Publications, London, page 16.

[16] *The Politics of Child Abuse* by Nigel Parton, Macmillan Educational Books, London, page 153, 1985.

While sociological explanations differ in important ways, 'they all argue that, for a variety of reasons, certain families are put under severe social and economic stresses, which predispose them to abuse and to be officially labelled as such,' writes Nigel Parton, a UK social worker and lecturer.[16]

Explanations of child abuse have been marked by lively debates about whether it is characteristic of a particular class and of a particular kind of culture. Some commentators biased towards a psychological explanation argue that it is classless and found across the board. The counter argument is that it is a characteristic of and found mainly, though not exclusively, among the poorer classes.

Available statistics of neglect and family violence strongly suggest the latter. But they have been largely gathered by social and welfare services which focus their attention on deprived families. Reinforcing the case for a class interpretation are arguments such that, even within the lower social classes, child

[17] *The Politics of Child Abuse* by Nigel Parton. Parton quoting L.H. Pelton, page 153.

abuse and neglect increase with the degree of poverty and, among the reported cases, the most severe injuries have occurred in the poorest families.[17]

Wealthier classes are rarely subject to investigation. They enjoy more privacy and are better placed to hide abuse. The wealthy can also pay for child abuse victims to be treated in private clinics. In Scott Fitzgerald's *Tender is the Night* Nicole, who has been sexually abused by her millionaire father, is sent by him to a Swiss psychiatric clinic to be fixed up.

There is also support for the view that child abuse and neglect are much more prevalent in western societies than current definitions of abuse allow us to see.

Child abuse author David Jones, writing of abuse in the UK, says that the more advantaged members of society may experience similar child care difficulties to others. But they either hide them 'behind a semblance of competence and respectability' or resolve them before crises develop, 'using knowledge or resources not readily available to the less well off, such as better use of the health services, sending the child to boarding school or employing a nanny or au pair.'[18]

[18] *Understanding Child Abuse* edited by David N. Jones, Macmillan Educational Books, London, page 22, 1987.

'The abuse of indifference affects many more children [than sexual or physical abuse] but we have no way to measure it,' Brian Roycroft, Director of Social Services in Newcastle told a London conference. 'It is characteristic of wealthier circumstances where money can buy care for one's children or supply them with diversions and where there is little development of affection between parents and children.'

The child victims of society's invisible forms of abuse remain uncounted as such. They are widely distributed among people labelled social failures – the drop-outs, suicides, drug addicts and occupants of counselling and psychiatric couches – as well as those accounted successes.

Rudyard Kipling captured the impact of emotional abuse on his own childhood in the story *Baa Baa Black Sheep*. Punch, who represents Kipling, is left by his parents in the care of a couple who continually rebuke and denigrate him. Reunited with his family he says of himself and his sister:
'It's all different now, and we are just as much Mother's as if she had never gone.'
But:
'Not altogether, O Punch, for when young lips have drunk deep of the bitter waters of Hate, Suspicion, and Despair, all the love in the world will not wholly take away that knowledge...'[19]

[19] *A Choice of Kipling's Prose* ed. Craig Raine, Faber.

Another issue concerning child abuse within the family is to what extent it existed before it was 'discovered'. For instance, was it as common in the more stable communities of pre-industrial times? Some people argue that there has always been widespread family abuse of children but historical evidence is sparse and unreliable. There is also so far little evidence of abuse, as it is commonly defined in the West, as a feature of the pre-industrial Third World, although it is appearing where traditional values and supports break down. Dr Robert Mushota, who has done some pioneering research into child abuse in Zambia, believes that there are fewer cases of child molestation reported from rural districts because such communities are still governed by traditional norms and habits which 'do not tolerate child molestation.'[20]

[20] *The Scope and Extent of Child Abuse and Child Neglect in Rural and Urban Zambia*; Dr Robert T. Mushota.

Neighbours, for example, are likely to intervene directly where child molestation occurs within the village but not necessarily in the urban areas where families are increasingly becoming nuclear rather than extended. 'Aside from the nature of the rural social set up, urban families apparently experience more socio-economic pressures leading to domestic conflicts than is true for rural families.'

The strong public focus on parental abuse of children distracts attention from abuse of them outside the home. Abuse suffered at the hands of their parents is likely to be compounded by the experiences of such children in society. Child victims of physical abuse and neglect commonly exhibit low self-esteem: in a culture where 'success breeds success', low self-esteem is perhaps further reinforced. Whether low self-esteem is expressed by the child as passivity or violence, it finds few sympathisers or admirers when the rewards go to confidence, self-control and 'forcefulness' of character.

Richie McMullen, an expert on the involvement of boys in prostitution in London, reports that adults who seek sex with children say they can spot a vulnerable child 'miles away'.

'That child's got a neon sign above his head which is flashing "victim". It's a non-verbal communication; it's the loss of self-respect, self-dignity.'

Children embroiled in prostitution find no shortage of trade in world capitals. Sexual abusers of children outside the family are to be found in all classes and include members of the most respected professions, particularly those which give adults positions of trust and power over children, among them the legal, teaching and child-care professions.

Other evidence of a wider disposition to act in ways that are severely detrimental to children, but which are not encompassed by the customary definition of child abuse, include the dumping of dangerous drugs in the Third World and 'the maiming of children from poorly tested anti-depressants or contraceptives'.[21]

The representation of child abuse as something that happens within families also distracts from a wider understanding of abuse which would point to the collective responsibility of society. Known variously as 'societal' or 'systemic' abuse, it refers to society's tolerance of large numbers of children being left to the care of parents in conditions that are well

[21] *The Politics of Child Abuse* by Nigel Parton, Macmillan Education, page 168.

Mother and child in accommodation provided for single-parent families in an old army camp in Britain
ADRIAN ROWLAND

[22] *Child Survival* ed. Scheper-Hughes, 'Child Abuse and the Unconscious in American Popular Culture' by Nancy Scheper-Hughes, Reidel B.V. Uitguery, 1987.

documented as damaging to health and general child development. Child neglect, which generally occurs in sub-standard environments of 'poor housing, insufficient food, inadequate clothing, education and medical care' is the main single cause of damage to children. In the US it accounts for 60 per cent of all child abuse reporting and 56 per cent of all related fatalities.[22] According to a National Institute of Mental

[23] *Treating Family Violence in a Pediatric Hospital: A Program of Training, Research, and Services – 1987* by Kathleen M. White, Jane Snyder, Richard Bourne, Eli H. Newberger. National Institute of Mental Health.

Health report: 'When harm to a child is severe enough to require hospitalisation or medical attention, it is one and a half times more likely to be due to neglect than to physical abuse.'[23]

In the UK there has been some media exposure (with little consequence) of children and parents on welfare payments consigned for long periods to 'temporary' bed and breakfast accommodation, despite accumulated evidence that it is detrimental to children's health and development. Latest figures showed 11,000 families in bed and breakfast. Mothers interviewed for a homelessness report described life in bed and breakfast in terms of a prison sentence. 'You can't lock your child in. And you can't leave your child alone in an unlocked room. You never know who is next door.

'Outside the room is the stairs. Inside, the room is so small an infant hasn't space to crawl or walk properly. When I take my kids up to the kitchen on the next floor to cook our supper, they go wild, the sense of space goes to their heads.'

[24] *Homelessness, an Act of Man*; National Federation of Housing Associations, London 1987.

Another mother talked of her fear of her own anger and frustration with her child. 'He cries and you can't stop him. Then people start banging on the walls. There are times when I want to kill him.'[24]

The share of the national income of the poorest fifth of households in the UK has fallen over the past ten years from 7.4 to 5.9 per cent, according to the 1989 National Children's Homes report, *Children in Danger*.

In the world's most powerful and wealthy nation, little or no power was exercised during the Reagan years to ensure the children of the poorest did not suffer from neglect directly related to their parents' impoverishment. A New York lawyer specialising in juvenile rights, Janet Fink, says: 'We have had children who have been stealing because they were hungry.'

Comments Trudee Able-Peterson, who works with the New York street children's programme, Streetwork Project: 'This particular (Reagan) Government has taken away from our children again and again and again – billions of dollars in cuts. It's ludicrous to deny it. They've gotten out of the housing business so that people have nowhere to live. There are homeless families and that creates homeless children. I'm ashamed to be a citizen of a country that does that to children.'

Nine-year-old **Shamelion's** judgement of the America she lives in is that: 'It's the pits.' Contorting her eyes so they appear to be about to pop out, she says of the towering ghetto that has been home: 'The ceiling leaks, no water don't work, no heat. Two rooms between six of us.

'It's crazy. They're always selling crack, on the stairways.'

*Shamelion (left) and
her friend Natasha*

The Brooklyn Arms Hotel is part of the flourishing welfare
hotel industry in New York. It used to be an upmarket hotel
serving a once prosperous part of Brooklyn but the area became
run down and the traveller trade shifted to other parts of the
city. However, property throughout the city has grown
increasingly scarce and valuable, putting it out of the reach of
the poor. The Brooklyn Arms, like many other hotels, has
found handsome profit in welfare housing.

New York's growing legions of homeless people face three
options (as do people in a similar position in the UK) – live 'on
the street', in a shelter or in a welfare hotel.

Shamelion lived in a shelter with her family for six months.
Asked what it was like she replies: 'You don't want to know.'
The shelters are run by the city authorities and by voluntary
organisations. Typically they provide dormitory accommodation
with no privacy, are highly regimented and regulated and have
no place for children to play.

'Sometimes the shelters are worse than living on the street
because people get abused in them, robbed, ripped off, so
they'd rather stay out on the street,' says Lieutenant James
Greenlay of the New York City Runaway Unit.

Welfare hotels are supposed to be a rung up the ladder but
residents of the Brooklyn Arms say they are fearful of living
there on several counts. The hotel houses 263 families packed
on to 17 floors. In August 1987 a fire almost turned it into a
towering inferno. Due to numerous false alarms, the police do
not routinely respond to emergency calls. The owners employ

private security guards to keep order. Nevertheless the hotel has a reputation for drug pushers and pimps. Residents complain they hang around the corridors and stairways. According to Jean Chappell, president of the housing crisis organisation, Parents on the Move, women residents and girl children in some of the welfare hotels are very vulnerable. 'The young girls are very enticed. What some of the security and maintenance guys do is they buy them jewelry and clothes or give them money and take them on the back stairs. A girl living in a hotel can't always have what she wants. So a guy will say: "Hey, I'll give you this or that, all you've got to do is have sex with me." Or they threaten.

'There's plenty of young girls, and I mean young – under 13 – living in hotels that are prostituting.'

There is no place in the Brooklyn Arms for children to play. A few linger aimlessly in the drab foyer. Others rush out into the street as if they are trying to leave the building behind.

Everyone arriving or leaving the hotel is scrutinised. Visitors are asked their business and required to sign in. Several people stand around looking vacant, 'like zombies, like they don't have nothing inside', as Barbara, a new resident puts it. The lift bells don't work. The shaft resounds with the calls of people shouting out the numbers of the floors they are waiting on to the bored elevator man.

Barbara 'at home' with one of her five children

Barbara's room is along a dark inhospitable corridor. 'I was

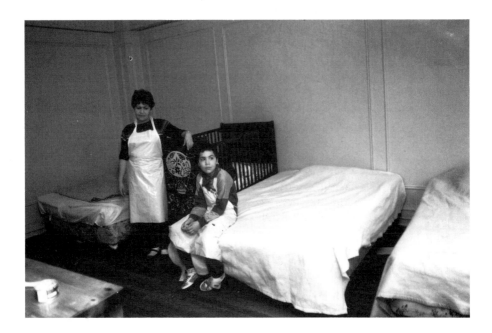

desperate for help. The man I lived with turned to drugs and was threatening me. The last straw was when a man he brought to the house tried to sexually abuse my daughter. She's only twelve. I've got five children. I asked for emergency accommodation for us.'

She had hoped to find something better for her children. Instead she found 'something more disgusting'. The room is desperately dreary. The toilet seat in the adjacent bathroom is broken, one of many signs of neglect. There is a refrigerator but no cooker: residents are not supposed to cook in their rooms and there is no common kitchen. For this kind of accommodation the city authorities pay the owners between $100 and over $200 a day per family.

A social services office is responsible for taking care of the emergency and longer term needs of the residents but cannot cope with the case loads and complexity of the problems. Arrangements are also made for schooling. But they tend to fail because of poor organisation and the recalcitrance of the children who have been shunted around from school to school.

'The kids here don't want to go to school. They are stigmatised, name-called: "Hotel kids", "you people", "welfare kids". Living in a hotel is a tremendous strain on the kids,' says Jean Chappell, who has survived with her five children for 18 months in a single room. Like the mothers interviewed for the UK homelessness report, Jean finds the cramped conditions tough on parents as well. 'If the kids get on your nerves you have no place to put them, unless you're fortunate enough to have two or three rooms – then you can put the kids in one room and you can barricade yourself, more or less, in another and ignore what's going on. But when you only have one it's hard.'

Yet even these living conditions are accounted a sort of privilege. The first 30 days in the Brooklyn Arms are a probation period which exposes people to the mercies of hotel officials. If a family is judged to be 'non-acceptable' they will be made to leave. 'Difficult behaviour' includes demanding too much heat, complaining and children being violent. Those who pass their probation may secure the privilege of being there for months or even years before something better is found. Shamelion's family was in the hotel for 18 months before moving on to individual accommodation. She still visits Jean's daughter, Natasha, and Jean is now hopeful that her own welfare 'sentence' will soon be over.

Over the road a Salvation Army centre doubles as a night shelter for homeless men and a day centre for deprived children, most of whom come from the hotel. Captain John

Rondon listens daily to the unfolding saga of bottom of the heap soap opera that forms welfare hotel life. He says many of the children are very confused. 'We teach children "Thou shall not steal", home teaches them, "You better steal". We say, "Thou shall love your enemies", at home they say, "Screw your enemies, don't let anybody get over on you".

'We tell them, "Your body's the most precious thing"; they get told, "Your body is the most sellable thing". So they're coming down the stairs and a woman's there having sex with a man and they don't see it as strange. They'll go right by, they see it as their way of life.

'If you say to these kids, "What would you like to be when you grow up?" they'll say, "Big and alive." They feel the pressure of almost dying, they really do. They have seen kids get shot, things that you and I only read about in newspapers and see on our TVs.'

Abandonment by society of the child to the fate allotted to the parent makes birth, where there are huge disparities of wealth, a form of lottery. Though the immediate 'instrument' of abuse is often the parent, it may be better understood in the context of a broader social negligence of poor and deprived people in general. In their paper, *Child Abuse and the Unconscious* Nancy Scheper-Hughes and Howard Stein argue that abusive parents, as the target of public rage, are being made the scapegoat in a downward spiral of societal and family abuse of children. Child abusing parents are blamed for what is a social and medical problem. Society's punitive reaction 'leads to a diminished sense of social relatedness and responsibility for the problem, and further reductions in social and economic support for parents with vulnerable and dependent children. This leads to increased stress, and frequently to increased abuse and neglect in those families at greater risk, who are seen as intrinsically bad.'[25]

[25] *Child Survival* ed. Scheper-Hughes p. 354.

Manuel Carballo (WHO) expresses a similar view: 'I think there's been an inclination in many circumstances to always blame the family unit for anything that goes wrong and not to take into account the stress that the family unit is exposed to in terms of unemployment, underemployment, poor education, poor environmental conditions, limited access to advice, limited access to any type of social support. I'm not excusing the family unit but we must understand the situation in which they have no function.

'There are certain circumstances in which parents have very little say in what happens to their children. Although mothers may know quite well what the child's needs are and nutritional

requirements are, they're simply not able to meet them. That's
what I'd call systemic abuse ... where the system creates a
situation in which the child is almost by definition neglected or
deprived of certain things. I wouldn't call that parental child
abuse at all.'

In the world's poorer countries this kind of abuse is so
extreme and extensive that the family's inability to secure the
survival and welfare of its children and child abuse are rarely
explained in other than socio-economic terms.

FAMILIES ON THE BRINK

Kamia, an 11-year-old street child, is the youngest in a family
of eight children.

*Kamia making his way
through Mathare
Valley*
JEREMY HARTLEY

His mother, Mary, once lived with her first husband on a small farm in Muranga in Central Kenya. They had four children. Though he was a caring father, he fiercely rejected a child she had had from an earlier relationship. He repeatedly urged her to abandon the child and this finally drove her to leave the home. In the old days she might well have been welcomed back on her family's land as a useful worker. But Kenya suffers the world's greatest population explosion. In many parts of the country people farm such small plots that they can no longer reap an adequate living.

Told by her relatives that they could not help, Mary followed the example of many others who have been displaced from the land. With her four children, she sought a future in the city.

Viewed from impoverished rural areas, Nairobi looks like a glittering centre of opportunity. But there is no gold in the city's pavements and the rich lifestyles, portrayed in advertising and the other media, are enjoyed by very few. There are no allowances or provisions for people shifting from the role of subsistence farmer to urban workseeker. The common destiny awaiting newcomers is to join those who came before them in unemployed destitution in one of the city slums. An aunt who had already made the move offered to give Mary and her children temporary shelter.

There was no formal work to be had but Mary started a steady relationship with a man who earned a living as a lorry driver. She had three more children by him, including Kamia, but she made sure that the children by the first marriage kept in touch with their father and visited him regularly.

Mary's second husband insisted on having two wives; she would not agree and so this relationship was also doomed. With

Mathare Valley

her children, she moved to Mathare Valley and her husband disappeared out of their lives.

Close to the centre of Nairobi, Mathare Valley is one of Africa's most notorious slums. It takes its name from the river that flows sluggishly between its flanks. The valley's slopes glisten in the sun – not with the sheen of young grass but the glint of old corrugated iron sheets. Beneath this crazed canopy makeshift structures of wood and iron house a population of a quarter of a million and each year more people arrive from impoverished rural areas hoping to find work.

Each day ushers in struggle: between employment and unemployment, hope and despair, social integration and the disintegration of individual opportunism, earning and crime. 'Home' in this setting carries little sense of refuge. The flimsiness and close proximity of the shanty dwellings exclude privacy. Step out of your shack and you are on a narrow footpath. Sewage and waste water are carried in crude open ditches along the side of the track you walk on. In the rainy season the maze of tracks and alleyways becomes a slithering morass of filth and mud which serves breadwinner, criminal, the diseased and the dying with equal disdain.

Jones Muchendu was born and brought up in Mathare Valley. Now he works with street children. 'Most families are large, with six to eight children. A lot have problems – unemployment, alcoholism, mothers coping on their own.' Relationships are put under enormous stress. Children find few opportunities to contribute to family income. There are many single-parent families. Not uncommonly, women must turn to prostitution to keep their children alive.

Mary and her children were so poor that the Mathare Village Committee gave them a tiny plot of ground. On this the older children constructed a home out of cardboard, waste wood and iron. Mary turned to brewing and selling sugar cane spirit, earning barely enough for the family to eat and for the older children to go to school.

She told Kamia and his youngest sister she wanted them to go to school as well and she tried to save. But there was never enough. Primary education in Kenya is free in theory, but uniforms have to be bought and a 'harambee' (community self-help) contribution must be paid to the school. These costs disqualify many poor people from giving their children an education. By this time Mary had even more mouths to feed; her eldest daughter, who was emotionally disturbed, had had three children and abandoned them in their grandmother's care.

In 1985 tragedy struck. Mary died of an illness which Kamia

calls 'swelling'. He was profoundly affected by his mother's death. His three older sisters had moved away. His older brothers worked on Nairobi's 'matatu' buses. One of them was soon in jail for a driving offence. The other did his best to provide for the six younger children who remained at home but they often went without food. For much of the day Kamia and a

Kamia in his family's house. The stove provides warmth but there is no food to cook
JEREMY HARTLEY

nephew, John, were left to their own devices. Increasingly they passed their time with other neglected children in the area and, at the age of eleven, Kamia finally abandoned the home to join Nairobi's street children.

There are variations on the theme of Kamia's story throughout the Third World. They are stories of people struggling to survive in zones of impoverishment and neglect or attempting to gain a foothold in the illuminated world of the wealthy

Progress has presided over an increasing separation of the rich and the poor. Though we talk of countries as being rich and poor or belonging to the North or South, the boundary between the worlds of affluence and deprivation runs across continents and through nations.[26] In the weathiest countries, there are sizable disadvantaged minorities. In poor countries development has been concentrated in the cities. Members of the urban rich elite may share the lifestyles and interests of the rich in wealthy nations more than they do those of the poor in their own countries. There is usually a small middle class and a mass of regular workers and under- and unemployed people. The heartland of Third World poverty is the rural areas. Even the inhabitants of the shanty towns have a call on government prior to that of the rural poor, holding as they do 'the ultimate weapon of all city dwellers, the power to riot' if food prices rise too high.[27] In his book, *The Greening of Africa*, Paul Harrison outlines how government and development policies have tended to meet the cities' demands at the expense of the rural poor.

In many Third World countries colonial and post-colonial industrial development has, by a mixture of deliberate policy and negligence, hastened the destruction of traditional ways of life and produced huge imbalances in the distribution of wealth. Traditional rural crafts have been undermined by cheap industrial products and subsistence farmers have been separated from their land, resulting in high levels of unemployment and underemployment.[28] Rural advancement has been largely limited to the establishment of large plantations and agri-businesses. It has promoted small elites, who are linked to the city power centres, and turned its back on the mass of subsistence farmers or peasantry. In India, poorer peasants commonly forfeit their land to the richer by taking loans – perhaps to see them over a drought or pay for a burial, or the marriage of a daughter. Interest rates are extortionate, making repayment very difficult.

Jayamma had to sell her children's labour to help pay for debts and interest repayments she has incurred. She and her family live in a small village in the state of Karnataka. They have a simple two-room house which, sleeping trestles apart, is bare of furnishings. There are four daughters and a son. The youngest child, Girijamma, is indulgently allowed to sprawl across her mother's lap as she speaks about her life.

The family has a small dryland plot. With a good harvest, it gives them enough food for four months, 'so there is nothing left over to sell'. Jayamma works as a wage labourer with road

[26] *Report of the Independent Commission on International Humanitarian Issues*; page 9, Geneva 1987.

[27] *The Greening of Africa*; Paul Harrison, Paladin Grafton Books, page 53, London 1987.

[28] For one account of this process read *Chains of Servitude, Bondage and Slavery in India* by Utsa Patnaik and Manjari Dignwaney, Sangam Books, New Delhi, 1985.

Jayamma and children: daughters Neelamma and Girijamma and son Srinivasa

repair gangs and on other peoples' land. Either job pays her four rupees (25 pence) a day. Her husband cuts timber and firewood, or works as an agricultural labourer – earning ten rupees a day. She finds about three months work in the year. He can get employment most of the time but his work exposes him to accidents. As Jayamma talks, he lies listening on his bed in the other room. 'He has been off work for several weeks with a bad axe injury,' she says.

From time to time she has to borrow money. A year or so ago her village committee recommended she receive a grant to repair the roof of her house. The amount allocated was not enough to pay for the work: money meant to help her resulted in her borrowing more, bringing the amount she owes to several thousand rupees. On this she pays a yearly interest rate of 500 (about £30) for every 1000 rupees borrowed.

She entered into a contract for her son, **Srinivasa**, and then her daughter, **Neelamma**, who was only nine, to go and work another district for a year. 'I was paid 1000 rupees (about £60) for the boy, for a year, and 500 for my daughter.' These small gains helped pay the interest and some of the capital on her loans but at the cost of losing her children's labour contribution at home. 'They slept and ate at their employer's. They worked at a great distance and I saw nothing of them. I started that three years ago but I have not sent them this year because I wanted a higher price and the employer wouldn't agree.'

The children were lucky; their employer, though exploitative, was not abusive. But as a result of their work they had no education. 'I felt lonely and homesick when I was away,' says Neelamma. 'I don't want to go anywhere like that again, I prefer to work for wages alongside my mother. I was expected to clean the house every day, collect cow dung for fertiliser and look after the goats and sheep. In the evening, I would wash the utensils used in the house, serve the food to the people of the house. Then I would eat my food and sleep. I can't remember any particularly happy day. I felt very bad when they scolded me. They would say, "We have given money but you are not working".'

The son's duties were to plough, operate a sugar crushing machine and care for the cattle. Apart from the money paid to his mother, he was given some token pocket money.

To Jayamma, sending her children away was 'like burning their umbilical cords on a fire'. 'However small the meal, the family should eat it together,' she says. She dreads having to sell the labour of her youngest child, **Girijamma**. But she accepts she may have to. The family continues to face problems – there is not enough to eat always, nor money for clothes. There will be dowry payments to be found for the eventual marriages of her daughters. And there is the interest to be paid. Her only other security is the family's lifeline – their land.

In parts of Brazil, peasant farmers and rural workers have been ejected from land farmed by their families for generations to make way for massive hydro-electric and road systems and large agricultural estates producing export commodities. Often those displaced have not been compensated or have received only inadequate compensation. Others have been expelled by powerful landholders who simply want to extend their property. At times the services of professional gunmen – pistoleiros – are used in land disputes. Trades unions of rural workers have mobilised to oppose such actions. More than 1000 peasants, rural workers and trades unionists have been murdered as a result of land disputes since 1980 and only three per cent of the killers have been jailed.[29] Developments that displace the poor benefit local and international investors and business interests and generally the wealthier classes. Poor farmers have also been displaced from the land by drought. Between 1960 and 1980 40 million peasants were expelled from or abandoned the land.

'Planners, politicians and businessmen often regard traditional land users as an inconvenience and a hindrance to economic growth, especially when they are tribal people with an apparently archaic culture,' says a report by the Independent Commission on International Humanitarian Issues in Geneva.[30] 'In many cases they are simply told to leave their land and are forcibly evicted from it. As a result, they must

[29] In his article 'Landscape of Death', Jim Hine outlines the causes of the displacement of peasant farmers from the land in Brazil. *Amnesty* No 37, British Section of Amnesty International, 1989.

[30] *Refugees – Dynamics of Displacement*; A report for the Independent Commission on International Humanitarian Issues, Zed Press, London, 1986.

either move to a new area and run the risk of conflict with the existing population there, or settle on marginal sites with poor soil, steep slopes or poor rainfall – the land that nobody else wants. Such incidents have taken place in every country of the Third World, and in countries of all ideological persuasions.'

Another crucial cause of rural decline and individual deprivation, and one for which the poor are sometimes themselves blamed, has been continuing high birth rates. Overpopulation contributes to the over-use and exhaustion of the land and helps define children as burdensome. But it too must be seen partly as a consequence of political and economic neglect; people have fewer children when the quality of life improves and they can be more sure that their children will survive.

When people lose their land, or it will no longer support them they must live from their labour. Agricultural work is poorly paid and seasonal. When work is short, labourers must migrate sometimes great distances to find employment, exposing family and community relationships to greater stress and uncertainty and breadwinners to additional risks, including the hazards of an unfamiliar workplace.

Ten-year-old **Kishore** once lived in a village near Bangalore, in southern India. His father, whom he speaks of with great affection, worked as a day labourer. At a time when there was no farm work to be had locally, he told his family he might find work at a coal mine in another state. 'I begged him not to go because in a few days it was my birthday,' says Kishore. Soon after the birthday word came that his father had been killed in a road accident.

Kishore reacted badly to the loss. He now had to work and his mother kept the money he earned. He became rebellious and earned a bad name in the village. One day the small child of a neighbour he was playing with lost a ring. Kishore was accused of stealing it. 'I didn't, but they wouldn't believe me,' he says.

With no father to protect him, he was seized by villagers, hung by his feet from a tree in the village and flogged unmercifully with heavy poles. His mother, possibly terrified that she too would be blamed and beaten, left the village during the assault on her son. After his release, finding his mother gone, Kishore crept aboard a bus to Bangalore to escape further punishment. Some city street children later found him in a bus station, semi-conscious and near to death.

Family and community violence, rejection by a step-father, the loss of the main breadwinner by disease or accident or violent death, or the breadwinner's abandonment of the family,

Kishore

are common themes in the personal histories of street children.

Also from a poor village, **Kumar** had an enviable start in life. Being the son of the village school teacher, he received regular education. The family also had some land. But then his father fell ill and died. His mother was able to keep him on at school because he helped her work the land. Then she was killed by someone who had a claim to the property.

Kumar brings his hand violently down and down again as he says: 'I saw it. I know the man. He used a sickle. My mother threw her arms up to protect her head. He cut her arm. After the killing I was put in a hostel. There I got a message that the man was going to kill me too. The police had been told but the man was still free. I was the only witness. I ran away to the city to save myself.'

The images of wealth, opportunity and success that emanate from cities are powerful lures to people trapped in an increasingly arduous, violent and uncertain struggle for survival in rural areas. Where parents do not make the move, children may be tempted to make their own bid to escape to a better life. This is all the more likely where poverty has eroded the capacity for love within their family or led to children being abused, neglected or exploited.

Domingas Vito Feliciano ran away from her home in Alagoas in the north-east of Brazil at the age of twelve to find work as a domestic servant in the city of Recife.

At the younger end of a family of ten children, she had automatically helped her mother with the work of the home and looked after the animals on the family smallholding from an early age. She started school with great enthusiasm but, within six months, her father announced she would have to leave to work full time.

'From the age of eight I worked with my father picking fruit on a plantation and on a plot my father cultivated as a sharecropper. I loved school and found the agricultural work very boring and heavy.' She continued to help her mother in the house. 'I and my mother were the strength of the home,' she says proudly. But from early on she began to experience severe back pains, if not caused then certainly not helped by the heavy work.

Domingas regards her parents as having been exploited by the landowner they worked for and as having exploited her in their turn. Perhaps out of concern for her safety or an old fashioned sense of morality, her father was very restrictive of his daughters. Domingas also sees him as mean. 'He never paid us for our work. He gave us what we needed. But it was never what we wanted. Either he or mother would buy our clothes. He made us wear petticoats and long old fashioned dresses.

'My older sister ran away because Dad beat her. He didn't approve of her boyfriend. He threatened but never hit me. He wanted to choose our boyfriends – he lived in those days still.

'He didn't want any of us to leave home to work. My parents wouldn't let me out of the house on my own. Any twelve-year-old wants to get out and go around and see places. They didn't let me dress in nice clothes, or paint my face or do my hair up. I wanted to feel free and do as I wanted.

'I suddenly decided to leave home and find work in Recife. When I went away I thought, "I have to work here at home. I

Domingas

will work elsewhere and earn money for myself." I wanted to be able to go out at weekends and buy an ice cream. I was under the illusion things would be better in the outside world.'

SLUMS AND SQUATTER CITIES

The drift to the cities provides urban employers with a welcome over-supply of cheap labour. But little or no attempt is made to help new arrivals, like Kamia's family, find their feet. Rather, the reaction of governments is often to bulldoze the simple shelters of migrants from rural poverty.

Hopes of a better life quickly yield to the realities of urban deprivation. Unlike the Wrights, whose move back to the

A slum near Recife

depressed north of England was between rungs far higher up the ladder of survival and in the context of a wealthy welfare state, there is no chance of a return journey for most of the Third World's rural migrants.

Deprived city areas include decaying inner city slums, the most insecure kind of peripheral shanty towns and other settlements where people have no formal services and no title deeds but have established some degree of permanency and sense of community. In Brazil the latter is called a favela.

The favelas in Rio de Janeiro are crazy skyscrapers of informal block, brick and timber dwellings, rising out of each other and clinging to the steep slopes of the mountains for which the city is famous. They reach right into the wealthy areas where work is to be found. Unlike many of the world's urban poor, Nilssa lives a stone's throw from her work as a servant – there are no bus fares to pay. Like so many other mothers she is separated from her husband, but she is in the relatively secure and considerate employment of a kindly liberally minded woman. Her employer takes an active interest in her and her children and the favela she lives in. It is one of the oldest favelas and has a developed sense of community. The school her children attend provides a free meal, which she therefore does not have to buy. There is a crèche she can send them to in the afternoons.

With these advantages and by 'improvising and making do' (a euphemism for a lot of self-sacrifice), she has so far managed to keep her three boys at school, despite an annual inflation rate of

Nilssa and Edson, in the home of Nilssa's employer

several hundred per cent. Her boys are aged eight, nine and eleven and her plan is to keep them in school by hook or by crook until they are old enough to find work and continue their studies part time.

But will they find work, with such high unemployment?

'I don't know but I have hope.'

What are her main anxieties?

'There are so many,' she says. She strokes her son's hair as she talks of them. There are health worries. Lack of adequate refuse removal, sewage provision and water supply and a large population of rats and other vermin in the favelas mean heightened health hazards.

'Above all I'm afraid of drugs and the sexual abuse of my children – both by individuals and organised crime. If I had girls I would be very afraid of prostitution.'

Until recently her area had been riven by two warring drugs barons. Then one was killed. Here again she was lucky. 'The one who died was very vicious. We were all very scared of him. Now our area is controlled by one big drugs dealer. We feel safe with him because he is very respectful on the sexual question and he won't allow children to be used as drugs couriers. He will call a parent in if he hears of a child involved in drugs and ask them if they do not know what is happening to their children.'

A large number of the people in Nilssa's favela work in the construction of the city's skyscrapers. Their main fear is of being rejected as neighbours by the owners and inhabitants of

Rio de Janeiro
UNICEF/
WILLIAM HETZER

the skyscrapers they build. Though their favela is 50 years old
there are no title deeds. The real estate value of the land they
occupy has grown with the city and attracts increasing interest
from developers. Every newspaper story about the eyesore of
the favelas, or the health or crime threat they pose is seen as a
softening up of public attitudes to allow the bulldozers to be
sent in.

The lives and welfare of the children of those on the margins
of the economy are held together by a frail thread of luck,
endurance and personal application that provides no assured
security.

Going out from the centre of Brazil's megalopolis, São
Paulo, by tube, then bus, then a second bus, you arrive nearly
two hours later at the outer perimeter of the city. Here is an
area of crude plain block structures and dusty roads and tucked
into open spaces are more informal shanty areas.
Accommodation may be rented not only by the week but by
fractions of a day. One example brought to the notice of a
community worker was of a family who were only able to rent
three boards in an otherwise empty room for just three hours a
day.

This is one area to which new arrivals come, most of them migrating from impoverishment in rural areas and other smaller towns and cities. Just 20 years ago 70 per cent of Brazilians lived in the countryside. Now 70 per cent live in the cities. São Paulo is a city of outsiders. Two thirds of the population originate from somewhere else. Rural migrants often lack every kind of advantage and support – education, skills, identity documents, networks of friends and relatives. They obtain the poorest paid, most insecure and most unwanted work and pay high prices to get to and from it.

Like migrant settlements on the periphery of cities in many parts of the world this area is so far from the work centres it is known as a 'dormitory'; life not gobbled up in working or work seeking is lost in travelling. 'Home' is where you snatch a few hours sleep between bouts of travel and work. In such areas workers and workseekers may have no choice but to neglect their children. Some parents are reduced to tying younger children to furniture for all the hours they are away to protect them from the dangers of the street.

Children in a Managuan slum left unattended. A major problem for mothers who have to go out to work is what to do with their children

Many children have no access to schooling. There are no facilities for them. Outside the room there is nowhere but the street.

'We would like to have space to play. Here we don't have any chance, either for working or for playing,' a black child from the Recife area says of life in a dormitory area. 'If we stay on the streets the neighbours complain. Here people complain about everything. Even our colour is criticised. Here many people don't like children. If you are playing with a ball and it falls in their yard, they just destroy that ball.'

'They fear we are thieves,' says a companion.

'They don't fear us, they are angry with us,' says a third. 'I have had my life threatened several times.'

Here threats to one's life are taken seriously. The economic violence of having to survive on terms that empty life of meaning is echoed by violence in the community, in vulnerable families and ultimately the hearts and minds of children. Having little to do with adults and no access to any facilities, children can easily become involved in drug-taking, stealing and prostitution. Beatings by parents, frightened by their own lack of control over their children, are commonplace. Children are also often beaten by members of the public, officials and police exasperated by high crime levels and mistrustful of their intentions.

Children, who would have worked alongside their parents in a rural setting, may find few legal opportunities to contribute to family income in a city slum. The opportunities that exist – scavenging for recyclable materials, portering and domestic work – take the child outside whatever protection the home has to offer into an immediately dangerous environment. Where a mother has no choice but to stay with her children the weight of supporting the family is born by a single breadwinner on insecure earnings.

'In the rural areas, the father sets an example and has status,' said Lygia Bove, who does voluntary work with neglected children in São Paulo. 'The only jobs open to him in the city are in the informal sector. Wages are poor and he can't afford food. The father loses his status in the family. He may abandon the family. The mother has to earn and may turn to prostitution for want of other work. The children are left on the street.'

The assault on individual identity and confidence is not just economic.

'When we come to the city we have to change our cultural identity, we have to renounce our customs and habits to be able to live here,' says João de Deus do Nasciemento, himself a migrant from a poor rural northern region and now working

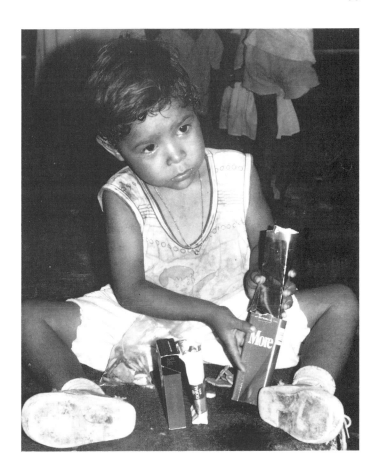

This child occupies himself while his mother is at work nearby in the market

with children in deprived areas of São Paulo. Many of the children have rural origins and are the descendants of black slaves from the north of the country or Indian people in the interior. 'One of the songs of street children is about having lost their cultural roots in the move to the big cities. Here we live a form of American culture but our spirit is in our own culture. Here the music is different, the food is different, the way of talking is different. We refer to ourselves as foreigners in our own country.'

Recife development worker Valdemar de Oliveira Neto, of the Luis Freire Centre, describes favelas as 'the final stage of a process of destruction of many very important ties in an individual's life, cultural, social, and psychological ties. Often the family is destroyed, the community is destroyed, the relationship with the land in the interior of the country is destroyed. It is a process of destroying these people.'

'THINNING OUT' THE CHILDREN

There was an old lady, who lived in a shoe.
She had so many children she knew not what to do.
So she gave them all soup without any bread.
And she whipped them all soundly and sent them to bed.

Victorian nursery rhyme

The biggest single danger to children is poverty and the living conditions that it imposes on parents and children alike. Six-year-old **Jelita** nearly died simply because her mother could not feed her properly. She had very little money and no knowledge of good nutrition. With the death of her husband,

Jelita (third from left) with her family

she was left alone to support four children. By selling fruit outside her slum home in Lusaka, Zambia's capital, she manages to make two kwachas (ten pence) a day. None of the family is properly fed but Jelita has twice gone into hospital with severe malnutrition. Subsequently her mother has been given nutritional training. 'But I can't afford to give them these foods. And the children still sometimes go without any food,' she says.

Fourteen million children in the Third World die every year from common illnesses and undernutrition and three and a half million are permanently disabled by preventable diseases.

Be it in the cities or in the countryside, poverty and social neglect can define children as burdensome to their families and expose them to great danger at the hands of their own parents. There are children who are killed by their parents, children who are abandoned, children who are neglected and allowed to die, children who are sold by their parents and end up in prostitution or dangerous employment and there are millions of children who go to work in conditions that damage their health and deprive them of an education and other vital development opportunities.

It would be easy to mistake such parents as being heartless or negligent or abusive. No doubt a few are, but the very acts that might expose poor parents to criticism are most often expressions of their deep desperation.

A young mother, Betty, brought her four children, two girls and two boys, into the Save the Children Fund office in Kampala and told the social workers: 'I love my children. I can no longer cope with them.' In a distraught state she asked the staff to look after them. 'I want to go on seeing them – to visit them regularly – and to have them home soon. It is only to help me over this difficult time.' The social workers, who face many similar requests, were sympathetic but firm. Wherever possible children should stay with their family. In any case the SCF-supported children's homes were full.

Betty explained that her husband had been killed by soldiers, leaving the family with no means of support. She was without a job but planned to earn a living by selling fish. Her landlord had allowed her to have a room rent free for a while but was now telling her to leave. She seemed so desperate that the social workers agreed to take in the older children, **Joseph** aged eleven and **James** aged seven, and the mother went away with her girls.

As they left the social workers remarked on how well cared for the children were.

A couple of weeks later Betty was back. **Eva** and **Mary**, aged

Eva, abandoned by her mother

eight and six, were with her. Again she was crying and begged the staff to arrange for the children to be looked after. Again her plea was turned down. She told the social workers that she had some matters to attend to and would be back shortly to collect the girls. She didn't return.

Two generations ago it would have been unusual for a mother to turn to a charity for help. As elsewhere in Africa the extended family would have ensured children were taken care of. But the impact of urbanisation and the post-colonial years of terror and death, from the beginning of Amin's reign in the 1970s to the coup that brought Yoweri Museveni to power in the mid-1980s, have left a swathe of destruction through Ugandan society and the economy. There are many widows and broken relationships. Just keeping body and soul together is extremely difficult.

In Uganda, as elsewhere, the reluctance of many step-parents to accept responsibility for children who are not their own is a major reason for child abandonment. 'Some mothers pretend they are badly off, they are so desperate,' says SCF social worker Rosemary Namutembizi. 'I said to Betty when she brought the children in, "You just tell me if you want to go and get married". She broke into tears and said, "I wouldn't abandon my children for the sake of a man. I just can't keep them at the moment".'

Anxious though the social workers are to trace Betty, it is not until some weeks later that they are able to find the time to set off with her oldest boy to look for her.

They locate her in a small, sparsely furnished but neatly kept room. Left to talk with her son she is clearly pleased to see him but also embarrassed and shy. Tentative smiles give way to a more open reconciliation.

She explains to Rosemary: 'I was tired of the children.' They had had nothing to eat the evening before she took them to the SCF office. 'There was no food and they spent the whole night crying. I was hoping you'd take them for a while so I could find work.

'My plan to sell fish didn't work out. Now I've rented a sewing machine and I'm trying to start up my own business. At present I can't cope with having the children back. But when I'm settled and have enough money I want to come and collect them. I love the children more than you do.'

She is persuaded by the social workers to go with them to see her daughters.

First steps towards reconciliation must overcome the mistrust and pain of children who have been abandoned. At first Eva and Mary say they do not want to go back to live with their mother but some days later there appears to be a change of heart.

Adults under stress are not noted for their grasp of how their actions are experienced by children. In cases of divorce, a father sees himself as leaving his wife rather than his children but the children may well see themselves as being abandoned. Where a child is truly abandoned by parents, the pain and confusion are great.

As an infant, **Matibo** was sent by his parents to live with his grandmother. He does not know why this happened but it is not unusual in Kenya.

For nine years his parents visited him and regularly sent money for his keep and education. Then one day the visits and the money stopped. Police attempts to trace the parents failed. Without the money the grandmother could no longer support him and he was sent far away to a charity for destitute children. He sees himself as abandoned.

Asked about his grandmother he replies: 'I think she is suffering a lot because of her situation.'

What did he think of his parents?
'I can't think of anything to say about them.'
Did he feel angry?
'Yes.'
Did he think about what had happened to him much?
'Yes . . . I don't feel well. I am feeling very bad.'

In environments hostile to the most basic needs of families, it would not be surprising to find mothers who abandoned their children to save themselves. And the younger, the more inexperienced and more isolated mothers are, the more this is perhaps likely to happen.

Matibo

[31] Report of the 'Woman's Action Group Workshop', Harare, October 1985.

A Zimbabwe workshop on 'Unwanted Pregnancies and Baby Dumping' raised the question of why women 'had to dump babies'.[31] Among the explanations were fear, in a context of changing values and customs, of angry rejection by parents or by the father of the child and, in the case of child mothers, fear of expulsion from school.

But children are often abandoned in ways that express the mother's concern for the child as well as her inability to cope. Like the caricatured single parent of Victorian England laying her bundle at the rich man's door, there are mothers who undoubtedly abandon children primarily to try to free them from their own fate.

Children are abandoned in hospitals, the lobbies of children's organisations, the homes of extended family members or of people known to be soft hearted – places where a child is likely to find concern and care. Other common choices, like busy streets and stations, would seem to betoken indifference but, in fact, may reflect the mother's sense of powerlessness and constitute the handing over of her child to the mercies of the community. Public places may also offer the advantage of enabling a fudging of the line in the mother's mind between the losing and abandoning of a child.

A young child, separated from a parent, even for an instant, in a busy Third World city is easily lost for ever. As a small boy, **Krishna**, now a Calcutta street child, became lost simply by wandering from his home.

'I came to a station. I clambered into a carriage and fell asleep. When I woke up I was in a different place. They asked me where I came from. I could not tell them. Some people asked me, "Who is your father?" I told them, "Dad". I never saw my parents again.'

A paradox of poverty is that while many children are simply abandoned by poor parents, they are highly prized by the unscrupulous for their value on the open market. Criminal gangs and 'agents' go to the trouble of abducting children for sale to the organisers of pornography, prostitution, begging, illegal adoption and slave labour. They are even taken for witchcraft purposes.

Children are rarely knowingly sold outright into danger by parents. Where one is sold in this way it is more usually to a middle man who falsely promises a better future for the children – for instance, placement in employment where he or she will learn a trade. This paradox may arise because, while parents see no other way forward, they are not usually interested in profiting from the abandonment of a child.

Krishna – lost as a small boy, he became a street child

[32] *Child Survival*, 'Culture, Scarcity and Maternal Thinking: Mother Love and Child Death in Northeast Brazil' by Nancy Scheper-Hughes.

Because a mother abandons one child it does not mean she abandons all her children or that she sees the abandonment as permanent. It may rather be that she sees her energies as limited and sacrifices one child, the better to ensure the survival chances of the others. Referring to the selective neglect of children, Nancy Scheper-Hughes reports on exploratory research into the behaviour of mothers in conditions of chronic scarcity and deprivation in Brazil.[32] The study was of women in a shanty-town of new rural migrants in the north-east; one of the many zones of extreme neglect to have emerged in the shadow of **Brazil's** now tarnished 'economic miracle'. **Such areas account for five million deaths of children below the age of five.**

Scheper-Hughes describes widespread selective **neglect of and maternal detachment** from those children who are perceived by their mothers to have a poor chance of surviving the conditions of slum life. In other words, the mother's concern for such children is withheld and they are left to die. The children so selected are most commonly already the victims of poverty-related diseases, thus the mothers effectively stand back and let the environment which is fashioned by political and economic negligence take its toll.

Their actions reflect an experience of life as a struggle between the strong and the weak. The mothers also act with a sense of needing to preserve their own depleted energies from the demands of non-survivors so as to be able to concentrate on children they see as fighters. This practice makes child survival a struggle of 'the weak against the weaker' – mirroring a society 'in which strength, force and power win out'.

At the same time the women do not find it easy to talk about the selective child negligence they feel forced to practice and it is clearly a source of pain to them. Furthermore a child singled out for neglect who disproves the mother's diagnosis and puts up a belated fight for survival will be gladly welcomed back into the protective custody and love of the family. Again, if an outside agency – such as a welfare or family support project – intervenes and improves the child's survival chances the mother may be delighted and show renewed interest in the child. Scheper-Hughes blames not the parents but the political economy that forces such decisions upon them.

Selective neglect of children has been recognised as a problem elsewhere. Trudee Able-Peterson (Streetwork Project) talks of 'throwaway' kids in New York:

'Their parents tend to be single parents who have four to five children. The 16-year-old is hanging out all night and doing drugs, and won't go to school and is endangering the younger ones. The mother says: "Take a walk, I'm going to take care of these small ones. I know you're robbing people, taking drugs."

'Fights erupt, the mother doesn't have the capabilities or the money to care for this large family and her husband is gone. She is a victim of society, too. That child becomes a throwaway, on the streets with no skill, experience, education.'

Referring to New York studies, Dr Mark Belsey, WHO chief of Maternal and Child Health and Family Planning, says: 'At the time when the family planning services and, even more so, when the Supreme Court ruling on abortion made safe induced abortion accessible to poor women – well-off women have always had access to safe abortion – there was a decrease in infant and perinatal mortality.' The numbers of children born underweight and of premature births also decreased and it was suspected that there was a decline in child abuse. 'By and large, you have a very low risk of battering and abuse and neglect in a family that is (a) prepared for child bearing and (b) wants that child.'

[33] *The Devadasi Problem*; William Carey Study and Research Centre, Calcutta, 1981–82.

[34] *Child Abuse and Neglect – Cross Cultural Perspective* ed. Jill E. Korbin, page 130, University of California Press, Berkeley, 1981.

There sometimes appears to be an undeclared cultural acceptance that parents may unburden themselves of children they cannot cope with. The Devadasi practice in a remote part of India allows an impoverished family to relieve itself of responsibility for a girl child by dedicating her to the love goddess, Yellamma. The daughter goes to live in the temple and there is made sexually available to a relatively wealthy patron.[33]

Hiroshi Wagatsuma[34] records that in Japan's feudal past infanticide was widely practised among impoverished peasants. The name given the practice, 'mabiki', meant 'thinning out', as in the cultivation of rice seedlings. The practice had some religious sanction in the belief that until the spirit of an ancestor entered the baby, an event indicated by its first cry, the infant was not human. Wet paper was placed over the new-born's face to smother it before the first cry. If a child destined to die in this way cried out before it was dispatched, it was allowed to live. Today in Japan there are very few unwanted children; Japanese parents rarely inflict any physical punishment on, or neglect their children and there is very little evidence of child abuse in the Western sense. However, there is a very high rate of child suicide, induced by parental and societal pressure to succeed, which amounts to abuse.[35]

[35] Ibid, page 121.

Infanticide is still found in parts of India, where cultural beliefs and practices define daughters as burdensome to their families and sons as positive assets. This bias exposes both young wives and girl children to great jeopardy in families that feel compelled to make survival choices between their members.

Under the dowry system, a girl's family is required to make payments to the bridegroom's family and to meet the wedding costs. The dowry payments demanded can be way out of balance with the earning capacity of the bride's family and dissatisfaction with the amount paid has given rise to the killings of young brides. (Official statistics for recorded dowry deaths are 999 in 1985, rising to 1786 in 1987 but a higher incidence is suspected.) Dowry payment is a major contributor to circumstances responsible for plunging families into debt

and embroiling them in repaying interest rates imposed by
money lenders.

In a remote area of Tamil Nadu and in some other parts of
India, female infanticide is practised to release poor families
from the crippling obligation of dowry payments. Some
childbearing families are said to cultivate poisonous plants,
usually oleander, to be in readiness to dispose of unwanted girl
babies. Though the practice is outlawed, it has been blamed for
a dramatic increase within ten years in the ratio of boys to girls.
Boys now account for 70 per cent of children under ten.[36]

Dowry both contributes to and expresses the denial of the
real economic value of girl children. It is part of the wider
cultural definition of women as having less value than men.

Jyotsna Chatterji, associate director of the Joint Women's
Programme in Delhi, says that while Indian parents generally

[36] 'Female
Infanticide – Born to
Die', *India Today*,
June 15, 1986, page
31 – cover story.

love their children 'when it comes to choosing between the girl and boy, it is the boy who gets the greater affection'.

'You can see the relative value reinforced in the popular media. For instance, in a TV serial a mother was singing a birthday song to her baby boy. She takes him and makes him sit and sings, "Whenever I think of love, it is you". She doesn't even look at the boy's sister who is sitting next to her – yet the girl needs love too.'

The bias works against women and girls at all class levels but renders girl children particularly vulnerable when a family is severely disadvantaged.

It operates even before the girl child is born. Pre-natal sex determination clinics using amniocentesis have proliferated. In a sample study it was found that of 8000 foetuses aborted 7999 were female. Though controlling legislation has been introduced in the State of Maharastra, clinics have opened in other states, according to material presented to a workshop on 'The Girl Child' held in Delhi at the end of 1988.[37]

The workshop identified other examples. Throughout their life cycle, females are fed less well than males. Girls get less milk, less frequently and for shorter periods of time. Though females are usually stronger than males at birth they account for just under half of the child population below the age of 15. Where there is a choice to be made the nutrition and health needs of girls will be neglected so that those of boys can be met. Girls are more likely to be denied an education than boys. They are commonly made into household drudges at home, both domestically and in the fields, until they are married, whereupon they enter a life of 'repeated childbearing and endless work'.

Both selective neglect of young children and infanticide have been explained as post-natal forms of birth control, resorted to by mothers who see their own capacity for parenting as undermined by poverty and too much childbearing. Its aim is to ensure the survival of at least some of the children. The abandonment of children may have a similar consequence. In many cases not to abandon a child in infancy is to expose him or her to inevitable neglect or rejection at a later stage.

'The most common reason boys leave home is that they lack a sense of belonging,' says Jones Muchendu, of boys in Nairobi. 'They think they are not wanted. Say a poor mother resorts to prostitution, a boy of 13 or so knows what is going on. Men come to the room and they're drunk. So whenever they come, the boy goes out. Even if he sleeps outside he doesn't seem to be missed. Gradually he moves out.'

Mothers may more actively contribute to their child's

[37] From a resumé of the conference carried in the Snehasadan Newsletter for Nov/Dec, 1988, Bombay.

departure. 'A mother can come to see her problems as being caused by her children. To relieve her feelings, she beats a child, who comes to think he's not wanted and so runs away.

'Mothers don't tell their children to go; their actions do it for them, even without their intending it.'

There is no more poignant example of what can happen to children who survive the early years of an impoverished childhood than that of disabled children in poor households. Lygia Bove, whose organisation in São Paulo, MAIS, specialises in helping children neglected in children's institutions and day-care centres, tells, among many tragic cases, of a blind child. 'She had no-one who talked to her or who took her for walks and, because she was left alone, she lost the use of her legs. Later she became mentally ill.'

There are rarely adequate support facilities for such children in rich countries. In the Third World provisions do not begin to meet their needs. (Of the approximately one million children in Kenya who suffer from some form of disability, only about 8000 are in special schools or care institutions and there are few programmes providing support in the community.) Such facilities as there are tend to be centralised, making it impossible for the poor to take advantage of them. So the disabled young go uneducated, unemployed and look to a future of dependency or beggary. Lack of opportunity to treat a particular disability often leads to a general disabling of a child.

In Kenya, **Florence** spends whole days lying in a simple wooden cot shut away from the sunlight in a dark one-roomed

Florence
JEREMY HARTLEY

slum house made of mud and wattle. Although the room is shared by a family of seven, Florence's cot seems surrounded by dead space. Sometimes she is left alone; at others in the care of a younger sister.

Born with cerebral palsy, she is now twelve and has severely restricted use of her limbs. She can do nothing for herself, nor does she communicate, except for the occasional cry and smile.

Florence's mother is out of the house a lot, making and selling baskets to help support the family. Her father says he often returns from his work as a poorly paid gate keeper to find Florence lying soiled and hungry in her cot. His wife has high blood pressure, he explains, and is not always able to attend to the child, though he feels she could do more. He does much of the housework, including washing Florence and doing the cooking. He says the family lives in debt. 'Sometimes I have to borrow from neighbours.'

'I have no time for Florence,' admits her mother.

The family lives in Kibera, where in the early 1980s a pioneering playgroup for disabled children was set up. Run by the Nairobi Family Support Service, with assistance from Action Aid-Kenya, it is open two mornings a week. Florence attends irregularly, depending on whether someone is available to carry her there. Although she is inanimate, she enjoys the atmosphere of the group and indicates her pleasure by laughing on the way there. Since attending the play group and receiving home visits, her eye focus has improved a little and she has become more sensitive to touch, but otherwise there has been little progress.

A social worker blames the severity of her disability on her having received no physiotherapy in the first few years of her life and subsequently only sporadic attention.

In impoverished conditions, disabled children who are not abandoned or lodged in children's institutions may find themselves abandoned within the confines of their own homes. Some spend their lives shut away, out of sight, almost starved of food. Even where parents take good care of their children physically, they may for reasons of ignorance or shame fail to meet other development needs. Marianne Kuitert, of Action Aid-Kenya, tells this story about a seven-year-old boy she came across in a town in northern Kenya:

'He is severely mentally retarded. Though he can walk, he can hardly speak. He has hardly any contact with people and you can see his skin is much lighter than that of his brothers and sisters.

'The mother is very attached to the child, she takes good care of him in that she feeds him well, washes him well. She gives her love in her own way. But she is so ashamed that she doesn't take the child on to the streets. That's why the skin is so light.

'Her boy gets no stimulation because he's always kept in the room behind a shop. There he sits on the floor, hitting his head, doing nothing. So we took him on to the street just to show the mother that if he had more stimulation he would stop banging himself. She was amazed by that and we hope she has continued to take him outside. But we still find a lot of children like that.'

Much disability in Third World children is born of poverty – its roots lie in the condition of the mothers during pregnancy and at birth; delivery problems; the child's environment in the crucial early years; preventable childhood diseases and malnutrition. Poverty also reinforces disability.

If the neglect or abandonment of disabled children are byproducts of the demands of the day-to-day struggle for survival they may also be underpinned by social and cultural beliefs.

Single mothers of disabled children may worry about their own marriage prospects, anxious that partners will be reluctant to take on what they see as a burden and fear the birth of more disabled children. In Kenya epilepsy is widely thought of as being caused by a curse. There are people who believe that if you touch a person who has fallen in an epileptic fit you too will contract epilepsy.

Neglect, abandonment or infanticide are all means resorted to by impoverished parents in order to improve the chances of their own survival and that of at least some of their children. Another and far more common means, where it is available, is to try to make children self-sufficient at an early stage.

DANGER – CHILDREN AT WORK

Ten-year-old **Minoti** gets up at four o'clock every morning of the week. She joins her friends, **Seema** and **Minu**, and they set off with other children of their village across the fields to Gutiarisharif Station, 40 minutes out of Calcutta.

They are going not to school but to work as domestic servants. Three hours of the girls' day are spent travelling by foot and train to and from the houses they work in. Invariably they are anxiously shepherded to the city and back either by Seema's and Minu's mother or by one of their older sisters, who also work in the city.

Minoti on the train to work

Minoti lives with her mother and smaller brother and sisters in a part of a village where most of the children work. The homes are crude tent-like structures made of mud and vegetation and cannot be locked or left unguarded. The people settled here unofficially as refugees from Bangladesh at the

Minu and Seema with Minoti

time of separation from Pakistan and there is some local hostility towards them. Some, like Minu and Seema's parents, lost land in the move. Most are now very poor and survive on the earnings of informal and casual work.

Minoti's income is vital to her family. Her father died two years ago. She has a younger sister who also works as a domestic servant. 'At first she was paid nothing because she was living there. Now they pay her ten rupees (50 pence) a month.'

Minoti's mother has to stay at home to look after her five-year-old brother. She makes popadoms at home for a city company.

Minoti works daily for four separate families. 'In each house I wash the dishes and clothes. I clean, sweep and grind the spices.' The cutting of onions and grinding of chillies is unpleasant work and harsh on the hands; so is the soap she has to use for washing. 'I like cooking but mainly don't get a chance.'

Minoti serving tea

Though working children risk physical abuse, none of Minoti's employers beats her, but some are unkind. Sometimes they keep her late, making her do jobs again, so that she misses her train. Either the others must then wait for her or she must go home unaccompanied. One old lady in particular bullies and shouts at her a lot and in another house, where both parents go to work, the children mistreat her. 'They throw water over me.' From the four households she earns 25, 35, 40 and 60 rupees respectively (together just £8) a month.

The trains she commutes by are very crowded and there is a lot of pushing and shoving. Recently she was hurt in a fall from the train and was off work for several days.

'When I get home in the early evening I prepare and light the tula (clay stove) and my mother cooks. Sometimes I clean the house a little bit, but mostly my mother does that. After we eat we sleep.' There is no time or energy and little opportunity for recreation. Minoti's workload increases at weekends in those households where her employers like to entertain.

Minoti went to school briefly when she was small. Like the other working girls, she would like to go to school again – 'but how can I? I have all this work.' She believes her brother will go to school, 'if he gets a chance. But very few boys, even, go to school from our area – only those whose parents have a permanent job.' Seven of the eight children in Seema and Minu's family do casual work of some kind. An older brother has to stay to guard the family's few possessions against marauding dogs and local troublemakers. Seema, who is about nine, has worked for only a year and earns £1.25 a month.

Their sister, **Mani**, started working in houses a few years ago at the age of six or seven. She now goes each day to the city to

Mani making poppadums

fetch spiced dough, which she brings back to her home to make into poppadums on a piece-work basis for a major manufacturer. If she makes three kilogrammes a day, she earns 50 pence. But she finds the work very lonely and arduous.

The children's mother, Bisanti, started working two years ago after their father became too ill to continue as a construction worker. That was the end of any of the children's education hopes. Bisanti works in two houses earning £4 a month and accompanies her own and other children in and out of the city each day and between the houses they work in, concerned that no harm befall them.

Asked at what age a child should start working, Bisanti says: 'Why should a child work? Children shouldn't.'

If she had the power to change something in her children's lives, what would it be?

'Why do you ask me this foolish question? If I had any power I would not have brought my children for this work. Why ask me this question?'

Child domestic workers who live in the homes of their employers are even more vulnerable to exploitation and they experience far greater loneliness than those who come and go each day.

When, at the age of twelve, **Domingas** Vito Feliciano ran away to Recife (Brazil) to escape a life of labouring on the land, she followed a course taken by many young girls with their parents' active encouragement. Her older sister had arranged a job for her as a domestic worker.

'Generally children are brought into the towns to work by an adult relative who is already working,' says Nila Cordeira dos Santos, President of the Domestic Workers' Association. 'Employers like it because the child feels some obligation to stay if a relative has helped them find the work.

'Child domestic work is a serious problem in Brazil, particularly in the north-east. It's because things are tough inland. People go hungry. Sometimes mothers will take their daughters to employers and say, "Just tell her to do whatever you want. Just take care of her." Really they are looking to the employer to be a second mother.

'So the child doesn't have much choice. The children often work without a salary; they get cast-off clothes from the employer's children; they get food – food is the big attraction. They start that way.' In the slums children as young as seven or eight are to be found employed in domestic work.

Domingas has had five jobs in four years. 'I spent ten months in the first house. There were six people. My job was to wash

their clothes, look after the children and cook. I had no day off
– I worked from six in the morning to ten at night. I would take
the children to school and give them their milk last thing at
night. I was given no pay; they gave me what I needed – food,
clothes and part-time schooling, but I never saw money. I was
allowed two hours in the evening to study but, when I got back
from school, I had to carry on working. I stayed with the class
for only four months. I was too tired to study.'

Children are vulnerable to sexual abuse in all kinds of
employment, but no more so than in domestic work. In her first
job, Domingas narrowly escaped sexual assault by a teenage
visitor to the house. 'He hid in my room when I went to bath.
When I got back something made me look under the bed.
There he was. I screamed and he ran out. I'm sure that if I'd
just switched off the light and got into bed he would have done
something to me. It is common for employers of young
domestics or their sons to rape them.'

In her second job, Domingas was paid a little money but her
employer would not let her study and began to make her do the
cleaning at a spiritualist centre in addition to the household
tasks. 'There were ten people at the centre. I had to wash
ceremonial clothes – there were lots of them – fancy white
clothes. I had to wash these clothes and leave them immaculate,
white and shining.'

Domingas left her third job soon after taking it because she
was frightened of the two teenage sons. In her fourth job she
worked as a nanny. Again she was expected to work a 16 hour
day and was paid less than the minimum salary and not allowed
to study. The people were 'nice enough, but they expected me
to hold this two-year-old child all the time and my back was
giving me a lot of pain. I left because I couldn't cart the child
around endlessly.'

'I'm in job number five now – with a neighbour of my sister's
employer. She is a very straightforward person. She pays quite
well. I work eight to five. I'm off from two on Saturday
afternoons *and* I get holidays.' Best of all, at the age of 16,
Domingas has at last found an opportunity to study part time.
She is also able to pool her earnings with her sister to rent a
simple, bare room and so no longer has to live in.

Are there any good things about being a maid?

'I don't really like this job at all. What I really hate most is
the washing up – it's endless.

'It's very lonely work. The husband and daughter go out to
work and the wife goes off to the houses of friends. Sometimes
I get frightened of opening the door because it's a flat and I
don't know who will come. Sometimes I will ask through the

door who it is but I don't understand the answer. Then I don't know if I should open the door or not. I open it trembling.'

It is not just robbers she fears. Some time ago a young domestic worker who opened the door to strangers was taken away by two men and disappeared. Despite energetic efforts by the Domestic Workers' Association to have her traced, she has not been found.

How would Domingas advise another twelve-year-old embarking on the same occupation?

'I'd say watch out for the working hours and make sure you can study and that you are not too tired to study – a twelve-year-old has to learn. I would like to work in another profession one day and I am doing the best I can to improve my level.'

What does she think of the employers who made her work long hours and would not let her study?

'I am ashamed of this profession. Employers dictate the conditions; we accept, or not. They live in the days of slavery. That is how they think.'

Millions of children work in different countries as domestic servants. No group is more vulnerable to the whims of employers but little is recorded of their lives.

Nila Cordeira dos Santos, who was herself a child domestic worker, describes the Cinderella-like existence. 'You play with your employer's children but if anything goes wrong it is your fault. The law which says children must study is not obeyed. The employers' children go to school. You get no schooling. Your employer may beat you or threaten to send you back to the interior if you don't do as you are told or come up to expectations. Your room is hot and cramped.

'The work is totally isolating. You feel desperate. There is no pleasure. You go out often but in your uniform and to look after children. You are always with the family but you don't participate. You miss your family. I cried a lot when I left my home.

'The danger of sexual abuse is not only within the employer's house. Girls in this situation are very vulnerable. They don't know anything about anything – they don't read. They may try to go out in the evenings. Then they are an easy mark to the first boy to show them affection. Many get pregnant; they can drift into prostitution. Some of those who do find they prefer it.

'These children are totally beyond the protection of the law – we see a few cases in the paper of a child being burned, or wounded or even thrown from a building, but nothing much comes of it.'

'Superexploited' by their employers, child domestic workers

[38] *Working Children*, Chapter 4 'Sellers and Servants', by Zimena Bunster and Esla M. Chaney.

may be tempted to steal from them. Whether they do or not they are likely to be blamed for anything that goes missing.

A report that looks at 'pitiful situations' of child domestic workers in Peru says that girls, many of them under the age of twelve, are commonly required to do the work of adults.[38] Under machismo cultural convention they may be regarded as sexually available to the males of the house. Some are severely beaten for minor misdemeanours, such as breaking a plate or forgetting to run an errand.

Poor mothers will entrust a child to an employer on a godparenting basis, giving the employer 'absolute rights of ownership' and an obligation to look after the child's welfare. Such children may be made to work long hours as domestic servants in homes and small restaurants for little or no pay.

Dr Philista Onyango, who headed a research programme into child labour in Kenya, also finds that children in domestic work are expected to do adult work and for far lower wages, to work beyond their physical capability and are daily confronted by their own exploitation. 'The child is disappointed because other children of her age are not working. She sees she is disadvantaged.'

[39] *All Work and No Play – Child Labour Today* devised by Alec Fyfe, A TUC Resource Book, TUC 1985.

A childhood free of work and devoted to a mix of pleasure and education is a modern invention that began in Europe in the 17th Century with the children of rich families. It became more general with modern industrialisation and the introduction in the 19th Century of compulsory education.[39]

Minding a roadside stall in the Andean mountains

Industrialisation in 19th Century Britain saw a particularly vicious exploitation of child labour and extensive child employment is still practised in the developed world today, notably in some southern European countries, particularly Italy, as well as in the United States.

Most of the children working in the US are Hispanic migrants illegally and exploitatively employed on farms and plantations. In 1978 it was officially estimated that a million Mexican children were working mainly in agriculture in the US.[40]

In Britain there have been occasional exposures of child labour in recent years but, though many children work part-time, it is generally thought to be in ways that do not interfere with their schooling and for 'pocket money' rather than essential family income.

This view is, however, countered in a report by journalist Caroline Moorehead.[41] She finds there is exploitation of part-time child labour 'on farms, in sweat-shops, in the kitchens of restaurants and above all in hosiery and leather garment businesses, especially among outworkers and small makeshift factories.' Most of the children are employed illegally.

An Oxford newspaper delivery boy says he is convinced some of the children who do paper rounds are under age. In his view the work is definitely exploitative. He earns £8.50 for what amounts to a seven hour week and has to carry loads weighing up to three and a half stone.

Conditions of child labour in poor countries today are often likened to the conditions in 19th Century England.

Working children are found throughout the Third World. In many countries you can see them working almost wherever you look – in the fields, on earthworks or tending animals in the rural areas; in engineering and auto repairs shops; in small roadside tea stalls, restaurants and hotels; in the streets washing cars, portering, hawking, on building sites, lifting and carrying heavy loads.

There are others who are less visible. They work in the privacy of their own homes. They do domestic work, mind younger siblings, do piece-work (like Mani's poppadum making) either alongside their parents or on their own. They also work in small factory establishments making string, recycled paper bags, electronic components and a million and one other products. In some areas they work in quarries and mines.

[40] *All Work and No Play – Child Labour Today*; Alec Fyfe, page 49.

[41] *School Age Workers in Britain Today*; Caroline Moorehead, Anti-Slavery Society, London, 1987.

Girl looking after a smaller girl

*Peasant children
recruited from North-
eastern Thailand polish
gems in tiny factories*
From 'Stolen
Childhood', a Cox
Newspaper report on
the exploitation of
Children
Picture: Rick McKay

Workers for a Managua coal merchant

[42] *Sellers and Servants – Working Women in Lima and Peru* by Ximena Bunster and Elsa M. Chaney, Chapter 4 'Working Children', page 171.

Even before they can walk, children accompany their working mothers, taking in the environment in which they may soon themselves work. 'Bundled babies are in a sense already sharing their mothers' work day. Sleepy baby faces, smiling baby faces, impatient baby faces, serious baby faces peek over their mothers' shoulders watch as the women coax undecided customers into commercial transactions,' write Zimena Bunster and Esla M. Chaney of Peruvian street sellers.[42]

Few large modern factories employ children. But there are whole industries which do so, like carpet making in India and Morocco. The gem polishing industry in Jaipur, the match-making industry in Sivakasi and the glass making industry at Firozabad are among those best documented in India as relying heavily on child labour. In India, as in most countries, there are laws regulating the employment of children. However, restrictions usually only apply to manufacturing units with more than a specified number of workers. Employers commonly organise their enterprises into small units of production, or farm work out on a piece-rate basis to people to do in their own homes to avoid being subjected to factory regulations, including those which bar the employment of children.

*Children from a fishing
village near Calcutta*

Child rural workers

India has the world's largest number of working children. It is officially estimated to have more than 17 million child workers below the age of 14, but 44 million is thought by many experts to be more realistic. In Brazil nine million children below the legal age of twelve work and a million of them are sole family breadwinners.

A distinction needs to be made between the practice of children working alongside and learning skills from their parents, as in traditional cultures, and their work in a cash labour market. In the former situation there was no formal education and work was the main channel for a child's development and socialisation. In the latter, children can find themselves in work environments that directly threaten their health and development and subject them to extreme exploitation. 'As soon as you have to go and work for money, it becomes a problem,' says Dr Philista Onyango. 'Family work wasn't for money, even though you could quantify it. But now the child works to earn a wage.' The work does not prepare the child for adulthood and prevents him or her being educated and the child must share the earnings with the family and 'so it becomes more like a business exercise. This is what I call exploitative'.

Throughout the Third World the transition from traditional rural to capitalist cash economics, marked by the displacement of people from the land and the undermining of traditional

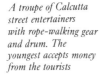

A troupe of Calcutta street entertainers with rope-walking gear and drum. The youngest accepts money from the tourists

skills, has greatly changed and continues to change the relationship between children and work.

Periswami is in the middle of this change process. He is a shy but eager young worker in one of the 300 granite quarries in and around Bangalore. India's fastest growing city, it is largely built of the local stone.

Hammering in the chisels – Periswami at work

The first job in Periswami's day is to help sharpen and re-temper the chisels, after which he is first in his family to get down to the work site. He works a full eight hour day and is often the last to return home.

Most of the quarries are leased from the State by contractors. Their wealth and power has grown with the city but the people who cut the stone have remained poor. The practice of labour bondage, by which a person agrees to work for a period of time on subsistence wages in exchange for a loan, has survived here, as elsewhere in India, despite being outlawed. Interest rates imposed on such loans generally make repayment very difficult. Some workers even have to extend their terms of bondage to their children. One bonded labourer said: 'Being bonded is like being a frog in a well. You go round and round and there is no way out.'

Periswami is now free of the likelihood of bondage. The workers at his quarry were able to seize control because they found that their boss was cheating the state and did not have a valid lease. So they applied for the lease without telling him and then gave him his marching orders. They were supported by a Catholic-backed organisation, the Worker's Centre of the Diocese of Bangalore, which has helped 'liberate' a number of quarries where bondage has been practised, prompting some of the established quarry bosses to provide better conditions for their workers.

Almost every quarry worker's story begins with a flight from rural poverty. Most come from unirrigated marginal or rainshadow areas, often great distances away from the state capital. The contractors send labour touts to such areas, particularly during a drought, with promises of a better life. They may offer a small cash token of good will. Those who take the offer move from desperation to deepening dependency.

Periswami's grandfather, Veraswami, was offered a loan of just 15 rupees (less than £1) to move from neighbouring Tamil Nadu state.

'In the beginning, I thought the quarry owner was a good man. I came with nothing and he gave me food. He loaned me materials to build a shelter for my wife and children – so, I agreed to work for him.'

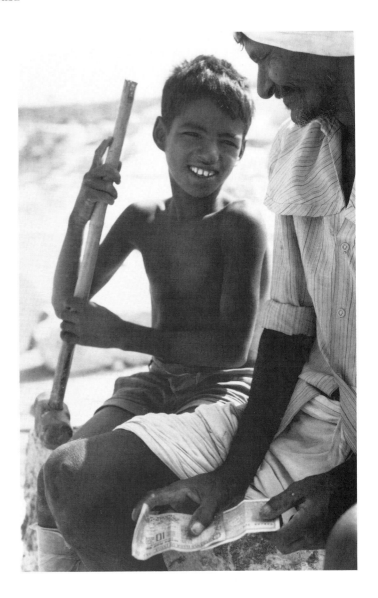

Periswami and his grandfather discuss their earnings

It was only later that Veraswami found that he and his whole family were expected to work every day, throughout the hours of daylight. Quarrying requires more than one pair of hands. It needs one person to hold the chisel while another swings the hammer.

'When I was bonded I worked as a slave,' says Veraswami. 'We were paid twelve rupees for cutting a hundred blocks. There was a fence around this quarry then and the master never let all the members of one family leave the enclosure at the same time in case they ran away.' Cutting 100 blocks can

take three days of preparation, blasting and cutting. It involves
the purchase of coal and dynamite. There were jibes or blows
for the workers when the contractor felt they were not
labouring hard enough.

Periswami is fortunate. The quarry where he works with his
family was liberated nine years ago and the workers now run it
as a cooperative. He and his grandfather often talk about the
old days of bondage. 'As free men, we can take a break when
we want to. When you are bonded, you are like an animal, not a
human being. We had no time to think. No time to talk to each
other.'

In a liberated quarry, working conditions are more
companionable and hark back to traditional family work
patterns. Families work in teams – wives and sisters hold
chisels or hammers, trusting the sure aim of their partners.
Everyone has a part to play, small girls learn from their mothers
how to chip stone to make gravel. They prepare food and bring
water for the family to have while they work.

*Children often begin to
work by copying their
mothers who have to
work and care for them
at the same time*

Periswami needs no coercion to put in a good day's work. He
enjoys the feeling that his labour contributes to the family
income. His family is proud of him, and he has the air of a
happy child.

But he faces many problems which may yet blunt his youth

and hopefulness. Though the quarriers earn more now that they are 'liberated' they are still poor and must work hard.

The work is dangerous as well as arduous. Cuts from rock splinters are common. More serious injuries can occur when the rock is blasted. Periswami's grandmother lost her hand in a blast.

The weight of the hammers and their percussion against the hard rock is punishing on a growing body. Heat and light blaze back from the blue rock. Like everyone else who works in this harsh reflected light eight hours a day, Periswami has difficulty while his eyes adjust at the end of the day. Most quarry workers suffer from nightblindness. Working surrounded by fine dust causes chest problems for some.

Since the quarry's liberation, schooling has been provided for the workers' children. The parents enthusiastically quarried the stone and built the schoolhouse. The Workers' Centre pays the teacher's salary and each child brings a contribution of a rupee a week. So far about 50 per cent of the children of schoolgoing age are attending the school.

Periswami's father, Kuppaswami, an active member of the workers' organisation, says he wanted him to attend. 'We suffered a lot not even being able to sign our own names,' he explains, but Periswami has chosen not to go to school. Asked why, the boy replies simply that scin ' is too hard.

But while he is missing the education that might give him other work options, his future as a quarryman may be shortlived. Though the quarriers now regulate their own working conditions they still have no control over the distribution and marketing of their produce. Contractors still own the lorries that take the granite to the city. The quarry people complain that drivers and contractor's agents frequently try to cheat them.

As worker organisation in the industry has strengthened generally there has been a new shift by the bosses with capital reserves towards mechanisation. Periswami's future may be a losing competition with machines bought from profits made on the backs of previous worker generations.

The industrialising process and impoverishment in the Third World have seen the erosion or loss of parental protection of working children. Even where children continue to work alongside their parents producing goods for the commercial market – such as matches, or sticks of incense – the process is not one of a handing over of skills so much as a joint working of a treadmill. Children employed in their own homes along with other family members on a piece-rate basis scarcely pause in

*Packing match boxes on
a project near Varanasi*

their labours to look up even when a stranger comes into the
room.

The main single reason families place their children in work
is impoverishment. The children's income is crucial to family
survival. Among other reasons are that there is no schooling
available in the area, or the children are not doing well at
school, or the parents believe that school will not improve their
children's ability to find work.

The mother of a sweeper, one of the lowliest occupations in
India, said: 'Why should I waste my time and money on sending
my daughter to school where she will learn nothing of use. . . .
My elder girl who is fifteen years old will be married soon. Her
mother-in-law will put her to cleaning latrines somewhere. Too
much of schooling will only give girls big ideas, and then they
will be beaten up by their husbands or abused by their in-
laws.'[43]

[43] From a study of
sweeper women by
sociologist Malavika
Karlekar as quoted in
The Hindustan Times,
October 2, 1988, *No
Time to be a Girl* by
Dr Neera Burra.

The mother's viewpoint would seem to have both objective validity and to be an example of how the poor get locked into a fatalistic 'psychology of poverty', as one development worker put it, that in itself becomes 'a major impediment to development'. There are also parents who place their children in employment to keep them away from the bad company of the streets. And there is a minority of parents who actively exploit their children's earning capacity.

Such is the desperation of poor families in Third World countries that many will place their children in work without pay, simply to secure a daily meal for them. This may help explain why some children start work as young as five. Others will hand their children over to an employer in the hope that they will pick up some skills that will equip them for better employment at a future date.

In such circumstances the scope for exploitation of child labour is virtually unlimited. While poverty deprives parents of the ability to secure the welfare and development of their children, many employers show themselves only too willing to put children to work on an exploitative basis.

[44] *The Working Children of Urban India* by Dr B.R. Patil, Indian Institute of Management, Bangalore 1986.

Surveys such as *The Working Children in Urban India*, conducted in Bangalore by Dr B.R. Patil, have shown that a large majority of working children would rather be at school. An even larger majority would, if they must work, like to be getting some further education and proper vocational training.[44]

A lot of child workers go to school part-time, but many if not most of the world's working children are employed on a basis that leaves them with neither energy nor time for studies or training. The majority are employed in unregistered establishments. It is not uncommon for children to double up as domestic workers in the homes of their employers after the day's work is done. Two thirds of the children in the Bangalore study worked eight to twelve hours a day. Ten per cent worked for more than that or had no appointed limit to their hours. The younger the children, the longer their working day tended to be. Many felt their employers were always wanting more work out of them. A majority felt they were treated unkindly and a considerable minority that they were ill- or harshly treated.

The desperation of parents for their children to secure a future may prompt them to support cruelty by an employer. A construction worker in Calcutta described his son's working conditions: 'He was eight-years-old when he started work at a garage. They paid him nothing but they gave him snacks and he learned something about filling cars that had been dented. He was working from six in the morning till nine at night. He then had to spend a long time washing because he was so dirty. He used to be beaten if he did a job badly. I forced him to go because I hoped he would learn something. I would chase him to work. When he complained of the beatings, I explained they were beating him for his future. After two years he left. He didn't want to go anywhere. He just wanted to sit with the other children at home.'

A Kenya study directed by Dr Philista Onyango, based partly on interviews with 21 child workers – in domestic, tea and coffee estate and forestry employment – found they worked for up to 16 hours a day without holidays. All 21 reported some kind of maltreatment by their employers; not being paid, being confined to the workplace and prevented from meeting with other children, being beaten and locked out. Nineteen slept on the floor at their place of employment. More than half the children had lost one or both parents and the majority of those working as domestics were sent by their parents to Nairobi from the rural areas without knowing they would be expected to work.[45]

[45] A Report on the Steering Committee Meeting of the Task Force on Child Labour and Health; World Health Organisation MCH/85.2.

Working children suffer abuse at the hands of both their employers and their fellow adult workers. A fifth of those interviewed for the Bangalore study admitted they suffered various kinds of physical abuse from adult workers inside and outside the workplace. In the hotel industry, children often had to sleep in the same room as adult workers.

Boy worker

[46] *Child Labour and Exploitation in the Carpet Industry*; Professor B.N. Juyal, Indian Social Institute, New Delhi, 1987.

Despite parental hopes, much of the work done by children does not provide a good basis on which to develop skills, nor does it give better assurance of employment in adult life. As in traditional subsistence economies, the bulk of the work done by children is helping, fetching and carrying. Little actual training is given – their terms of employment, says Dr Patil, constitute 'a denial of education and training'.

Two thirds of all the carpet weavers in an Indian regional survey were found to be children. Ninety per cent were completely illiterate.[46] While the children were being trained in carpet making skills they were employed within an industry that favours the employment of children over adults (employers justify the use of child workers on the grounds that small nimble fingers are necessary to the making of fine carpets). Extensive child employment takes place in a context of extensive adult unemployment and while that situation lasts there is no guarantee that a working childhood will lead to a working adulthood. Meanwhile illiteracy leads to an adult life as an unskilled labourer, a category that is already greatly oversupplied. Many a labouring child is destined to grow into a parent dependent upon the earning power of his or her children. Because it takes work from adults, child labour recreates the conditions for its own perpetuity.

The development of girl children is even more cribbed and confined by work than that of boys. Parents expect girls to marry and be supported by their husbands. Particularly in India, where the girl leaves the home upon marrying while the boy stays and is viewed by parents as their 'old-age insurance',

Child rural worker near Calcutta. This little girl had at least three kinds of work, making fishing nets, making envelopes and bags out of used paper and helping with household duties

[47] *No Time to be a Girl* by Dr Neera Burra, *The Hindustan Times*, October 2, 1988.

[48] *The Working Children of Urban India* by Dr B.R. Patil, page 44.

[49] *Working Trends: Current trends and policy responses* by Assefa Bequele and Jo Boyden, ILO, Geneva, 1988.

[50] *The Working Children of Urban India* by Dr B.R. Patil.

[51] *All Work and No Play – Child Labour Today*; Alec Fyfe, page 46.

[52] *Child Labour and Exploitation in the Carpet Industry* by B.N. Juyal.

there is little to be gained by investing in girl children. Fewer girls than boys are given the chance of an education. Because of their illiteracy, they are forced to take the lowest paid and least skilled work.[47] Parents may also be reluctant to let girl children work outside the home between the attainment of puberty and their getting married. In India girl children who go out of the home to work do so at a younger age than boys and are later withdrawn, giving employers even less motive for investing in their development than they do that of boys.[48]

Much of girls' work goes unrecognised as such even by their parents. They help their mothers in low-paid piece work and carry out home duties to free their parents for other employment.

Children are favoured by employers over adults because they 'can be easily laid off when business is slack; they cost less; and they have no rights as workers and cannot join trades unions'.[49] Studies have shown that the profitability of those industries that employ children goes up by more than 25 per cent. Such industries tend to be labour intensive, low cost and to use low technology. Because children are inefficient, it is generally unprofitable to employ them in capital intensive industries.

Children often go unpaid altogether or are paid only nominal wages for a 'probationary' or 'training' period which may last for a number of years.[50]

Those involved in bonded labour (more usual in rural areas) may work for years virtually without pay until the sums advanced either to them or their parents have been repaid with interest, if ever. The bondage or sale of children is not peculiar to India. In Brazil children are reportedly sometimes placed by their parents in domestic work as a way of paying off debts. In Italy, in 1976, the suicide of 14-year-old shepherd boy Michele Colonna temporarily shocked the Italian public. He had been sold to a farmer at the age of ten by his father and tried unsuccessfully to return home several times.[51]

There have been extreme cases in the Third World of children being either abducted or bought from their parents by agents or criminal gangs and kept in slave like working conditions. Writing about 'coercive labour' conditions in the carpet weaving industry, B.N. Juyal, Professor of Sociology and Rural Development at the Gandhian Institute of Studies, Varanasi, cites an incident in which 114 children were rescued from carpet weaving businesses. Some bore marks of beatings and physical torture, inflicted for mistakes in their work, some had been branded for trying to escape. At night they were locked up.[52]

Children are easily cheated by their bosses and by other

older workers. Money is deducted from their pay for 'mistakes', failure to meet work quotas and other real or imagined misdemeanours. There are cases of their being taken on as casual workers and then sacked on some pretence just before they are due to be paid. In plantation work, the quantity of crops they have harvested may be under-rated by supervisors.

Investigations into scandalous working conditions of children in 19th Century Britain's textile mills in the early stages of industrialisation found children with nervous disorders, deformities, stunted growth, digestive complaints and tuberculosis. Such complaints are still common among the world's working children today who also face many additional hazards. They are commonly exposed to dangerous materials, chemicals, manufacturing processes and equipment.

Sugar cane crushing – many child workers are exposed to unguarded machinery

53 'Glass Factories of Firozabad' by Dr Neera Burra, *Economic and Political Weekly* November 15 and 22, 1986.

Dr Neera Burra, the author of many detailed and descriptive reports on the conditions of children in industries in India, compares them with those in 19th Century Britain. She describes child workers in one of the less salubrious factories in the Firozabad glass industry, where in 1986 almost 50,000 children below the age of 14 were working[53]: 'The whole factory floor was strewn with broken glass and naked electric wires were to be seen everywhere. The noise in the factory was deafening and there was hardly space to move without bumping into somebody or other. At least 30 to 40 per cent of the labour ... seemed to be made up of children of the ages 8 to 13 years.'

Glass factory workers,
Firozabad
RICK MCKAY/
COX NEWSPAPERS

[54] 'Child Labour in
India: Poverty,
Exploitation and
Vested Interest' by
Dr Neera Burra,
Social Action Vol 36
July–September
1986.

In this environment, the children scoop molten glass from
fiercely hot tank furnaces and carry it on the end of long poles
to adult workers for shaping. Burn injuries and accidents to
children are 'frequent'.

She describes another factory, lit by kerosene lamps, without
ventilation and full of soot, where children work for twelve hour
stretches crouched over acetylene flames joining bangles. They
suffer from 'enormous eye strain' and 'a high incidence of
tuberculosis'.

In numerous industries children are put to work in cramped,
ill-lit, unventilated and damp conditions. Child diamond
workers who labour in such rooms in Surat are sacked when
their eye-sight begins to fail.[54] Young children who work
joining fine wires together in micro-computer factories and in
the embroidery industry suffer eye-sight damage within a few
years. Children are also prone to accidents in the workplace, for
various reasons including their inexperience and the fact that
they work with implements designed for adults.

Labour increases nutritional requirements and many working
children are badly and erratically fed. Dr Mark Belsey of WHO
says working children divert energy into work instead of growth,
stunting both their physical stature – by up to 30 per cent of
their biological potential – and the stamina they will have in
adulthood. 'You're consuming your adult capital,' he says. P.M.
Shah, also of WHO, writes: 'Severe malnutrition, anaemia,
hard labour, fatigue and inadequate sleep make them more
susceptible to infectious diseases.' He adds that children are

[55] *Child Labour and Health: Problems and Prospects* ed. Usha Naidu and Kamina Kapadia, *Working Children: Health Problems*; P.M. Shah. Tata Institute of Social Sciences, Bombay, 1985.

given the dirtiest jobs and exposed to insanitary conditions.[55]

Employers generally like to think of and present themselves as the benefactors of their employees and the employers of children are no exception. The conditions in which children work often deride such pretensions. But, although the employer may be the immediate exploiter of children, he must be seen as operating within an exploitative system. Nabi Ahmed, who suffers from severe breathing troubles after many years of working in electroplating, has now stopped doing the work himself and employs others. Asked by Neera Burra why he did not employ his own children, he replied:

'So long as I am alive, I will never let my children work. Look at my condition. I cannot even breathe easily. I do not let my children even enter the premises. Both my boys are studying.'

Children in a
Managua market

[56] 'Exploitation of child workers in the Lock Industry of Aligarh' by Dr Neera Burra, *Economic and Political Weekly*, 11 July 1987.
[57] *Sellers and Servants – Working Women in Lima and Peru* by Ximena Bunster and Elsa M. Chaney.

However, Ahmed has to employ other children to avoid his own children working. That he described as 'the way of the world'.[56]

The readiness of some employers to exploit the children of the poor contrasts shabbily with the motivations of working children themselves. Periswami is not alone in the pride he takes in his contribution to his family. Ximena Buster and Esla Chaney observe in children in Peru a deep affection for their mothers and strong feelings of solidarity with their families.[57] The children 'explain at length that they work because they love their mothers and they want to help them'. Two children they quote said – 'I work for my mother, to help her, otherwise we wouldn't have any food to put in our mouths,' and 'I give my mother all the money I earn; I'd like to give her more because I have so many small brothers and sisters and my father and I are the only ones who work'.

Sadly, in time working children can easily begin to see their parents as their exploiters.

In some cases they are right.

Interviewed for the periodical, *Child Workers in Asia*, Thai child demolition worker, Dum or Tid Wiweklum, said he was paid less than the legal minimum wage by his boss. Though he pays a proportion of his earnings to his father he has to race him to the pay office or, 'I get nothing . . . He takes all the money for liquor. I have to go off somewhere and stay out of the way. If he asks me for money and I don't give it to him, I get kicked.'

Children leave their homes prematurely for a variety of reasons. Most commonly in industrialised nations they are abused or neglected or feel unwanted; some are just bored and strike out to claim a more exciting future than life with their parents offers. Child boredom can be as much a feature of wealth as poverty – the runaway daughter of a multi-millionaire told a New York police officer she had left home because she was bored. Some children flee the pressure of the parents' or another mentor's expectations of what they should be. Some are lured away by peer groups and the false promise of the bright lights. Some succumb to regular drug taking, making it impossible for them to stay at home.

Says Mark Raskin (Day Top Drug Rehabilitation Programme): 'A child is a child whether the parents have a lot of money or don't have a lot of money. Children need the same things. They need love, they need attention. As they're growing into adolescence . . . the children's rebellious side comes out. That's almost normal for any teenager. That is where the communication breaks down. The parents lay the law down because they're the parents, it's "their house". Then the child thinks, "I can't talk to these people".'

In the industrialising Third World, young children leave their homes for similar reasons. But more commonly the home has simply been overwhelmed by poverty and social change in its ability to support and protect them. A parent or parents die prematurely. Children are abandoned or they abandon their homes. Some leave with the idea of helping their families. Working children may see themselves as escaping the exploitation of their parents.

A worker with street children in Bangalore believes the latter to be a major reason why children end up on the streets. 'They fall to thinking, "My parents are only there for the money. I'll go away and work for myself."'

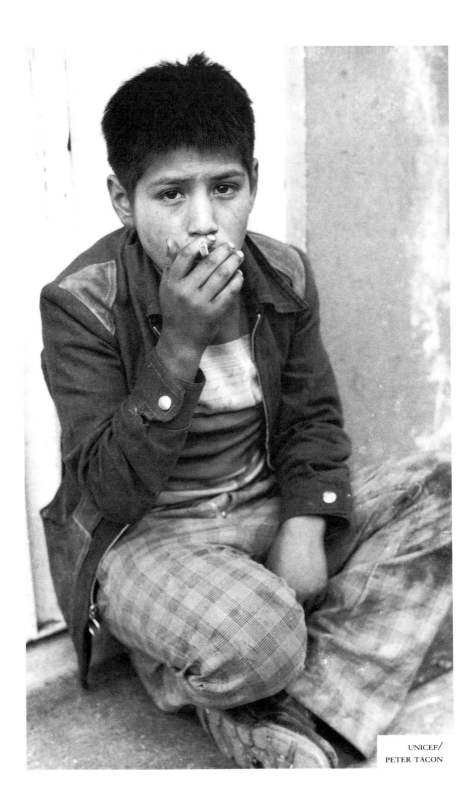

Artful dodgers

At first it was very hard sleeping out in the cold. But I got used to living on the street and did all right. I liked being able to do what I wanted. But sometimes I felt really bad because I needed my mother.

Carlos, a Colombian boy, speaking of his life on the streets at the age of eight

The child is hungry and sees much food everywhere in supermarkets, sleeps in the streets and sees churches and houses that are empty. He or she is half naked and sees all these clothes – what greater violence is there than that. It's one that affects the person psychologically, internally.

Father Armiro Amigo, Brazil

Walk around New York City and you'll see what you see in Calcutta. You'll see people dying on the streets and you'll see people stepping over them. Many of them are not children but some are. You won't see a lot of the children, they're crawling in and among everywhere, the different bus and train stations, in the subways, burnt-out buildings, tenements, houses – surviving those type of conditions that are very prevalent in the Third World.

Elizabeth Burnell, Covenant House, US

KAMIA, KUMAR AND THE STREET CHILDREN

Kamia

Kamia stirs beneath his covering of waste plastic and rubs his eyes. The world he awakes to is that of an eleven-year-old alone in Mathare Valley. Home is the confined roof space of a smelly public toilet. Hardly desirable accommodation but finding a safe place to sleep is one of the biggest headaches for Nairobi's street children.

Kamia is not overburdened by possessions. He dresses in one half of his worldly goods. He owns two pairs of trousers and two torn T-shirts which leave patches of his flesh exposed.

He clambers down from his room in the rafters and, carrying a large plastic bag, sets off for Ngara, a plusher part of the city with stone and brick houses. If he has money, he takes a bus. Otherwise he walks the four kilometres. There he meets up with street friends, shares cigarettes and chats, and searches the rubbish bins for charcoal. Fuel for cooking and warmth is expensive in Nairobi. Street boys can earn small sums by rummaging through rubbish tips for bits of charcoal that have not burned away completely. 'I'm always looking for charcoal wherever I go in the city. But Ngara is the best place for it.' Kamia goes about his activities with a paradoxical air – at once mischievous child and earnest man of business.

In the afternoon he goes to see a 'mzee' (a respectful term for an older man). The man had once seen him sniffing petrol. 'He told me it was bad for me and I should stop. He would help me if I did. He gives me money. He thinks I need it for food.' Instead Kamia takes it to a garage where he buys his 'bhangi' (marijuana). The boy makes a serious attempt to fill his charcoal bag only on days when the mzee sends him away empty handed, saying, 'Come tomorrow.' When his bag is full he takes it back to Mathare Valley, his small arms struggling with the load.

Crouching beside the public toilet he sorts the lumps into small lots. 'The people I sell to can't afford to buy new charcoal. I get about two and a half shillings (11 UK pence) for four litres.' He doesn't need the money for food. Other street children have shown him how to survive by going to Asian homes and hotels and pleading, 'Mama give me chapatti'. He lives on leftovers. Life on the street is cheap; most essentials can be got free. But cash is needed to impress other boys and to pay for enjoyable extras, such as the cinema, the universal favourite of street children.

Charcoal gathering is dirty work and Kamia's grubbiness exposes him to police harassment. 'They say, "You! You are a

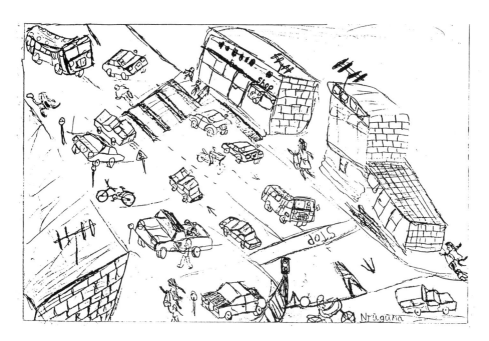

Street child's drawing of Nairobi, depicting several thefts

bad boy, you don't listen to what your mother says. Whenever you are sent to buy water for her, you run away with the money,"' – a hurtful reproach as his mother is dead. 'They say I smoke bhangi, that I sniff petrol and steal side mirrors from cars.' He gives a sheepish smile as he admits that he does in fact do all of these things.

Poorly paid work, crime, prostitution, scavenging for rubbish, begging are the survival options of street children. Most try several of them before they begin to specialise. Kamia is encouraged to steal by adults at a garage. 'Whenever I go there with a car mirror they tell me to get more.' They pay 50 shillings (£2.20) for the big ones (20 times what collecting four litres of charcoal yields).

Kamia's identification of himself as a street child is reinforced by the attitude of the police. They taunt him with the tag 'parking boy' – a name used for hardened street children who direct motorists to parking places and keep watch over their cars in return for tips.

He no longer goes to what is left of his family home. The lifestyle he took up after the death of his mother made him dirty and he smelt of bhangi. 'I started sleeping above the toilet because I was afraid I might be beaten up by my brothers.' Before going to bed Kamia has a smoke. With the sweet anticipation of an old man filling his evening pipe, he carefully prepares a joint and lights up. The bhangi makes him feel 'very high. My head goes ding, ding, ding, dong, dong, dong, like drumming. That's when I feel good and I sleep.'

Although he is alone much of the time, Kamia's nephew and friends are always close at hand when he wants company or support. He belongs to a small group of boys. 'It isn't a gang,' he says, 'we are good friends, we feel OK together.'

Some groups of street children in Nairobi are more formal than others – there are groups who even pool resources to rent a slum 'room' in which to sleep at night. Some are more like street gangs. Groups vary with the personalities of the leaders. Either way, they help give their members a sense of identity and of belonging. Occasionally groups clash. Fighting is considered part of the excitement that street life offers – it is stuff of the moment rather than a concerted battle for territory.

Street children have developed a slang, 'Sheng', which helps individuals from different parts of the country and different tribal backgrounds to establish a common bond. A blend of Ki-Swahili, other African languages and English, it also enables the children to communicate privately between themselves in public, at times to warn each other of danger. On the street the children are always alert to danger, real or imaginary.

'Life in the streets is like a game of hide and seek from normal society,' says Jones Muchendu of the Undugu Society which helps street boys. Contacts with the police are potential flashpoints. 'The boys are a nuisance to the police. And the

Nairobi street gang

boys fear the police. When they see somebody they suspect is a policeman they duck into the back streets.' One of the children's greatest fears is that they will be arrested and sent to a remand home.

It is hard for children to find a half-honest means of survival. Unemployment is high and even the most poorly rewarded work is seized upon by adults.

The 'work' of parking boys was developed by street children and the phrase has stuck to them. At one time many boys took it upon themselves to guard cars. At night, they could commonly be seen sleeping on the pavements, protecting themselves against the cold with plastic sheets or cardboard.

But parking boys have increasingly been elbowed out by more powerful adolescents and adults. At the same time, an upsurge in crime has made the city centre more dangerous. The risks of physical and sexual assault and of being set upon by guard dogs are high.

Fewer children now operate in the centre of Nairobi. Younger ones move in during the day, usually to make money by begging. But they retreat to the slums to sleep. Those who do stay late – to tap cinema and night club goers – may arrange to bed down near a night watchman, rather than risk a dangerous journey to the slums. For their part, watchmen are usually only too glad of the company of an agile youngster who might help raise the alarm in case of trouble.

Collecting and selling charcoal is one of the few ways street boys can earn money. But the returns are very poor. The temptation to turn to crime is great.

'Give me money'

Kamia had been on the streets for six months when another boy offered to take him to the Undugu Society. 'He told me, "You can get clothes, food, and have somewhere to sleep there." I don't like this charcoal work or living in a toilet, so I thought, "I'll give it a go".'

When **Kumar** took flight from his mother's killer, he began a journey that was to find him later in the day, like many other children before him, alone and penniless on Bangalore's main station. Each day the station sees a few new arrivals add to the city's population of street children.

Kumar noticed ragged children doing various kinds of work, hawking food, shining shoes, begging, offering to carry passenger's bags or summon them a taxi or a rickshaw.

'I watched the other boys and then I asked a man if I could carry his bags but a coolie (licensed porter) chased me away,' says Kumar. 'So I asked another man and he let me carry his bags and paid me a few rupees. After that I worked every day at the station.'

Station children with pet monkey

Kumar was quickly absorbed into the fraternity of the 'station boys'. 'I slept at the station – sometimes on a train, sometimes

inside the station, sometimes under the trees outside. When the police came at night we'd wake up and run away. I'd never even heard of street children, until I became one.'

Bangalore alone is said to have 25,000 children on its streets. Not all come into the city from the rural areas. Many drift into street life from deprived urban areas. Some are in regular contact with their families. Others have no contact at all.

Generally street children are regarded by the police as nuisances or potential petty criminals. In sharp contrast, the children see themselves as workers, and they occupy an elaborate if very informal world of work, moving into any gap in the market.

Street children in Calcutta

Indian people are 'film mad'. There is no going to buy your ticket for a hit movie on the night. Box-offices open in the mornings to queues – too long for workers to snatch a few minutes off to buy a ticket. Street children have become professional queuers, waiting two hours or more for tickets which they resell at a profit later outside the cinema.

In Bombay's efficient but over-crowded rail terminals, station boys have established a seat reservation service. Working in pairs, they jump aboard the unreserved compartments of the

Station child. This boy moved between trains, trying to sell travellers a pair of earrings

trains as they speed into the station. One boy occupies a seat, another stays at the door. In the scrum for seats, passengers hurl themselves into carriages even before the trains have stopped. As the carriage fills to bursting, the boy at the door will offer to sell latecomers the seat his friend is occupying. UNICEF worker Gerry Pinto challenged a boy who offered him a 'reserved' seat: 'Do you think you own this compartment?'

Back came the reply: 'No, sir, this is the Government of India's.'

'What business have you to ask me ten rupees (50 UK pence) for this seat, then?'

'I reserved the seat, sir.'

'What if I catch hold of you and hand you to the policeman over there?'

'No problem, sir. Half of what you give me is for him.'

Children who work unofficially as station porters will tip official porters to keep them off their backs.

Like birds who snatch their living from the shoreline, street children must develop an acute sense of when to advance, when to stand their ground and when to run, in their relationships with more powerful adults. They soon become skilled manipulators, learning to bribe policemen to leave them alone and to pay adult work rivals for the right to tout for work on their patch.

But the children's bargaining power is precarious. The ground rules can suddenly change. A police purge may be ordered and children rounded up whether a bribe is offered or not. The street child's ultimate defence is flight.

Station child's drawing of porters

Some of the work relationships established between street children and adults take a more paternalist, less purely exploitative form. The small backstreet dealer, to whom the ragpicker or paperpicker sells his waste, can protect as well as exploit his young collectors. He exploits them financially, but may also defend them against bigger boys. He will manage their money and may pay them when they are too ill to work. However, to keep them on the hook, he may never quite pay them all he owes.

Waste recycling dealer

It is too simple to think of small dealers as the villains of the piece. Rather they are just part of a wider system in which survival is secured by exploitation of the weaker by the stronger. Some might even be characterised as collectors who have 'made good'.

But while it is not clear the dealer is a villain it is clear that the children are exploited. The major cities are haunted by hosts of solitary grey grubby children with dirty sacks on their backs who shuffle unnoticed along the gutters, heads averted, eyes seeking out refuse they can turn into money.

Paperpickers tend to stick to a particular beat. 'A paperpicker

has a mental map in his head,' says Rosario Anselm, who runs a project providing a night shelter and sorting centre for them in Bangalore. 'He knows where to get his food. He knows where to get his paper and where to sell it and he knows where to get his entertainment.

'Yet if you ask a boy at the bus station, "Do you know where the City Market is?" it becomes clear that, though he is on the street all the time and may know there is a market, he has no grasp of how the city is knit together outside his patch. He's afraid to go beyond it – afraid, for instance, that if he does bigger boys might beat him up and steal his paper.'

Paperpickers perform a valuable public service in the

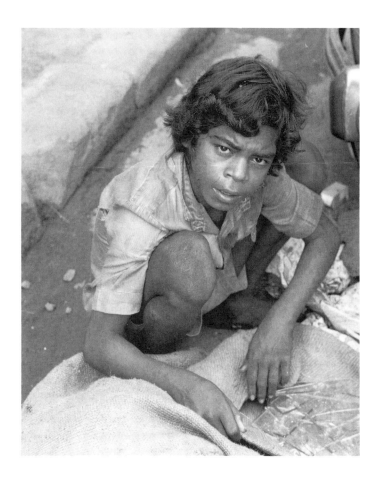

Ragpicker crouching and filling his sack

recycling of refuse and run considerable risks of injury and disease from the materials they handle, but their work gains them little recognition.

Kumar lived and worked as a porter for only a few months before a police clean-up drove him on. 'They began to check us out more often and caught more boys. I ran away from the station and went to the market. There I met a boy paperpicking. I became a paperpicker.'

He did his work at the station, where he already knew his way around and where he was part of a group that ate and slept and went to the cinema together. 'I did paperpicking for about a year. At first I earned about five rupees (25 UK pence) a day. Within two months I was earning four times that because I'd learned how to sort the paper and knew what paper paid best.'

Not uncommonly, a child will earn 20 to 30 rupees (£1 to £1.50) in a day.

A ragpicker's collecting bag doubles as his sleeping bag

At night those who have no slum home to go to climb into their collecting bags and go to sleep where they are, in a street subway, a nook in some building or simply on the pavement.

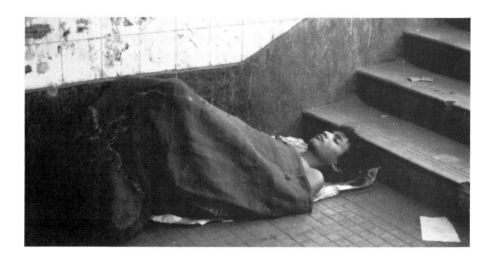

Street children come to identify themselves with their type or place of work. They refer to themselves as paperpickers, station boys, market boys, bus station boys, airport boys, harbour boys, tourist boys (working on commission as hotel touts and freelance tourist guides).

Girls are rarely to be found living on the streets independently of their parents. One reason may be that they simply are not allowed to be alone on the streets for long – the police or a concerned member of the public will question them and an attempt be made to trace their home, or put them into care or protective custody. A further reason is that in a country in which women are severely restricted by taboos, girls are less likely to run away from home or an institution in the first place however abusive it may be. Away from their parents they would risk being abducted and sold to brothels.

'Even with the boys, you have to remember, it's the more adventurous and courageous who end up as street children,' says one project worker. 'The less spirited would not leave home on their own initiative and they would not survive street life. They'd end up being caught and put in a remand home, or something worse might happen to them.'

As in the conventional employment market, the occupations of street children are accorded varying status.

Begging is acceptable as an occupation only of the very young (under ten) or the disabled, otherwise it is shunned. 'Very few

Begging in Calcutta. The boy's mother was begging nearby

boys will beg from the public,' says the project worker. 'Begging from house to house, the boys have a name for that – "carvala". Absolutely no-one would like to be told he is doing that.' Why? 'Because they like to earn their money. They will do that only if there is nothing else.'

Ragpicking is just one step up from begging. A hotel boy – though probably employed on abusive and exploitative conditions – might say derisively: 'I'm in the hotel business. You're just a poruki (a picker).' Yet even within ragpicking there is a pecking order; there are gatherers of the raw materials, sorters and small-time dealers.

Tourist boys enjoy high status. They work as commission agents for hotels, restaurants, prostitutes, drug dealers and illegal money changers – anyone willing to pay to be put in touch with a customer – or they offer their services to visitors as city guides.

Street children usually operate in groups based on the work they do. Membership changes as friends fall out, get arrested, are injured or even killed or simply move on to other cities. The groups offer some measure of protection and support and a sense of solidarity.

Members will warn each other of danger – say a police raid – and will share a wide range of information. If a boy is sick or has not made any money that day, others in the group will share food or money with him. If a boy is arrested or sent to a remand home, the group might even go so far as to try to bribe officials or otherwise attempt to rescue him. Bus station boys in Bangalore refer to members of their groups as 'partners' and it is understood that you share everything with your partners.

Street boys with dog

Many a group will have a pampered pet – a dog, cat or monkey – as a kind of mascot.

Duties and responsibilities may be allocated to group members. **Suresh** is ten and works as part of a fish procuring and selling operation in one of India's major port cities.

'I help the porters push the fish trolleys up the platform. I have a bag in my shirt and, as I push, I will take one fish and put it in the bag.

'The man pulling the trolley knows that I take a fish but says nothing. He knows I will take only one from each trolley and he pays me very little for helping him. At the end of the day the other boys bring their fish to me and I go out on to the street and sell them.'

The group believes that, as the youngest and most winsome, he is least likely to be harassed by the police or other traders.

A boy in another group has the job of collecting food, going around restaurants when they are closing and throwing out unsold food. He has no other duties, the rest of his day is spent sleeping, idling about or going to cheap movie houses – other group members pay him part of their earnings.

Projects trying to help street children have to come to terms with the fact that such children do not see themselves as hapless victims waiting for someone to rescue them. They are actively engaged in the business of surviving in the conditions that society has provided for them and they come to place a high premium on their freedom.

'Many have traded whatever protection home offered them for freedom,' says Anselm. Projects have been disappointed to find that the street children will take what they want from services offered – what is immediately useful to their lives on the street – and leave the rest.

Offered the chance of informal education, for instance, a street child may insist on learning English, not as a way of advancing out of street life but as a way of advancing within it – English will enable them to communicate with tourists.

Gerry Pinto tells the story of an eleven-year-old boy who he encountered while working for a programme trying to help street children in Bombay. 'The boy said if we had to send him to a school, we should send him to learn English. We found he had studied English for two years – so he was not from a poor family. He'd run away from a stepmother – the usual story. We made an exception and fixed him up at an English school. He did very well for a few months. Then he ran away. There are no locks on the doors, so there is nothing to prevent a child leaving. Two weeks later he was back – "Sir, I want to go back to school." OK. Three times he does that and the last time he doesn't come back.

'Later I see him outside the station. He waves and calls, "Hallo, sir. How are you?" I ask, "Why did you go off? You got what you asked for and even got an acceptance back, twice." The home was no fun, he says.

'"What kind of fun do you want?"

'"Sir, I like chicken every night. I don't like vegetarian. I eat when they empty the kitchens at the Rex Hotel – three star, sir. And I don't like school – suppose I go to school for ten years, will I get a job? Now I make 25 rupees (£1.25) every day or more." "That's a big story," I say.

'"No. There are these Arabs who come from the Middle East. I ask them what girl do they want. If they'll pay 100 rupees I'll take them to Colaba (a famous tourist area), if 50, Flora Fountain. The girls always give me something."

'"But where do you sleep?"

'"No problem, the whole of Bombay City is mine." And where do you wash?" "The sea is right there."'

Though Indian street children have established a complex world of work, their approach to work is informal and unstructured. They are essentially pleasure seeking and live within the limited perspective of a child's mind. Most live for the present, doing just enough work to meet the day's needs – a few cigarettes, a special snack and entertainment.

They are insatiable film goers. 'If they have the money, they will go to all three shows a day. It's not so much that they want to see a particular film,' said one night shelter worker. 'It's a way of spending three hours in another world, where they can be the hero, where everything becomes possible. Movie actors shape the lives they imagine themselves to be leading; they function through the hero's brains.'

Long after the actual screening has stopped the film enjoys a lively existence in the dreams and conversations of the children. 'At night the talk is only of films.' The world of films and the world of the street merge in the minds of the children, sometimes in a very direct sense. Rashid is able to earn money by staging street karate displays. He kicks, leaps and strikes alarmingly at a throng of imaginary foes. He has never had a karate lesson, outside the front row of the stalls.

Street child's self-portrait, reflecting typical film hero image

Some children will never be weaned from the streets – they are too successful at surviving on them.

Sachin is a veteran. At seven he absconded with other boys from a children's home where an older brother had placed him after the death of his parents, and where he was often beaten. He arrived at V.T. Station, Bombay and that has remained his base. Now he is twelve.

'At first some bigger boys bullied me, but later we became

Sachin cleaning window

friends. The station police used to make me clean out their offices. They didn't pay me but didn't arrest me either. I like the station – it's better than living with my brother and much better than the children's home I escaped from.

'Once I worked as a ragpicker. Now I do some work for a hotel, emptying the rubbish morning and evening. The owner lets me sleep on benches left out when the restaurant closes. He pays me 60 rupees (£3.30) a month. I also work at weddings – clearing and serving – and get about 30 rupees a time. I do other things; cleaning windows at a church school.

'I go every week to the Pavement Club (a charitable weekly event for street and slum children). I go because there are games and they give you some food and sometimes clothes. There is another place I've heard of, a home where you can stay and get some education. Some boys go there . . . when they can't get any work or are sick. But it's too far from the centre of the city. You can't earn any money there.

'I get on well with the man at the hotel. He is kind. He says one day he will give me a full-time job.'

Like Sachin, **Seena** is also unlikely now to leave the streets. He is a tough looking lad in his late teens. By working as an unofficial porter at the station he has managed to save 6000 rupees (about £300).

When asked to do a drawing of his home, he drew a plan of the streets around Bangalore station, with himself and a tiny

Seena's drawing

'special friend' depicted as porters. The lines at the top of the drawing are porters waiting for customers, he explained. He wrote his name on each street. 'That is my home,' he said.

TERMINAL SURVIVAL

The Observer
13th April 1979

Runaway schoolgirls who play a dangerous game

Ghost army of the missing children

The Observer
30th October 1979

Western countries like the US and the UK are slow to acknowledge that they have a street children problem. Yet in the US between a million and a million and a half children run away from home, or care, each year, many of them ending up for longer or shorter periods among the homeless. In the UK some 75,000 to 85,000 children go missing annually.

At a conservative estimate New York has 10,000 children on its streets; some are there for less than 48 hours, others for several years or until they die. They are there for different reasons. 'We deal with four specific types of children – the runaway, the throwaway, the abandoned and the homeless,' says Elizabeth Burnell, a worker for Covenant House, which provides emergency shelter and assistance to children and young people.

The New York Port Authority Bus Terminal is point of arrival for many of the city's street children.

It is a multi-level conduit of hallways, corridors, escalators, ramps and stairways, which not only serve the bus bays but also sustain their own human ecosystem. Tides of bonafide travellers sweep through its rows of shops and cafes daily, obscuring and, by and large, determinedly ignoring various kinds of stranded or scavenging humanity.

A woman in haste for a toilet cubicle steps unflinchingly over a sleeping child curled up uncomfortably on the floor.

There are few seats in the terminal; a deliberate policy, it is said, to discourage non-travellers from 'hanging out'. Police patrol, usually in twos, and tell loiterers to move on. There is a small, special department, the Youth Services Unit, which has the specific task of looking out for child runaways.

Out in the cold in New York
COVENANT HOUSE

Despite these impediments, the terminal shelters a non-travelling population of pimps, prostitutes, paedophiles, drug pushers, the homeless and runaway and local children. 'You know what it is? It's a park – a place to meet friends, that's heated, air-conditioned, has telephones, bathrooms, restaurants,' says Sergeant Bernard Poggioli, of Youth Services.

Susie is the street name of one of the youngsters staying at the Port Authority. Sitting on some steps, commuters bustling around her, she agrees to talk about life at the bus terminal. She is attractive and her hair and clothes look freshly washed. She looks about 16 but will not divulge her age. Though running away from home is not a criminal offence, the police are required to check on children who may be under age, defined varyingly from state to state as being between 16 and 18.

'I came to New York seven months ago. I had problems at home, arguments with my mother.

'At first I felt OK, I had a place to stay with a friend. I felt I was going to get on my feet. But things didn't work out as I planned, it was harder than I thought it would be. I've had a couple of jobs, working as a waitress and a shop assistant, but mostly I've been unemployed. I've spent two and a half months on the street, based here at the Port Authority with nowhere else to go to.

'When I got to New York I thought, "Hey, I can do what I want now." The funny thing is I did more of what I want to do when I was home. I can't go out and party for instance.'

Life at the terminal imposes its own restrictions and routines.

'We get up early, at five, six or seven – we don't want anyone to know we're here. We walk around inside until about ten, by which time we'll have eaten something, we'll have scraped some money together by then. Some people steal – many have committed crimes, mostly to do with drugs.

'At about ten, we leave the building. Some days I have appointments, say looking for a job, sometimes we go out for fresh air or to see friends, so we don't get too used to it here. I don't want to get any lazier. That's when I'd start looking like I belong.

'Usually we're back within three hours. We walk around and then go out at about four when the cops get busy hustling the homeless to clear the way for the commuters.

'When we come back later we usually end up staying. We walk around and then disappear – mostly upstairs where the buses arrive. Some people sleep on the buses, – there's a real easy way to open them. A lot of people sleep on the stairways but I wouldn't trust doing that, there are crack-heads around. You have to watch where you sleep, we've heard of dead bodies being found.

'A couple of weeks ago I went to a cheap hotel for a night, just for a break.'

What does she do for money?

'We have a lot of friends who give us money and vice versa. I wouldn't stand up and beg. People in some restaurants take care of us so we don't have to worry about food.

'The main thing that bothers me here is to see the way people are treated, especially by the cops. Sometimes they take away all your pride. When you comment back, they may handcuff you. The Youth Services police are a little better – you can complain to them. With the others nobody cares, it's your word against theirs.

'It really bothers me when the police treat me with no respect. I'm just as good as them. It could happen to anyone, being here. They beat people up for no reason. I got hit with a baton twice by a male cop and males aren't supposed to touch women.

'Once they get to know your face – that's trouble.'

Susie's monologue is interrupted by a policeman ordering her to move on. She leads the way to a cafe. En route she points out an area where gay men hang out – different groups of non-travellers favour different parts of the building. Two girls aged about 13 walk past, one carrying a baby.

'She's probably staying at Covenant House,' says Susie. 'It's got a programme for young mothers and their children. You see quite a few girls of 13 or 14 here, pregnant or with kids. Sometimes you see a father with them, but that's rare. I think it's sad. What's the kid going to get out of it. A lot of mums are on drugs. I feel sorry for the child. I was adopted myself.

Passers-by ignore a boy asleep on a Manhattan pavement

'This is not a place for young people to hang out.'

At the cafe Susie is joined by a young friend, Peter. He looks

very tired and a bit dishevelled. Within minutes he's asleep in his chair, slouched over the table. Susie looks at him sympathetically.

'I don't get much sleep, because every time I put my head down a cop's chasing me, telling me to move or to stand up or whatever.

'If I'm lucky, in the middle of the night I'll get a couple of hours sleep. They don't care, they've got their homes to go to when they're finished. Because I'm up so much, running from the cops, I have shoes on like 24 hours. Now my feet are getting swollen, well not swollen but they look bad. They're not my feet.

'Recently I've been getting shaky. The building's extremely cold and I sleep on a cold floor. Then there's all the pressure inside of me. I think that's what's making me shiver so much. It's like a rock of pressure in the middle of my chest that's just exploding, it's like it's trying to be released but it can't be released, no-one's giving it a chance to get out.'

Susie's belief in herself is like a high wire stretched across the grey space of the terminal. She measures her self-respect by keeping her balance when there is a long way to fall.

She has rejected frequent approaches from both drugs dealers and pimps. 'When pimps see you on your own, that's when they push you. You've got to be strong and tell them to get lost. They feed you a lot of dreams. Some people fall for it. One of my friends worked for a night. We got into a big argument and she told me it sounded so good, a lot of money.

'I'm proud of myself. I still have the power to say no. I've seen a lot of others losing their pride. I've seen kids from the same good homes as I've come from start to kill themselves. They go straight out on crack and they look really bad. They steal from their friends, they don't take care of themselves, they don't wash, their clothes are brown that used to be white. I can't understand that, how you can let yourself get so low.

The Reagan years have added many families to the drug addicts who used to inhabit America's skid rows, reports Martin Walker

Homeless scandal bites hard in Washington

'I like to keep my appearance up because if I let it go down I'd start to feel I was going down. I still care as much for myself as I did before. I can get cleaned up at the Streetwork Project (an outreach project for street children).'

Susie also feels sustained by the support street children give each other. 'Everyone looks after everyone. People come and bring you things. Kids staying at Covenant House will bring you food. When one person has money they'll throw this person a dollar or whatever, back and forth. So it's nice. It's like I have no money and I eat three meals a day, well maybe not three but enough. I've never fainted from lack of food. I've become pretty close to these people.

'About five of us hang around together, I consider them like a family. We chant reggae, making it up. We crack jokes. So there are some good times. Sometimes we talk about what this person did in the past. When we're chased by the cops we sometimes laugh about it.

'I'm so close to these people that if I was to get a large apartment I'd take a good amount of them in to stay until they could get on their feet. All a lot of these people need is somewhere to stay until they can get on their feet.'

Doesn't she ever feel down?

'A couple of times I've just sat and cried to myself. I was observing everything around me and I'd ask myself. "Am I ever going to get out of here?" When I felt like that I wanted to get out that minute. I wanted to go and lie down on a bed, take a shower like I used to. Sometimes on a Friday night or a Saturday night I'll sit back and think of what I'd be doing if I was still at home. It got to the point I was thinking of every possibility of a place to go, even home.

'People tell me, "You're lazy, you don't need to be on the street if you don't want to be." But it's not that easy to get up and be off because if it was I'd be gone. I come from a comfortable home, unlike some of these kids who've been struggling their whole lives. I'd never have thought I'd be out here because I had so much. Before I came, the nearest I got to this life was the TV or the movies. I'm determined to get out of it. Every day you hear kids saying, "I want to get out of here", but they rarely really try. I try hard but I get lazy sometimes, like with looking for a job.'

But she is investigating other opportunities.

'When I first got to New York I didn't want anyone to know who I was but now I'll let people who can help me know.'

She mentions another project – 'The Door', a community service centre for young people which provides a wide range of educational, recreational, medical and counselling services. She's thinking of going there to study for college entry qualifications. 'I wanted to be a lawyer. I studied law in school.

But now I want to be a musician.'

Does she ever really regret leaving home?

'The arguments with my mother weren't worth leaving home for. She'd take me back but I feel I must accomplish something before going back. I'm very stubborn.

'My mother and father are actually separated. Neither knows I'm on the street. I haven't got the guts to tell them I'm doing so bad – they think I'm studying, got a job and have my own place. My father would have a heart attack if he knew. That's why I'm going to keep trying. And I don't want to hear my mother saying, "I was right".'

For several months Susie didn't contact either of her parents but now phones both occasionally.

'I called my father recently and said I need some money. It should be in the mail by now – to a family friend. I just got frustrated one day and called up. It's something I should have done a long time ago.

'I hope to have a job next week in a record shop and get a room.'

Susie is ready to go and stirs her friend. Peter, she says, is a song writer. He agrees sleepily to write out one of his songs as a memento.

> *This is the Port Authority living, living*
> *This is the Port Authority living, living*
> *You have the batiman*, sadamite*, crack head and them not*
>   *leaving,*
> *Say, what a feeling, feeling*
> *We'll have to reach far because we have ambition,*
> *We'll have to work hard to reach the top.*
> *batiman – dealer   *sadamite – lesbian

DANGER AHEAD

The attempts of children to survive street life may partly explain the slowness of governments to act and the public to protest effectively over their growing numbers in many parts of the world. 'If they were dying on the pavements, the government would react strongly,' said Gerry Pinto, of UNICEF in India, speaking a few years ago. 'They don't even put themselves across as needing pity. They'll say they're enjoying themselves. Perhaps the government thinks, "OK, they're grubby and a nuisance sometimes but they're coping". The magnitude is not understood.'

Unprotected by caring adults, children are exposed to

A Nairobi street boy sniffing glue

immediate dangers arising from their lack of knowledge, their lifestyle and what is a generally exploitative environment. They risk drug addiction, sexual abuse, prostitution, crime, imprisonment, dangerous work conditions. Referring to sexual exploitation, a New York cop says, 'There are adults who look at a child as a dollar sign.'

Children are taken or recruited into organised begging rings and there are reports of deliberate maiming to make them more effective as beggars. Street children in Bombay have been offered up to 30,000 (£1500) for a kidney to be used in a transplant. They have no idea of the kidney's function and for them this would be an enormous amount of money.[58] In Brazil and other countries the corpses of children have been found with vital organs skilfully removed, feeding fears of an illegal trade in spare parts for transplants.

[58] *Snehasadan Newsletter*, Bombay, September 1988.

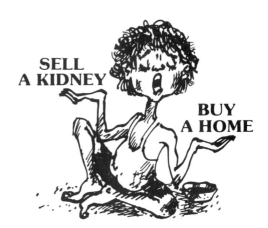

**SELL
A KIDNEY**

**BUY
A HOME**

*A cartoon from an
article in the
Snehasadan newsletter
about the kidney trade*

Children are also duped or forced into criminal activity.
They are used in housebreaking and to smuggle drugs past
police or harbour checkpoints, or make drugs drops to
customers, and to carry illicit liquor.

'What makes you streetwise is you've experienced assault or
rape, or your money has been stolen,' says Police Officer
Eugene Lewis (Runaway Unit) of street children in New York.
'You don't get streetwise by standing around and looking at
things, you get streetwise by the experiences you have and
generally speaking they're negative. If everything was wonderful
you'd still be as stupid as you were, or naive as you were when
you stepped off the bus. You get streetwise by getting knocked
around.'

Street children run many health risks and are poorly placed
to recognise and remedy disease; they have little or no access to
health services or grasp of the basics of good health. They have
many sexual partners and sexual diseases are rife. They and the
adults who use and abuse them live in the shadow of the AIDS
time bomb. A 1987 survey of 50 'high risk' children at
Covenant House (New York) showed that 38 per cent were
HIV positive. The project's founder, Father Bruce Ritter,
describes street children as the 'third great wave of AIDS
victims' (after male homosexuals and intravenous drugs
users).[59]

[59] *Amtrack Express*,
April–May 1988.

It is easy to be fooled by the ingenuity of street children and
the face they may present to the public. No children pitching
their courage against the odds of survival on the streets and
playing heroes in their heads will readily admit they are not
coping. The public rarely sees such children at the point of
crisis and failure. It is the survivors – the Kamias, Kumars and
Susies – who give interviews about their lives.

The freedom of street life is too often the freedom of

self-indulgence and offers little opportunity for self-development. In time its attractions pall. 'The cinema!' protested an older Indian boy listening to younger children talk excitedly about a film. 'I see films, too. It is just a way to pass time.'

The film-enriched fantasy world of many street children is in sad contrast to the indifference with which they are regarded by society. Their bravado barely disguises their assailed self-images. 'If I was a policeman,' says Kamia, 'I would tell off boys who pick up charcoal.' Other children talk of going home one day – but only when they have made a lot of money, got a regular job, or otherwise proved themselves.

Though they may work, few street children do so in a disciplined way. Without outside guidance, fewer still plan and save. The Sachins and Seenas are exceptions.

The children's approach to work – that of plucking an apple from a tree to satisfy an immediate need – is poor preparation for the rigours of adult work. The work options of the street child give little opportunity for advancement. Most lead nowhere but to the prison of an illiterate, impoverished, powerless adulthood. The financial needs of the adult are greater than those of the child but, as he gets older, the street

Brazilian boys held in a centre of temporary internment while their cases are being processed

child may find his accustomed work opportunities dwindling. The traveller who will hand his case to an unofficial child porter will be less trusting of a grown man.

The occupations of street children are a nudge away from their criminal potential. Bag carrier easily translates into bag snatcher; guarding cars provides information about owner behaviour that precisely equips the car thief; showing tourists the city brings far higher rewards if it is linked to pimping or illegal money changing.

A drift into a life of crime and prostitution are among the greatest dangers facing the children of the streets.

'THIEVES AND ROBBERS'

Snake sits apart, declining to be photographed. He gazes out at the polluted sea, head erect, jaw set, with the look of one who knows that there is nothing to be done but spit on the ground and pit his inner reserves of indifference against those of the world.

He has the build of a twelve-year-old but is closer to 14. He is already into gang crime and has been seen carrying a gun.

That puts him in the category of the most at risk of Brazil's 30 million deprived children. The danger is not only from the official police or gang rivals. A majority of the 120 or so people killed in a year by 'justice committees' (death squads) in the northern city of Recife have been under 21 and have had a background of criminal activity.

Snake's friends are talking about how they live. There's **Sal**, the group's joker; **Prince**, a tough looking boy with a closely shaven head and broken nose and a tendency to scoff and swagger, and **Roberto**, bigger but more wistful than the others.

They are on a beach near Recife. Just out of sight is one of the city's slums. Robbers are known to keep an eye out for opportunities to relieve unwary bathers of their belongings and tourists are advised not to use the beach. The youngsters sit among crude wooden chairs and tables under a weather-worn canvas canopy. A couple jig in a desultory way around a box-wood dance floor to music from two monstrous speakers. Behind the beach cafe are cubicles used by prostitutes and their clients. In the shade of the canopy a large black woman and a smaller man compile the day's fish stew in a huge cooking pot over an open fire. They alternate layers of whole fish, onion and potato.

Sal is saying he cleans out cars at a garage at weekends. 'I earn a hundred cruzados (about 33 UK pence). I give it to my mother.' He is 15 years old and made it to the second year of school. Like all his friends he is from a big family. 'I have six brothers and two sisters. My mother doesn't work. I steal as well as work – watches, bracelets. I steal in the city. A fence gives me 300 cruzados a time. Friday is the day we go. We usually go for women. We run from behind and catch them. All of us are afraid we will be caught.'

If he could choose how to earn money, what would he choose? 'I'd like to be a policeman,' he says. He is rewarded by an explosion of hilarity from his companions. He pauses and then drawls: 'What I want is plenty of money, plenty of women and plenty of cars.' There is more laughter.

Prince says: 'We steal watches and wallets. Before we go on a job we usually smoke marijuana. I try to get as high as I can to be able to go out when I may not come back.'

Weren't they afraid of being caught?

'All of us are afraid.'

'I get as high as I can to go out to live or die,' says Snake matter-of-factly.

One boy shot a tourist dead on this very beach, says Prince. He warned him with a gun but the tourist tried to punch him. He shot the man but the man still tried to get him. So he shot him again. The tourist is dead and the boy is in jail.

Another boy, says Sal, went out to rob with a gun for the first time. 'He found a tourist on the beach, a big man. But he was very small. To look bigger, he stood on the sea wall and challenged the man from there. The tourist looked down the gun barrel and saw there were no bullets in it. So he grabbed it and the boy let the gun go and ran off into the slum.'

'Keep your voices down!' warns Snake, breaking up the laughter. 'Cops – just behind us.' Two policemen have appeared and talk to a man on the other side of the dance floor.

Roberto says he earns some money selling newspapers. He boasts of having double charged a foreigner for a newspaper.

How did they think rich people get to be rich?

'Some inherit money,' says Snake after a pause. 'The rest . . .' – he completes his sentence with a gesture of the hand that signifies both stealing and accepting backhanders. 'Rich people are mean – not like poor people,' says Roberto.

'I worked in a building yard for a while,' says Snake, 'loading sand and blocks. But they never paid me.'

Was it right to take money off rich people?

Roberto: 'It's right. They have a lot of money and they have taken it from someone else themselves.'

Prince: 'The best thing is to get a gun, shoot them and take their money.'

Roberto: 'Whenever we assault or steal, we are afraid for our lives because we are afraid of the police. The cops are very strong, very violent and they torture a lot.'

Were the police honest?

'They are not honest. They are robbers,' says Prince. 'When they catch people with stolen goods, they keep the goods. If they catch us with drugs they keep the drugs and smoke them when they are out of uniform.'

Prince has been arrested and held three times in the police stations and once in Febem, a state-level institution that deals with abandoned and delinquent children. In some states, Febem is reputed to be both repressive and paternalistic, though in Recife there is now an attempt to reform it.

'I was caught by the police in the city. I had fallen asleep on the pavement on my way home from the beach. In Febem I was treated well. I was hit on the head and if you don't get up at five a.m. they throw a bucket of water over you. In the police station I was hit on the palms and my back with a big stick. I was put in cells with adults.'

Snake: 'Those cops who were behind us just now, they are ones who take us robbers. They beat us up when they need money just for a good night out. They take our money and let us go.'

'Last week a friend of ours was wrongly accused of stealing a watch,' says Roberto. 'The police beat the shit out of him and let him go.'

'When we suffer beatings from the police or hear of them I get very angry and want to kill them,' says Snake. 'One day I will go to São Paulo. I have a sister there. She will send money.' (Dreams of finding a brighter future in São Paulo usually end in the vast slums that ring the city.)

Didn't the police come from the same kind of community they came from?

'From the favelas? There are policemen from our group. But the bandits and thieves hunt them out. I wish they'd go and die,' says Snake.

A younger child stops briefly at the table, is asked rudely what he wants and told to push off. His visit prompts an intense conversation. He was a street child. While sleeping on the street he witnessed a burglary. The burglar, fearing identification, tried to kill him with a knife. The boy survived but has since lived 'only to sniff glue'.

Three girl prostitutes, none more than 13 years of age, seat themselves at the next table. They are in the money and ostentatiously order some lunch. The boys ignore them.

Was it right this life of stealing?

'It's wrong to steal but it's right to work,' says Roberto.

'I steal because there is no work. I have tried asking people for money and they don't give it to me,' says Snake. He practises blowing on his lower lip to make it tremble in an ugly, intimidating way. He explains that he works as a look-out person for a gang who have guns. His job is to check out the situation before an attack. Is the victim alert? Is he alone? Is he armed?

'But they don't give me any money so I'm thinking of getting out. This stealing and smoking marijuana is a mug's game. I'd like to work; any work as long as I get money. Not joke money. Real money.'

What was real money?

'Around 600 cruzados (£2.25) a day.' The others laugh. Few of the jobs that children might do will earn them that in a week.

The boys fall to talking about identity documents. Without such documents they say they can't get regular employment, or schooling or hospital treatment. To get documents you need a birth certificate, a photograph, to leave your fingerprints with the Department of Security and pay a fee.

If they were writing a book about children which would be read by rich people what would they say?

Prince: 'Tell them we need work and we will work. That sometimes we sleep in the street and at times we have nothing to eat. Most days we have nothing to eat. We beg and steal – but mostly we steal. We go to the market every Friday and Saturday to steal food, enough to last the weekend. The reason people steal is they don't have work.'

If they could talk to the people they robbed what would they say to them?

Prince: 'If they'd listen I'd say help poor people.'

Snake: 'If they would listen, I would say I just want a job. Not one like recycling rubbish. Collecting rubbish you work like an animal and get no money.'

What did they think of the youngsters in poor areas who chose to work rather than steal?

Snake: 'Those who collect rubbish? Those guys are all fucked up just like us.'

A van with the two policemen in it tries to turn in an open area next to the cafe. The rear wheels spin and burrow into the soft sand. The police get out and push the van in the midday heat. Everyone watches. No-one moves. The police seek no help.

Again the conversation turns to the need for work.

'We should change the government and get some work. The prices go up. The poor are fucked,' says Snake.

'Let's do some business,' suggests Roberto after a thoughtful lull in the conversation. 'Would you like to buy a gold chain – pure gold?'

How much?

'Forty, perhaps fifty dollars. Pure gold.'

Where was it?

'We haven't got it yet.'

The boys leave the cafe and walk back along the beach. They perform Capoeira, a form of foot fighting developed in Brazil by enslaved Africans. Banned by the colonial authorities as unarmed combat, it survives as a dance. Today it enjoys a revival as part of a popular movement to restore the cultural values of the poor, an umbilical cord to a pre-enslaved past.

The boys strip off their shirts and plunge into the sea. Bits of weed and plastic bags catch around their limbs. Snake surfaces next to Prince and gestures excitedly to him to make a sling with his hands. He steps into the sling and hurls himself into a backdive. The young robbers frolic in the polluted waves.

Graffiti protesting at arrests of children: 'tourists bring lots of money, they don't want to see bad things.'

Within months of this meeting Prince was picked up at night by police and badly beaten up. A judge urged him to make a formal complaint but he declined, fearing for his life.

One of his brothers was also arrested and beaten up. Another young boy from their community was stabbed in a gang fight but survived. Some weeks earlier he had replied to the question, 'what did he see himself doing in ten years' by saying: 'In ten years I think I will be dead.' An older brother of his was later shot dead in his bed at night in a gang killing.

Community workers in Brazil express dismay at the violence visited upon 'marginal' children. At a public meeting about street children in Recife a worker described the arrest of a group of children: 'They were doing nothing except glue sniffing. Perhaps they had stolen before but they were not stealing now. A police wagon screamed to a halt and several policemen jumped out with automatic weapons. They pushed the children to the ground, ordered them to lie face down spreadeagled, as though they were very dangerous criminals.'

Armed police will turn out in strength to surround a whole neighbourhood and sweep through it, conducting house to house searches for arms and drugs.

'Once you have been caught by the police, you become marked and then you can be killed,' says a young boy who relies partly on theft to support his family.

There are no official records of the number of children killed by police or in acts of violence in the home or community in Brazil but the issue of violence towards children is coming under increasing scrutiny from a variety of community workers and academics. Allegations of torture, beatings and shooting are commonplace. Lawyer Valdemar de Oliveira Neto, of the Luis Freire Centre, a community development support organisation which does legal and other work in the Recife area, says: 'The police rely on confessions to secure prosecutions. They haven't the training or the resources for investigation of a crime, so the extraction of a confession is how they secure convictions. Some have the attitude that if children behave like adults and commit criminal offences then they deserve to be treated like adults.'

But what violence there may be from officialdom takes place in the context of a wider acceptance of violence against children. 'We have so many complaints that we take legal action only in cases of murder,' says Oliveira Neto.

'We live in a city, a state, a nation afraid of its own children,' says Irene Oliveira Siffert, of MAIS in São Paulo.

Talking about their lives, children on the borders of criminality are disarming. They will say they would like to have had a proper schooling or would rather be working. Asked what kind of jobs they would like to do, they name practical jobs – engineers, doctors, nurses.

A young girl listening to a group of boys talking in a slum, answered the question saying without hesitation: 'I would like to be a sailor. It's such a beautiful profession.'

AN UNBEAUTIFUL PROFESSION

[60] *The Sexual Exploitation of Children* by Judith Ennew, Polity Press, page 77, UK, 1986.

'Sexual exploitation is part of the wider spectrum of domination, in which rich exploit poor, males, females, whites other ethnic groups, and adults children.'

Judith Ennew[60]

'My parents were always busy and they were always tired. They were both on public assistance and with seven of us children things were difficult for them. We'd come to New York from Puerto Rico when I was six months old and it wasn't much of a new start for them,' says **Angel**.

'I wouldn't say I was really a neglected child. I think my parents tried to pay attention to me but I didn't give them the time. I'd lost all respect for them. They used to argue constantly.

Angel started prostituting in New York at 13

'Then my brothers would come up to me and say, "You're adopted, we found you in a garbage can," and I started

believing them. They were playing a joke on me but I didn't understand. I got upset and said, "How come I look like my mother and you don't. They found you in the garbage can and I look like my mother and you look like nobody, so drop dead." Then we'd fight and I'd say, "Forget it, I don't want to talk to you," and walk away.

'I liked to fight, and one of my brothers taught me how to box. Once I had a boy on the floor, choking him, and my brother said, "You fight like a boy, you're not a girl, you're a boy." I said, "I might as well be one, I've got five brothers and one lousy sister." I used to come home with black eyes.

'My sister's got green eyes and light blond hair and everybody thought she looked cute and I hated her for it. I used to try to rip her eyes out with my nails. My father loved her the most; if I smacked her I'd get beat, if she smacked me I'd get beat. My family used to say I was ugly and I stopped looking in the mirror. When I look in the mirror I don't look at myself, I look past myself and see somebody else.'

At ten Angel was sexually abused by a close relative.

'He used to come into my room and touch me and have sex with me. It went on regularly for a year. I told my sister and we tried to tell our mother, but she wouldn't believe us. She said it was the TV getting to me.

'Before the age of ten I was always in front of the house playing with the kids. But after ten I started hanging out harder, taking drugs without my parents knowing. The first time I took them was at school, in the bathroom. Friends came up and said, "How are you feeling?" I was upset and they said, "Here smoke this, it'll make you feel better." So I took the reefer and got high, and all I could do was laugh. Finally I came down and I looked around wondering what I was saying. All I could do was mumble and laugh. So they kept on coming back almost every day looking for me so they could see my reaction, and soon I was buying, taking pills and heroin as well as marijuana.'

'My parents didn't really notice a lot of what I was doing; they were always busy with the others. At night I'd sneak out when everyone was asleep and go round to my friend's house and get high for a while. She was a few years older than me and was always taking drugs. She paid for them by stealing from her mother.'

One night when Angel was twelve she was stopped by six youths. At first she wasn't worried because she recognised them, but it turned out they had a grudge against one of her brothers.

'They started hitting me and I was fighting back and finally they hit me on the head and knocked me out. I was gang raped.

'And I actually got pregnant. I realised it at about five months when talking to some kids at school about menstruation not coming. They said, "Fine, you're pregnant" and I told them not to say nothing.

'To disguise my pregnancy I started wearing tighter pants and baggy clothes, and I always carried a lot of books to cover up. My parents didn't see me as much as they wanted, I never let them see me, and they didn't notice. When I started getting bigger I started playing more hookey from school. But I was taking drugs and actually forgot about being pregnant, jumping around like kids do at that age.

'One day I got pains, contractions. I didn't understand it, so I went to my friend's house and lay down. That's when the baby came down. My friend was in shock; I was in shock. Finally we went to the basement of an abandoned building. I was crying and screaming and she covered my mouth so no one would hear. And it came out and she looked at it and I was laughing at it and saying, "I'm sleepy, I'm high I know it." Yet it was true, I'd given birth. But the baby was dead.

'My friend had a knife – she always carried a knife – and she cut the umbilical cord and said, "Push one more time and see what happens, if there's any more baby,' and the afterbirth came out. Fortunately she'd brought some sanitary pads; I was bleeding a lot.

'We buried the baby quickly and we buried it deep. There was already a big hole in the floor so we laid the corpse in it, put in some dirt and placed rocks on top. We didn't throw the rocks, we placed them on lightly just in case the baby got hurt.

'Back home the reaction set in. My mother saw I was behaving differently. I said, "Don't worry, there ain't nothing wrong, I just don't feel like eating a lot." I wasn't speaking with them, especially my brothers, and hardly laughing. They noticed I'd lost a lot of weight and that I was sleeping a lot.

'They kept on watching and worrying over me but they never guessed.'

Angel spent longer and longer periods away from home. For a time she was put into care, but ran away. At 13 she occasionally earned money prostituting. Through street life she met and became involved with Slim, a 19-year-old.

'At first he treated me nice but soon he was making me black and blue. He was drinking a lot and we were both taking drugs.

'Soon after we met, I moved in with his family, but one day I got fed up and started hollering at him and his father told us to leave. I said, "I'm going to my mother's, I don't know about you." Finally my mother said we could both move in and he didn't lay a hand on me until we left to move into an apartment he'd found. Then we started fighting more and I kept on walking out.

'After the summer vacation I should have gone on to high school. But the school had lost my records. I was so frustrated I gave up all hope. Slim would see me and get upset that I wasn't going to school, and that would end in another fight.

'If I looked at someone else he'd hit me. Or if he looked at a girl and I just looked at him I'd get hit too, and we'd start fighting. Then at Christmas I realised I was pregnant and his fighting got worse. I used to laugh at him and say, "Don't hurt me, I'm so used to your punches." So he started taking me by my hair and throwing things at my stomach.

'Every time he stopped getting drunk he was nice but when he got drunk he started getting violent.

'Finally I gave birth. I was just fifteen.

'Soon he started noticing his punches didn't do nothing and took it out on the baby and wouldn't let me near her for three days. But then he got so drunk I snuck in and I saw the baby. She had two black eyes. I turned round and he was right there and he just punched me and I looked at him and laughed and said, "Are you going to hurt the baby more? I'll kill you, I hate you for what you just did."

'When things calmed down I got someone to call the cops. They said, "Tell us who beat the baby," and Slim looked at me as if to say I should lie for him. I smiled at him and said he did it, that he used to beat me and the baby. Finally he confessed, and was eventually sentenced to six months in jail.'

Angel's daughter was taken to hospital and put into protective custody. She had serious injuries and brain damage. Angel was taken by the police to Covenant House where the staff wanted her to stay for her own protection. 'But I got sick of it and would awol back and forth, going to 42nd Street, the Port Authority terminal, hanging out, hustling for money, robbing people.

'I was in shock. I didn't know what I wanted to do. I just did what I wanted for the moment not caring what anybody said. During that pregnancy I'd stopped taking drugs but I started up again even worse.

'People used to say I didn't belong on 42nd Street, there was something about me that was different from everybody else. They got me angry 'cos they wouldn't explain. So I tried to be like one of the crowd and started mugging. I played the role of a prostitute and a guy called out, "You're special," and I said, "Forget about special." Next thing I knew my friends jumped him. And it was like exciting, and we got five hundred dollars that night.

Times Square

'It was easy so we started doing it more often. I'd take a man to an isolated place where he'd talk to me and put his arm around me. Then my two partners would jump on him and steal his money, his credit card, and we'd run off.

'As it was my face the man had seen, I obviously got the most money. I stayed in the same hotel as my partners but we had separate beds, I really don't like to sleep with guys.

'One by one they were getting busted but I wasn't – I was escaping faster. I usually ran to a train station or the Port Authority and would put on a hat, put up my hair, put on some make up. Sometimes I'd switch clothes with a friend who'd be waiting for me.

'New partners came in but the money got less and I got sick of it and after about two months, and about 25 hits, I quit. I changed my role to prostituting.'

Despite her previous experience, she was nervous. Her first client told her he was a lawyer.

'This man approached, very handsome and young and dressed up nice. He said, "What you doing tonight," and I said "I'm doing nothing but walking." He said, "Do you want to spend some time with me?" and I said, "Fifty and up." And he said, "Fine." So we went to the movies and on to a motel and he left me with two hundred dollars.

'He started seeing me almost every day. He was just being nice, I know he felt pity for me, I was crying that first day he came up, thinking about my daughter. I liked him a lot and would have liked to get married but he was happy to waste his money. Then I realised guys were out to mug him, seeing as he had money, and I told him, so he stopped coming around.

'I continued to hustle and got into asking for an identity card to make sure the men weren't police officers, because I didn't want to go to gaol. They sometimes thought I was a police officer! And I'd say, "How could I be, I'm young." When I told them my age – fifteen – they got more excited. They love teenage girls.

'Some of them were nice, they talked to me about their problems with their wives, their children. And they actually gave me money for that. They just wanted somebody to talk to for a while, they just wanted to take somebody out, not always to have sex.

'Also, guys started phoning me at the Port Authority saying they wanted to see me, so slowly I became a call girl. You give them the number, tell them what time to phone and that you'll be right next to the phone.

'Other times a man approaches you and you go off together for a short time to a hotel or to a peep show where there are booths. And then you come back and the other kids start realising what you're doing but they usually won't say nothing. Some kids, though, were shocked at me and would say, "Are you crazy?"

'I tried to keep the fact that I was prostituting from my boyfriend. I'd wait until he went out to get some money and then go off myself. After a time he started getting more suspicious 'cos I kept on coming back with more money and I was gone longer. But then we got heavily involved with drugs again and when that happened he didn't mind how I got money.

'I liked to hustle at the end of the week and weekends, that's when there's money. That's the only time I really did it until I started getting heavily into drugs and then I did it every day.

'Everything was perfect until the pushers introduced us to crack. We actually got addicted in three days. We did like over a hundred dollars a night and then we started getting more expensive with it. They were making us more hungry for it. They'd put the crack in your face and say, "See what I've got, do you want to come along?"

'To make more money I'd go to a nice area of Manhattan, like Avenue of America and 50th Street. High class prostitutes worked the area but there were guys looking for young girls. I'd walk around and they'd see me and I was dressed up decent and they were spending 200 dollars for half an hour. So I said, "I'm doing this more often". Sometimes they'd asked me to stay with them and I started lying to my friends as to where I was, making more money. The money went into my socks. I'd walk around with maybe 500 dollars stuffed into them.

'I didn't actually like prostituting. It was the money I enjoyed, it was easy money. I started feeling disgusting, having sex with all sorts of men that I didn't know, didn't know what they might have, how their wife feels, if they did anything to their daughter 'cos often I was the same age as their daughter.

'When I took up prostituting I stopped having sex with my boyfriend. He didn't understand why and I wasn't about to explain. I was so disgusted with myself for having sex with other people and then with him. But I was already pregnant by him.'

One day on the street, Angel met Trudee Able-Peterson of the Streetwork Project.

'She said, "You know you're pregnant?" I said, "No I'm not," though I looked it. I wasn't paying attention to myself, always thinking about drugs. Finally she took me to a doctor and he said I was five months gone. Then she told me about a place for pregnant girls where I went to stay. But I continued hustling on and off.

'At first the dates didn't notice that I was pregnant, then when they did they said, "Good, pregnant girls are better in bed than the non-pregnant ones," and they started giving me more money. I only stopped prostituting when the baby was getting ready to come.

'She was born in hospital, and I lost custody of her.'

Angel spent most of the next few months staying with various friends but then moved back into street life.

'I started getting more wild, more dependent on drugs and making lots of money.

'After giving birth I'd stopped hustling. Then three months later I decided to have sex with the baby's father and immediately got pregnant. I had an abortion, but not long after I was pregnant again, and when we were down on money I went back to prostituting. I did it behind his back. He wanted to make money and I wanted to make money, but he'd take for ever doing whatever he was doing – I was never quite sure what it was – and I was tired of living on the streets and sleeping in movie theatres.

'Those days my role was changing. I'd say to a trick, "Are you sure you want me, she's cuter than I am?" pointing at another girl. "Do you want me to introduce you to her?" If it was yes, I'd say, "Fine, give me twenty dollars." They'd go off and later the girl would give me a something. That's how I started pimping girls. At one time I had three regulars working for me.

'I never myself worked for a pimp. Men were always asking but I wouldn't.

'I knew I was suffering emotionally. I was also thinking about when would I die, like, "I hope my life goes by fast." I was wanting to kill myself but I was willing it so much that it didn't take no effect on me. When you back down that's when it really happens, I've heard that a lot. There were many times I wanted to kill myself, since I was young I've been trying, I did it a lot of times over stupid little things. I'd think, "If I die, nothing else could go wrong."'

It was at this point that, through continuing contact with Trudee, some things started to go right.

Just how many children are involved in prostitution in Western countries is far from clear. Frequently quoted US guestimates range from 300,000 to several million. Whatever the number, it is a lot of young lives, and people who work to help them in several of the major cities believe the numbers are growing, and that younger children are becoming involved.

In the rich world, because of compulsory schooling and relatively extensive welfare provisions and policing, children below the age of 15 are rarely to be found leading a street life. However, as in the case of Angel, prostitution may begin at an earlier age.

One of the major worries of Trudee Able-Peterson is the increasing number of young boys who wander down to the notorious Times Square area. She tells of two she found standing by a fast food shop. 'They were small, I thought they were seven or eight but it turned out they were nine and ten. I walked up and said, "What are you doing around here? It's really dangerous, somebody might try to hurt you." And one of them began to cry and they said they were very hungry. They'd missed their school meal and grandma didn't have enough to feed everybody in the family so she fed the little kids first. These boys were so slight they were obviously undernourished. I said, "Why did you come to Times Square?" They said, "We heard you could make money."

'They really didn't know how they would make money, but they had heard they could – maybe from older kids in the neighbourhood. Now had a paedophile got to them before I did he would certainly have fed them and then asked them to participate in something sexual or got them off somewhere where they would have been in danger of being raped or sodomised. I fed them, got them back home and gave them a stern lecture. I think they're not so unusual.'

Children who look as though they should be at school are picked up by the police Truant Squad. But many slip the net. The New York Runaway Unit frequently finds boys of between ten and twelve hanging out in known paedophile pick-up points.

'We call them throwaways,' says Lieutenant James Greenlay. 'They come down, hang around the arcades, perform oral sex on men and they get ten dollars. So, if they do four, they make 40 dollars. To these boys who come from a low economic area that's a lot of money. They hang around for two to three days maybe, sleep in abandoned buildings or in and around the area with their friends, then they go home and their parents never report them missing. The kids don't see anything wrong with it – it's money for games. They don't realise the dangers.'

While Runaway Unit officers generally patrol in cars, Trudee spends much of her time going on foot through the Times Square area and knows all the 'nooks and crannies and corners' where children hang out.

Most of the children she works with are from the city. They are hardened to street life and either feel they cannot go home or have no homes to go to.

'The kind of kids we make contact with are street couples, they're both hustling. We deal with a lot of boys, as many or more than girls.'

Trade is not confined to the evenings. There is a booming lunchtime demand from businessmen who will pick up a boy and take him to one of the lower class hotels to have sex. A boy on the game can make $200 to $400 a day (though children tend to exaggerate their earnings).

Runaways fresh to the city naively expect to get a job – in a boutique, record shop, or cafe. Most have rudimentary notions about money, the cost of living and, more particularly, survival in a big city.

What confronts them is a highly competitive employment market and an urgent need for money, for everything from food through to accommodation. They find themselves in a short-term poverty trap and some will turn to prostitution as a way to survive.

Ironically, protective bans on the employment of youngsters below the age of 16 increases the vulnerability of street children to becoming involved in prostitution or criminal activity. Begging or busking increase the risk of a child being picked up by the authorities. Unable to sell their labour, children have only their bodies to sell.

Asked about survival on the streets of London, **Mark** said: 'Survival? Imagine you're on the street. Sleeping in sleeping bags, in doorways, on church steps. Cold and hungry. Would you be able to survive? You've got to learn.'

He'd heard about the rent boy scene shortly after arriving in London.

'I thought, "That's one thing I'm not going to do." Then one Saturday I thought, "Sod it, I'll do it once." I felt good when I had some money in my pocket. But I felt disgusted because it was with a bloke. I had my morals – otherwise I would have done it earlier.' From 'once', Mark went on to become a rent boy.

The sex industry doesn't wait for children to fall on hard times but actively seeks out new recruits to feed the market's demands. Stepping off a bus at the New York Port Authority building can be the first step into prostitution, depending on who you meet and where you stay.

'They're right in the seamy area of Manhattan. Some never get out of a ten-block radius,' says Lieutenant James Greenlay. 'I would say the majority of girls who are gone from home for a week will get involved in prostitution unless they have a place to go.

'Firstly street people take advantage of them, steal their money, take their clothing, steal their suitcases. They are made to pay higher prices in hotels because the desk clerks know they're runaways.

'Then there are the paedophiles, the pimps and the peer group.'

A child who has just left home is in a particularly insecure emotional state. 'On the surface you've got a sense of personal liberation and freedom,' says Richie McMullen, who has pioneered recognition of the plight of rent boys in the UK. 'But linked with that – and hidden very often so that you can survive emotionally – you're actually denying rejection; that you've been rejected by the family or by the education system or by friendship groups.'

Prostitution often has little to do with making a lot of money, says Richie. 'There are kids who will go with someone for a cup of coffee and a bag of chips.

'Imagine you haven't eaten for a couple of days, you're bitterly cold and very lonely. You're depressed and the chances are you've seriously considered suicide. Then someone says, "Would you like a coffee?" You think of the warmth of the cafeteria, the warmth of the coffee, the human contact of someone who seems to care for you. And the man says, "Would you like to come back and stay the night?"'

Some paedophiles and punters (clients) can be very kind and protective: 'The kid melts.' In the phrase of another counsellor, 'They kill them with kindness.'

Not all homeless or runaway youngsters succumb to the pressures on them to start prostituting. The Central London Teenage Project, which runs a safe house where runaways can take refuge, estimates that 15 per cent of London's homeless youngsters resort to prostitution.

Trudee Able-Peterson thinks this estimate too low for a major city. A study of children helped by the Streetwork Project in New York showed that 86 per cent had been involved in prostitution in some form, at some time. 'Kids don't always admit, and we don't always look at the subtle forms of prostitution. What about the girl who's on the run and lives with one guy one month and another guy for two weeks, and another for two months, moving in and out with guys who'll take her in? They may not give her money but kids do use sexuality as a way to survive and that's prostitution.'

Studies suggest that a disproportionate number of children who become involved in prostitution were previously victims of sexual abuse. **Barry**, who became a rent boy at Piccadilly Circus, was first seduced by a man in a park at the age of twelve. The man paid him. 'I already knew sex was fun and here was money as well,' he said. Neglected by his mother, he began to hang around the parks and toilets near his upper-middle class home in the south of England. His mother knew little of his activities.

'She knew I was having relationships but she didn't know it was prostitution. Often I would have 40 pounds in my pocket but I never let her see the money. She didn't want to know anyway.'

The experience of the New York Runaway Unit confirms a correlation between sexual abuse and prostitution, as does research conducted by Trudee. 'At least 70 per cent of youngsters I've worked with, both boys and girls, were sexually abused before entering prostitution, usually by a family or surrogate family member. It isn't that all abused children become prostitutes but that those on the run, alone, hungry, who've already experienced abuse, usually do.'

Drug taking among youngsters on city streets is another major contributory factor to their turning to prostitution. Trudee believes the crack craze has resulted in an increase in child prostitution. 'They start using it, they start selling it, they start selling their bodies. They'll sell anything to get crack. They're using it desperately, they'll turn five dollar tricks to get a small bag of crack. We even know of young kids who are trying to get off crack by shooting heroin.'

Punters and pimps have a nose for damaged and vulnerable youngsters and are skilled at manipulating them to their own ends. A pimp boasted on an American TV programme that he could spot a potential prostitute instantly. Within minutes he could bring her under his control. His technique was to become 'everything' to her, father, mother, psychiatrist, boyfriend – whatever the child felt deprived of.

According to members of the New York City Police Runaway Unit pimps exploit children's dependency, their fear of going home and their self-delusions about what is happening to them:

'Few girls consciously decide to prostitute themselves. They come in with low self-esteem. The pimp is a smooth talking, worldly-wise guy who can easily impress a child. He builds you up and he knocks you down, then builds you up and knocks you down – psychologically and physically.

'He'll tell you how gorgeous you are and persuade you you're somebody. This is a child who has been rejected at home and at school. He'll use phrases like, "Baby, you're fine", or, "You've got a gold mine there". He'll try to build up your self-worth in dollars.

'The more money you make, the better you are and the more status you have with the pimp. Girls can be manipulated to a point where they measure their value in terms of what they do for "their man". They'll say, "You see that Jaguar, I bought that for my man". It doesn't matter to them that they bought it by selling themselves, that they're walking and they don't have a car.'

The mockery of love and respect pimps offer young girls is usually enough to give them control but where it fails it may be readily backed up by violence.

'Pimps have been known to burn girls with heated wire hangers or put them in boiling tubs. They've been known to take a girl's clothes away for two to three days and bring their friends in and maybe just have her mortified by making her stay around without any clothing on. I'm talking about a girl of 13, 14 years old.

'At other times pimps will treat her very well, for instance buy her fancy clothes and maybe take her to Miami. For a young girl it's got to be an exciting life if she doesn't displease her man and doesn't get caught.

'Most girls deny having a pimp at all. But it's not true. If they didn't, other girls would be kicking their butt off the street because there's competition out there. It's also dangerous and a girl looks to her pimp for protection.

'A girl believes what she wants to believe. One of the myths is that a pimp is putting money into the bank for her. Many a girl will tell you she's going to open up a boutique when she gets back to her small town. They live in dream worlds and these guys lead them on.

'The whole scene is deception. A girl convinces herself that this isn't her life or that this is the only thing she can do, or that she's not going to be out there for ever. And we know that unless she quits very soon she will be there for ever, get to be an old prostitute – that's if she survives.'

Drawings by a former rent boy. In his mid-teens Adrian, the artist, was taken by clients to Malaysia and several European countries

Much more attention has been paid by researchers and the media to female than to male prostitution. But worldwide millions of boys are sexually exploited.

In London rent boys generally work independently of pimps, and can sometimes earn considerable amounts of money and ply their trade in different countries or be taken on holiday by their clients.

Hotels rarely ask questions when a man checks in with a boy. The average age of punters is 40 to 45, 'so it's the perfect age if you're picking up a youngster to appear to be a parent,' says Richie McMullen. 'And it's a kind of fantasy some of the kids wouldn't mind, because they can fantasise that the man really is Dad.'

Boys usually take the passive role in sexual acts, to satisfy the paymaster's need to dominate. But they like to think that they hold the reins of power in their relationships with clients.

Despite the money they can earn and the notions they have of being streetwise, involvement in prostitution almost invariably further diminishes a child's sense of worth and self-confidence.

Adrian reviews his years as a rent boy, saying: 'When I was at school I was in the top stream, getting "A" in everything. Now I find it hard to write a letter. I can't even do a crossword anymore. It's crazy, I've not done anything for four years. It's done my head in, warped my mind.

'I'm ashamed. I can't go back home to my mum; a "friend" told her about me prostituting. When I go to job interviews I cover up, when I meet people in general I cover up. That will be with me all my life, what I've done. It disgusts me in a way, I'm attracted to women. I'm not even bi-sexual. I did it because I needed the money.'

Trudee Able-Peterson finds that many children believe they deserve what's happening to them. 'They say, "I feel like a piece of shit, I hate what I have to do to survive, I'm nothing, I'm nobody."

'They don't just say it. They do it in their actions, by abusing their bodies with drugs and tricking and not using condoms. Our kids are in real danger of getting AIDS. Their immune system is ripe for contracting the HIV virus.

'I don't know anybody who has a worse diet or worse sleep patterns or who has had more sexually transmitted diseases. I don't know anyone who sleeps with more people and has more unsafe sex: they sleep with their tricks to get money to survive; they sleep with each other because they don't know how to just hug to give care; they go home occasionally and sleep with old boyfriends, girlfriends and sometimes their parents.'

Her attempts to persuade children to take better care of themselves meet a wall of indifference. 'They say things like, "Why are you telling me about things that'll kill me in five years when I might get killed tonight?"'

According to Richie McMullen children involved in prostitution blank out the dangers they face. 'You deny you're going to get ripped off, get beaten up, get killed, get AIDS. You have to blank out these possibilities, otherwise you'd be a nervous wreck, and you can't afford to be a nervous wreck.'

Police Officer Hazel Walters (New York Runaway Unit) believes many children are on a self-destruct course. 'What do you say of girls who get into cars with strangers, who get their throats cut, get stabbed, get pushed out of moving vehicles? It has to be a suicide mission. We tell girls what might happen. They admit they might run into a crazy person but they're taking their chances.'

On the wall of the Runaway Unit office is a board of press cuttings. Young faces peer out of snapshots. The photographs are of the kind normally found in family albums or residing proudly on mantelpieces. But this is a death board of prostitutes killed by clients.

'Right up there, that girl.' Police Officer Velma Hamilton points at the board. 'We placed her in a runaway shelter. Then the pimp convinced her to leave. Her parents and everybody were waiting to take her home. Next morning the homicide detectives came here with a picture of her. She'd had her head blown off.

'The girl who was with her got grazed by a bullet, but she was out on the street again the next day.'

[61] *Trafficking in Women and Children in India* by Sister Rita Rozario, Joint Women's Programme, New Delhi, 1988.

Child prostitution in India is a 'silent' problem, according to Sister Rita Rozario. A qualified social worker and member of the Good Shepherd Congregation, she conducted research for the first nation-wide report on prostitution.[61] The story of **Meena** which follows, is her rendering of the account of one of many girls and young women she has interviewed.

'I was born in a small village in Andhra Pradesh, in the south of India. There were five of us; my father, mother, older sister, younger brother and myself.

As a little girl I used to see my father go off to look for work early in the morning. Some days he would return home after only a short while. Then he would sit in our hut in silence. Other times he would return late in the evening, exhausted but with a glitter of victory in his eyes at having been able to provide us with food.

My father had owned a few acres of land. He cultivated it and also worked for others. We had enough. But then he got into debt and was tricked out of his property by a greedy brother. I cannot think of one happy day in my house after that.

My father continued to work the land but now only as a coolie (a daily labourer). On the days he had no work he stayed at home. I think he was ashamed to show his face to the other villagers. He also felt bad that he could not provide meals for his family. I grew to hate my unjust uncle.

At this stage my elder sister reached puberty. It was celebrated according to our tradition with a family feast and festivities. Money had to be borrowed.

Soon after the celebration my sister was married. Her marriage meant more borrowing and her dowry took all the remaining family valuables. My sister left for her in-laws and my parents seemed relieved to have done their duty. But I was miserable. I missed my sister very much. Also we had many debts.

Creditors began coming.

There came a stage when my mother could not borrow even a single meal from the neighbours. My little brother would cry from hunger until he fainted or fell into an exhausted sleep. I could not bear to see him cry and so went around the villagers and begged for food for him.

We had become beggars.

Then one day I met a young man at a house in the village. He seemed a respectable person. He told me that in a nearby town many families needed helpers and domestic servants. If I went with him he would help fix me up with work. He would be leaving that day from the bus stand. If I wanted work I should join him there.

I thought that if I went I would be able to save up enough money to come back and open a small lentil and rice shop. This would pay for the family's daily meal and maybe make some extra. There seemed no other way to end the suffering of our family. If I asked permission it would be denied.

I went to the bus stand.

In the town the gentleman took me to his home – he had a big room full of books, he turned out to be a lawyer. There were three other rooms – two occupied by two women and the third he gave to me. I was delighted to have a room of my own.

After I had washed and eaten, the gentleman called me. I went to his room thinking I should obey him to return his kindness. But when I got there he grabbed me and raped me. I was shocked and humiliated. I felt hopeless and disgraced. My dream was shattered.

Over the following weeks the man repeatedly raped me. There was no way of escape. I battled with him and demanded a decent job. At last he seemed to relent and offered to send me for work. He bought a suitcase, gave me 300 rupees (£15) for 'expenses' and sent me with an old man.

I was taken to a house in a city in a different state. It turned out to be a brothel.

That was two years ago.

The owner is a 'rowdy'. He has several girls. He raped and beat me to force me to go with the customers. He takes photographs of us and sends them out. If a girl tries to escape she is badly beaten. One was burned with cigarettes. Anyway we would not know where to go.

He keeps us shut up in a room. There is a fridge-like door through which we are allowed out to attend to the customers.

My health is ruined. Still the customers are forced on me. See my hands. The sores itch. I think it is the food.'

Meena was 15 when she told this story. After three years of being forced to satisfy men's sexual desires, the child who had set out to save her family was infected with venereal disease and was alone, frightened and heart broken.

But for Sister Rita's chance visit to the brothel, Meena's future would have been one of advancing illness until she was of no further use to the pimp or his clients. She would then have been thrown out onto the streets to beg.

The man who abducted and raped her and many of the other men who used her probably remain respected in their communities.

'Children? My God, repeatedly the girls I was meeting were children. All cases are very pathetic,' said Sister Rita, profoundly moved by the experience her survey had exposed her to. A great majority of the 1100 prostitutes she and her researchers interviewed – mainly encountered in unannounced visits to brothels – were either children or had first been sexually exploited as children. Nearly a third of those interviewed were under 16. 'Only a few were lured into prostitution by sweet talk – the rest were all forced in some form or other.'

Most of the children came from poor families and had little or no education. Most of the men who used them – at least while they were still young and could attract a high price – were comparatively rich. 'Generally the customers are upper class people and the whole system is initiated, sustained and perpetuated by moneyed people.'

There are close parallels between accounts of child prostitution in the Third World today and those of 19th Century Britain.

Following several visits to England in the 1820s and 1830s, French traveller and observer Flora Tristan wrote a journal about social conditions in London. Referring to a statement of the Society for the Prevention of Juvenile Prostitution she noted:

It said there were large numbers of men and women whose business it was to sell girls between ten and fifteen years of age whom they had caught in their traps. These children, enticed on some plausible pretext into collecting-houses or brothels, were kept in close confinement for a fortnight or so and thus forever lost to their parents.

Victorian cartoon of procuress offering a child for prostitution
FÉLICIEN ROPS

[62] *The London Journal of Flora Tristan*; translated, annotated and introduced by Jean Hawkes, pages 92 and 98, Virago, London, 1982.

She quotes the Society's founder, Mr James Talbot:
The other modes by which infamous houses are supplied, as death, disease or demand require, is that the keepers employ agents, young women of about eighteen years, to perambulate the streets, and decoy any children they may meet with, under pretence of taking them to see a relative, or going for a pleasant walk, or inviting them to the theatres, or getting them a place of service. [62]

In many countries abduction remains a stock-in-trade technique of those who procure children for prostitution and sometimes for labour. In her report of research between 1983 and 1986, Sister Rozario refers to an article in *The Times of India* telling of police taking action against a powerful inter-state gang alleged to have kidnapped several thousand children. [63]

[63] 'U.P. Thrives on "export" of kids'; *The Times of India*, March 24, 1984.

A third of the girls and women interviewed for the study said that some relative had been involved in their procurement for prostitution. Some had been abducted. Others were tricked, for instance, into fake marriages to men who turned out to be procurers or by promises that they would be placed in work. Family complicity was 'almost invariably that of an uncle or a distant relative and sometimes a drunkard father or brother. Sometimes a neighbour is responsible. It is very seldom the mother'.

Another researcher into prostitution, in a red light district of Bombay, Priti Paai, said 'You find women who have been forced into prostitution by their own parents – sold because the parents had other daughters lined up to get married. Their attitude is, "What else could I do? There was this person ready to pay me for my daughter – instead of ruining all six daughters I ruin one person's life to save the others."'

Sales of children into prostitution by parents occur most often where the family is breaking down under the pressures of poverty, according to Jyotsna Chatterji, associate director of the William Carey Study and Research Centre, and head of the Delhi-based Joint Women's Programme, which commissioned the Sister Rita study.

'We came across firm cases of girls of 13 and 15 who had been sold into prostitution by rich landlords in the rural areas and businessmen in the slums, whose inhabitants are mainly migrants from drought-ridden areas. These men would take the girls in exchange for money lent to the father or guardian and not repaid,' said Jyotsna. Most of the girls are from poor families in the dry-land areas of the more backward states.

Some girls and women who have been raped may be more easily persuaded into a life of prostitution. A woman in a brothel in Bombay told a social worker she had been raped as a child by a shopkeeper in her village. Her father later went blind and so couldn't earn. The family, with five daughters, was very poor. 'After the rape a woman came from Bombay and said I would make a lot of money if I went with her. "Your life is ruined anyway because you have been raped," she told me. "You will have a better life and you can send money to your sisters and at least you will save them."'

Sister Rita's researches uncovered evidence of some inter-state trade and an elaborate pricing structure. A virgin from the south fetches a higher price in the north and vice versa because differences in appearance and manner make her seem more exotic. A Nepalese girl with characteristically 'chinked' eyes and a fair complexion is very much in demand in Bombay and South India. The plump girl typical of Tamil Nadu or Andhra Pradesh might be sought after in Delhi but in the red light area of Puna might fetch very little. Prices paid range from £50 to £2500.

The girls may be traded through a network – if a Calcutta brothel needs a girl from Tamil Nadu they will contact a centre in Pondicherry and the girl will be sent. 'A brothel will have a variety of the girls to meet the taste of the clientele. It's the clientele that decides the kind they want and the girl's value is set by demand,' said Sister Rita. Virgins command a special price and are sometimes auctioned to customers by brothel owners. Competition to be the one to deflower the child is stimulated by a myth that intercourse with a virgin is a remedy for venereal disease. There is also a belief that the younger child is pure and clean; after her first menstrual cycle she is mature and unclean.

The trade in children is not confined within national boundaries, says Jyotsna Chatterji. 'We found girls are being sold to the Middle East, some to Hong Kong. You find Indian girls in Nepal and Pakistan, just as you find Nepalese and Pakistani girls here. We believe there is an international ring which procures little girls from Asian and other Third World regions.'

Initiation of young girls into organised prostitution is usually brutal and designed to convince them of their powerlessness. The pimp or brothel owner who has bought a child is concerned only to hold on to his or her investment and to get a quick return on it.

As soon as the female is decoyed to a brothel, she is no longer allowed to wear her own clothes, which become the prize of the keeper; she is decked with second-hand trappings, once the property of some wealthy lady. The regular clients are notified, and when she no longer attracts customers to the house, her master sends her to walk the streets, where he has her closely watched so that it is impossible for her to escape, and if she attempts it, the spy, often a bully or a procuress, charges her with stealing from the master of the house the clothes she wears on her back. Then the policeman arrests her, and sometimes he takes her to the station-house, but more commonly he gives her up to the brothel-keeper, who rewards him.

Flora Tristan, writing of 19th Century England[64]

[64] *The London Journal of Flora Tristan;* quoting from the 1836 Annual Report of the Society for the Prevention of Juvenile Prostitution.

Sister Rita's study found that on arrival at a brothel a girl is likely to be ordered to undress. Then she will be made to hand over her clothes and any other possessions. In return she will be given some scanty clothes and some cheap make-up. That is all she will have. The girl will be told that thousands of rupees have been paid for her: she will have to accept customers in order to clear the debt and pay for her keep.

If the child continues to resist or tries to escape, food may be withheld and she may be beaten or tortured. The girls who resist are raped as a matter of course.

'Some are branded or cut with a knife. Some are mutilated. One little girl of nine was whipped and kept in a closed room for nearly two years, whipped constantly but forbidden to make any noise or tell anybody. After the whippings she was raped. After two years she broke open the door in the man's absence and was able to escape – I met her in one of the children's state homes. There were burn marks on her body, a lot, made with rods.'

Children are held as virtual prisoners, some literally locked up in rooms. 'Most of those kept in bondage are children,' said Sister Rita, who has sometimes entered brothels and huts at a risk to her own life.

The blend of brutality and isolation in a brothel can destroy a young girl's belief in an alternative life in the outside world. She may have no knowledge of the neighbourhood, let alone the city or how to get from the city to her home. Pimps in the street would quickly inform the brothel keeper if a girl appeared to be leaving the area. A child who had been abducted from her home might rightly conclude that going home would not put her beyond the power of the pimps anyway. By such means children are brought to accept their fate.

Physical bolts and bars may not be necessary. One little girl aged below ten was in a bondage of terror to a blind beggar.

'He used to bring her on to the trains. She would thrust out the begging bowl for him. She wore a soiled dress and had matted hair. When she came into the care of social workers, they tried to give her a bath and found her private parts were infected. Her owner was one of a group of blind beggars who made young girls beg for them during the day and put them to prostitution at night. The children charged about two rupees (ten UK pence) a time and the beggars insisted the children bring them each ten rupees a day. If they failed to do so they were thrashed and burned with bidi (cigarette) butts.

'I came across so many distressing stories like that. The extent of such abuses of children must be great because, within so short a time, I have been able to get so much information.'

The odds for a long life are dramatically shortened as soon as a girl becomes engaged in prostitution. Her health is likely to deteriorate through frequent sickness. Venereal disease is particularly common, but Sister Rita found a huge ignorance of it among young prostitutes in her sample: most were infected without understanding what was wrong with them.

'I used to ask if they had relevant symptoms. But I stopped asking because I could feel it immediately, you could tell just sitting next them. They were spitting blood, some of them. Some had leprosy also. Some couldn't use their limbs.

'I found a 15-year-old girl who had been brought to Karnataka from Andhra Pradesh who thought that maybe the food didn't agree with her. I interviewed other girls in the same brothel and then I brought in a lady doctor. They all had venereal disease of different kinds – young children.'

In contrast, the AIDS scare is showing signs of getting through, even if the information is not always correct. 'In Bombay some of the youngsters were asking me about it. "I'm afraid to kiss", they'd say.'

When the young women become well known to all the regular clients and no longer excite their fancy, they are passed on to a second-rate house and after a year or eighteen months the wretched creatures die in hospital or are left to fend for themselves on the streets.
from *Flora Tristan*[65]

[65] *The London Journal of Flora Tristan*, page 93.

In the most abusive establishments, a girl is made to work round the clock whenever there is a customer, until she sickens – in body or mind – or is no longer marketable. But in many brothels once a child gives up resisting and accepts her enslavement, relations with a brothel owner may improve.

Pimps may encourage the girls to become mothers and will even withhold contraception until they do have a baby. They know a child will give the mother something to live for and a reason to work harder.

'These girls long for a lasting relationship,' says Sister Rita. 'They are basically insecure. They long to get married. They long to belong to somebody and to have a family of their own. They endlessly search for a man who will love them sincerely.'

Few prostitutes are able to save, least of all those in bondage. In India they have first to repay the price paid for them by the pimp and money is extracted from their earnings for accommodation, food, clothing, contraception and so on. They have to borrow from the madames to pay for medical treatment or cover them in times when they cannot work. Debt bondage takes over as the need for incarceration falls away. The debt is rarely paid. When they can no longer draw customers and have outlived their usefulness they are just thrown out. One of Sister Rita's respondents was given 100 rupees (£5) and put on a train to nowhere in particular. 'She was not able to stand, let alone walk, she has a growth in her neck but, until the day she was put on the train, she was in a brothel.'

The involvement of children in prostitution is illegal in India and there is little official recognition that it occurs. Allowing for regional variations, Sister Rita's findings coincide with those in countries where the problem is both more extensive and more investigated – such as Thailand, the Philippines and Brazil.

A brothel in Thailand. At the sound of a bell, prostitutes line flood-lit benches wearing numbers so customers can select from them.
RICK MCKAY/
COX NEWSPAPERS

Prostitution is essentially deprivation dressed up as pleasure. It is the byproduct of poverty and an abuse of power, by both the procurer and the customer, which treats human beings as consumer items. The link between abusive power and poverty is luminously captured in a description by Sister Mary Soledad Perpinan (Third World Movement Against the Exploitation of Women) of the arrival in Olongapo City, the Philippines, of 5000 US sailors. At anchor in the bay is the starkly destructive reality of their nuclear capacity warships. In the city's recreation areas a flimsy veneer of gaiety cloaks the reality of poor women selling their bodies to a rich nation's men of war.

'Everything looked plastic under the garish colours of neon and strobe lights. As we wove our way in and out of the disco dens, clubs and bars, everybody appeared like objects of the entertainment world. A certain weirdness permeated the air – of men unwinding after being cooped up in ships and of women, cheap and giddy, prey of pressing economic needs.

'That night it was the entire sickly system that glared at me – the nauseating dominance of one nation over another. The people in the joints and street were but pawns playing their pathetic roles.'[66]

In the context of this market a German citizen feels free to address a clinical inquiry to his country's embassy in Bangkok: 'For the duration of my stay in Bangkok, I would like to hire a Thai girl. Since I do not wish to return to Germany with the clap or syphilis, I would like her to be examined by a dermatologist. I would therefore be very grateful if you could give me the address of a reliable doctor. . . . Or is there an agency in Bangkok that guarantees its girls are healthy?'[67] Commenting on protest in his country against commercialised sex tourism in Asia, the president of a Japanese travel agency is

[66] *Tourism, Prostitution, Development*; The Ecumenical Coalition on Third World Tourism, Bangkok, page 19, 1983.

[67] *Tourism, Prostitution, Development*; page 7.

*Boy selling
pornographic
magazines on the
streets of Manila,
Philippines*
DEXTER TIRANTI/NEW
INTERNATIONALIST

[68] *Tourism,
Prostitution,
Development*; page 7.

[69] *The Worm in the
Bud, The World of
Victorian Sexuality* by
Ronald Pearsall,
Weidenfeld and
Nicholson, page 430,
Pelican 1971.

quoted as saying, with apparent resignation: 'In the capitalist system it is unavoidable that the weak will fall prey to the strong.'[68]

The readiness of adults to exploit children sexually is not peculiar to this century. Ronald Pearsall wrote of 19th Century England: 'The extent to which children were looked upon as direct sexual objects was frightening.'[69]

It still is, but the power of money now enables men from rich and dominant nations to treat some poorer countries as sexual playgrounds offering freedom they would not enjoy at home.

A few years ago a bilingual Thailand Tourist Guide presented a *Which* magazine-style appraisal of the country's centres of sexual diversion. Under 'Group 5' it said: *If you fancy*

It is illegal for bars in the Philippines to employ anyone under 18, yet many do. For a fee, the bar where 14-year-old Merlin works will allow its dancers to leave with customers

RICK MCKAY/
COX NEWSPAPERS

extremely young girls or, generally speaking if you want something for which you would get 'hanged' in your home country, you can find it in the places of this group without the risk of being hanged. You can even expect a nod of the head, the Asian clasp of hands, accompanied by a thank you.[70]

[70] *Tourism, Prostitution, Development*, page 46.

'What is terrible is not that a ten-year-old girl will work as a prostitute to survive,' says a prominent spokesperson for prostitutes in Brazil, Gabriela Silva Leite. 'It is that we have reached a state of sexual repression and hypocrisy where men feel attracted to ten-year-old girls – even rape their own children – and where porn movies are shown in which children are made to create a fantastical world for masculine pleasure.

'Prostitution is society's creation. It can be understood only in the wider context of society's morals and ways in which men and women can relate. In macho, christian societies women are deeply divided into two camps – the wives of men and mothers of their children who must be pure and saintly and the others, prostitutes or lovers.' Men are also subject to conflicting expectations. 'The man must live out the serious role of worker, husband, father, along with the notion that he is somehow more a man if he has many other women in the street. So prostitution is one of the legs that supports this concept of family.'

Gabriela believes it is unsurprising in such a context that men can retreat from the challenge of finding a more creative relationship with women into increasingly self-absorbed carnality, ultimately reflected in the use of children.

In his writings about 19th Century England, Pearsall noted that 'at the other extreme' from the view of children as sex objects, little girls were looked on with a 'reverence that would have been applicable to angels'.[71]

[71] *The Worm in the Bud*, page 431.

Considering the organisers of prostitution, Sister Mary Soledad Perpinan distinguishes between 'small and visible' operators and the 'big and invisble'. Visible sellers include

Pagsanjan, the Philippines. A broken sign warning off visitors in search of the sexual services of boys
RICK MCKAY/COX
NEWSPAPERS

[72] *Prostitution: Survival of Slavery*; 28th International Congress. International Abolitionist Federation.

relatives, recruiters, pimps and go-betweens, such as taxi drivers and tour guides. 'Protectors of the business,' she says, 'are reputedly policemen and supposed law-enforcing officers.' The invisible sellers are those who directly and indirectly hold responsibility for the prostitution phenomenon and who can be found in business and government centres of power.[72]

A major contribution to the market for prostitution is the commercial abuse of power that separates men from women in the form of migrant labour.

In the process of extracting the natural resources of Peruvian

[73] *International Children's Rights Monitor – Special Edition*, 1984.

Amazonia 'short-term migrant workers live in camps or enclaves and companies supply prostitutes for their sexual needs. It has been reported that the demand for very young girls (12 to 16) is very high in Iquitos and that virgins are offered as gambling prizes.'[73]

Gabriela says girls as young as ten are introduced into the compounds of some mines in Brazil to service the sexual needs of migrants who live apart from their women folk. Women cannot be persuaded to go into these compounds, 'where there are so many men subjected to oppressive conditions'.

She adds that migrant workseekers who come into cities find it difficult, and cannot afford to establish relationships with city women – 'girlfriends are more expensive than prostitutes'.

Commercial advertising and pornography are important means by which sex is promoted as a commodity. Child pornography ranges from soft-porn to 'snuff' movies, in which children are actually killed and hard-porn periodicals which are sent out through paedophile networks. A magazine produced privately in the US but distributed internationally had a section headed 'Kiddie Torture' which starts: *Child abuse is a sublime pleasure. All the great extremes – genital torture, forced unlubricated rape, butchering; all these pleasures and more reach their pinnacle when the victim is a small child . . .*

[74] *The Sexual Exploitation of Children* by Judith Ennew.

At the softer end of the porn market, interest in adult/child sex is reflected and encouraged openly and creeps into brand name advertising.[74]

The Sex Maniacs' Diary 1988, which was sold in bookshops and garages in the UK, carried several advertisements for known paedophile organisations with addresses in the US, including one which is said to have a membership of 10,000 and has the slogan 'Sex before eight; otherwise it's too late'.

Sometimes parents are involved in making children available for pornography and may also be the photographers. Other children are recruited through networks by word of mouth or by advertising. In the UK, small ads angling for teenage boys are common in gay, naturalist and soft porn magazines. The wording, says Richie McMullen, is usually very simple. 'It will be a tiny little ad stuck in a corner saying X magazine seeks models for lucrative modelling work.' The respondents are youngsters usually already involved in prostitution.

As with prostitution, some children are sold or abducted for pornographic purposes. They may be forced to take drugs to secure their cooperation.

Trafficking of children for the purposes of sexual exploitation is thought by some to be big business but there has been remarkably little in the way of solid research into it. This is probably partly because most of the children involved are from poor homes in Third World countries who have little call on the attentions of the authorities. It is also likely to be because the organisers are powerful gangs or individuals who know how to secure their interests in the corridors of officialdom.

Certainly the demand is there, the rewards can be high and it is also remarkably easy to move children, even across some international boundaries. The UK television Cooke Report exposed the ease of moving a child across the Brazilian-Colombian border in a programme about the abduction of children for illegal adoption. The Turkish press reported babies being taken at birth to be sold to couples in the country and abroad; mothers were told their babies had died.[75] In Guatemala police discovered a nursery with 14 babies bought even before they were born.[76]

[75] *International Children's Rights Monitor* Vol 1, No 1; Defence for Children International.
[76] *Report to the Council of Europe on the traffic in children and other forms of child exploitation*; September 1987.

Adoption from Third World linked to prostitution and pornography

Netherlands acts to tackle world trade in children

The Guardian
10th October 1987

There have been reports of orphans procured for the trade in several countries. The readiness of rich childless families to buy children illegally for adoption purposes promotes structures that might also be put to more sinister uses. Federal police in Brazil estimated that 3000 children were illegally exported from the country to childless couples in Israel, Europe and the US for sums up to £12,000. Children acquired in this way may go to caring homes, but there are fears that illegal First–Third World adoption has also been one of the guises by which children have been procured for prostitution.

77 *The Sexual Exploitation of Children* by Judith Ennew, page 43.

While the reports of sex trafficking capture public attention, some experts argue that with children being available locally for sexual purposes, there is little cause for trafficking. Making this point, Judith Ennew writes that exaggeration of the trade in children does a disservice to those 'in petty sordid relationships which are the day-to-day reality of the majority of cases of child sexual abuse and exploitation'.[77]

INTERPOL, an information sharing service available to the police forces of its 146 member nations, is a unique barometer of international police priorities. The agency sees signs of a revival of concern in some north-European countries about child pornography and trafficking but very little information is requested or offered by national police forces.

Chief Superintendent Helmut Sipple, of INTERPOL, argues that policing priorities are dictated by various pressures, including public concern. Current preoccupations are organised crime, violence, terrorism, drugs. 'They (national police forces) concentrate increasingly on the intelligence gathering work of very important crimes and the day-to-day small crimes are increasingly handled by police in uniform.'

At this level offences tend to be dealt with as if they are a national problem.

'If you are an ordinary policeman and you come across porno cassettes – your investigation is directed against the last person who sells the films, but he is only at the end of a process. You try to establish that he sold them – and he will be punished in a very small way for having sold banned pictures and that will be the end of the matter.

'I think there are many investigations of this kind all over Europe without the information being shared or requested internationally. You can't find out who has made these films and most investigations stop within national boundaries.'

'Prostitution is the same – there is nothing that obliges the investigator to deal with it as an international case. Again it is regarded as a very small offence not warranting a lot of police investigation – to take it further would require a lot of effort.

'I think things are changing; there have been some investigations on an international basis, especially in the area of hard pornography, against people who have been working together producing and selling films. In the manufacture of these films it is our growing impression that children under 14 are misused. There is now some international interest.

'Where we have been missing international interest up to now is in child prostitution. Perhaps there is a hangover from the 1960s view that prostitutes are normally more than 18 to 19 years old, but if you go to certain parts of Paris or Hamburg you will find children of 14 to 15 years. You didn't find this ten years ago. Things have changed but I don't know if police perception of things has changed yet.'

But also child trafficking is likely to be 'a crime without a victim'. The child will not usually be in a position to complain. Parents who sell a child won't complain. Investigation into the abduction of a poor child in a remote part of the world by ill-equipped police facing a tumult of problems is unlikely to extend beyond national boundaries.

'It is the old police problem – if you have a crime without a victim, you have little opportunity to go into investigation, if the police don't act the crime doesn't exist. So we need the official interest of the public – and people to become aware enough to notice abnormal behaviour and inform police of their suspicions. Out situation in Europe is that all things related to sex are more and more allowed. No limit is set.'

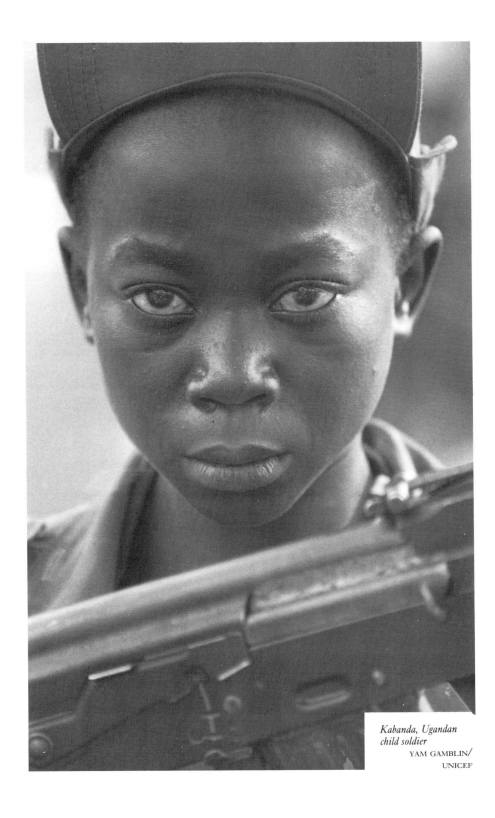

*Kabanda, Ugandan
child soldier*
YAM GAMBLIN/
UNICEF

Children of conflict

[78] *Report of the Independent Commission on International Humanitarian Issues*; page 9, Geneva, 1987.

The psychological distances between the strata are in imminent danger of reaching the point where the only form of discourse between top and bottom may be open conflict, often violent . . . occasionally punctuated by outbursts of charity.

Independent Commission on International Humanitarian Issues[78]

We have in Nicaragua around 12,000 people who are fatherless because of the war. We have many children who have been shot in the war, who are legless or armless because of the war. And this is the question we ask everyone: What has a child done so that he is fatherless, what has he done so that he has no leg.

Ajax Delgado, Secretary General of the Asociación de Niños Sandinistas

Soldier, it is a bad thing. It is good if you are a child and they killed your mother and all your brothers and sisters. But when it is peaceful, I would not go in for being a soldier.

Kabanda, a corporal in the National Resistance Army, Uganda.

FAMILIES IN THE FRONT LINE

Maria Neles looks down at a photo of Ignacio, her child who died fighting

Maria Neles treasures the photo she has of the son who went off to war at the age of twelve. It is mounted on a board with pictures of other members of the family. Except for her memories, it is all she has of him. She speaks of him with happiness and great sadness.

Ignacio Ramon Olivas Torres was a hard-working, bright boy. At seven he laboured on the family farm while pursuing his schooling. At twelve he was teaching adults as part of a national literacy campaign. When President Somoza was overthrown in

1979, most Nicaraguans were illiterate and the new Sandinista government started trying to make up for lost years. There were not enough adults to do the teaching, so the campaign relied heavily on children.

It was a policy of the US-backed Contra forces to threaten the civilians who helped with the literacy campaign. Ignacio was one of them.

The family lived close to the Rio Coco in the lush, fertile mountains of Jinotega district. This area is near the border with Honduras, a host country to the Contras, and when they started their offensive in 1981 the family was in the front line.

Maria Neles says her son used to help out on a neighbour's farm. One day a band of Contra appeared. 'They threatened Ignacio about his teaching activities and said that he was the son of a well-known Sandinista. One said "I'm going to go to your house and I'm going to kill you and all your family."

'That was when Ignacio left home. He felt his family was in danger if he was there. As he left he said, "Don't worry about me but I'm going to help with the army."

'We really thought he was going to die, and he thought so too. He told us, "You have a son who wants to defend his fatherland."'

His mother saw little of him over the next five years. 'All around he was in battles. I wasn't afraid because I believed in God and believed that he would keep him safe. It was important to help in the defence, but I was also sad, but that was my problem.'

On April 10th, 1985, Ignacio was killed in battle. He was 17.

During the mid 1980s, death and destruction in the Rio Coco region persuaded many families to move to safer areas. Ignacio's family went 80 kilometres south to Matagalpa Province to join 16 other families from their region in one of the cooperatives set up for people displaced by the war. The cooperative is now named after Ignacio.

'Some of us came here because the war was too close to our homes, others because we have lost family members,' says Aide Gonzalez Centeno, who lost her husband and almost lost a son, **Abercio**.

The boy's father had been a teacher and encouraged him in his studies. Like Ignacio, he helped with the adult literacy programme and so became a Contra target. Abercio also joined up with the army. His mother tried to dissuade him from leaving home. 'I was very sad because he was only twelve and so little. I struggled with him for many days. His battalion was a long way away so I didn't have contact with him.'

Abercio survived. Now aged 20, he is production secretary of the cooperative, in charge of organising labour, purchasing supplies and marketing produce. Swinging in his hammock he talks in an understated way of his years as a child combatant.

'The Contras were looking for me, so I volunteered to help with the defence. There was a battalion near my home and I was taught how to fight. When I joined up I was doing what everyone else was doing right away.'

Did that mean he had been involved in combat?

He dismisses the question with a look of mild disdain. 'We were right in the front line near the Honduran border. Of course I used a gun. It was necessary, and there were casualties.

Abercio

'I was in many battles. One lasted 15 days. There were 3000 Contras in the camp we were attacking. Other battles lasted maybe five days, some one or two hours.'

When Abercio was 14, he heard that his father had been killed by a Contra mine. 'After his death I just had more courage in fighting the Contra.' He continued to fight until he was 16.

His days as a child soldier have left him with a damaged eye. 'I think something entered it, like a mortar splinter.' He also suffered what he terms a psychotic breakdown. 'After so many battles just a little thing would set me off. I had a terrible sadness, I worried a lot and I had a lot of pain in my head. I'd think people were running to fight. I'd think about being in combat. I had a lot of nervousness. Sometimes friends didn't seem like friends.'

Now he helps to support his mother in bringing up his younger brothers and sisters.

In the cooperative's small schoolroom, children talk of the loss of fathers. An eleven-year-old begins to recount an attack in which his father and 18-year-old brother were killed. 'I saw it all,' he says, swallowing back tears. Another brother who survived the attack takes up the story. 'Six hundred Contras attacked our community. Sixty of us tried to defend our homes. The fighting lasted five days.

'I was coming back with the militia to defend our part of the

Four years ago this 18-year-old fought alongside his father and brother who were both killed. Now he helps guard the 'Ignacio' cooperative

community. My father was killed by a grenade. His body was badly mutilated. My brother was also dead. I had to run for my life. I stayed away four days. Twenty-five members of our militia were killed in the attack.'

After speaking, he sits slightly apart, calming his troubled young half-brother.

Ten-year-old **Carmen**, one of a family of five, grimly gives witness to his father's death. 'The Contras came to the house, opened the door and killed my father. I saw them . . .'

Away from the children, his mother explains: 'We lived on an isolated farm. We'd been afraid the Contra might attack. My husband was doing his national service but, at the time, was back home with me and the children.

'A Contra came to the door and asked me for a meal. My husband, sensing danger, tried to escape through the back of the house. But there were more of them outside and they threw a grenade to stop him. They then attacked him. They robbed and stripped him and mutilated his body. They cut off his genitals.

Carmen – 'I saw my father die'

'They took the children outside and burned the house.

'The children saw everything. Sometimes they talk about what's happened. They'll cry and say how terrible it was that their father was killed. And they ask, "Why?"'

Like children everywhere, the youngsters of the cooperative have moments of playing and laughing. But they are also unnaturally subdued and weary.

Over a few years, with the help of government extension services and aid agencies, the families have managed to build up a vegetable farm from nothing. They have done so despite stringent shortages and marketing difficulties. Most of them have their own houses. A member of the cooperative has been given training to provide a basic health service. There is a school, a water supply, a shop and a store for agricultural implements and produce.

But again the families feel threatened by war.[79] A change in

[79] These interviews were conducted immediately after the announcement in March 1988 of a 60-days cease fire. The families were sceptical that it would be adhered to.

Carmen's younger brother and sister

Contra strategy and an improvement in their supply network has seen a wider dispersal through the country of small armed bands.

'It wasn't dangerous here in the early days but now it's different,' says one woman. 'The Contras walk around all over this area and attack when they have the opportunity, when there aren't many men around. They haven't come here because we're well defended.' The army is nearby and the cooperative has its own small militia.

Ignacio's younger brother, **Xavier**, is one of 20 men and boys who guard the families. He volunteered to join the militia

Xavier

when he was 14, two years after Ignacio's death. His mother was nervous but resigned: 'It's important for the defence.'

By the end of 1987, 455 children were known to have died as a direct result of the war in Nicaragua; 1502 had been injured. But there were probably many others in less accessible parts of the country whose deaths and injuries went unrecorded. Also, there was a sharp increase in the numbers of child victims of the war in the months of heightened conflict from January 1988 to the declaration of the cease-fire in March.

Children have been involved in the fighting on both sides but most of the child casualties have been unarmed, the victims of attacks on civilians or of land-mine explosions.

Kitty Madden, an American social worker based on a state farm close to the 'Ignacio' cooperative, says cooperatives have been prominent targets and attacks on them are essentially attacks against women and children. Because of mobilisation many of the men are away fighting. Having spoken to a lot of victims of violence, she says the Contras have had 'no qualms about throwing grenades into homes when they know children are there.'

Accounts of atrocities are legion and accusations are made on both sides. What firm evidence there is points to the Contras as being responsible for most hostilities directed at children and it has been acknowledged Contra policy to treat as targets civilians who help keep the government in power or maintain government services. For its part, the government concedes that there have been some attacks on civilians by its soldiers, but claims that they have been breaches of policy.

Some atrocities appear to have no motive other than

intimidation. Carrie Parker, of Witness for Peace – an American organisation documenting attacks on civilians, tells of a 15-year-old boy, a 'helper around the church', who was taken out of a parish house. 'The Contras laid him down and shot him for no reason. Nobody knows why.'[80]

Mines – which have been planted by both sides – are particularly dangerous to children. To warn civilians, the Sandinistas have marked some areas they have mined with small signs, reading 'Minas', but these provide no protection to young children who cannot read.

Alfonso, a seven-year-old Sumo Indian, and his two brothers were injured by a mine boobytrap left near their home by Contras operating in the remote north-east of the country. The children found and started to investigate an object that had been wrapped up to look attractive. It blew up, leaving Alfonso with a damaged eye and shrapnel wounds.

[80] Witness for Peace is one of several American organisations and individuals in the country opposed to US support for the Contras.

Alfonso

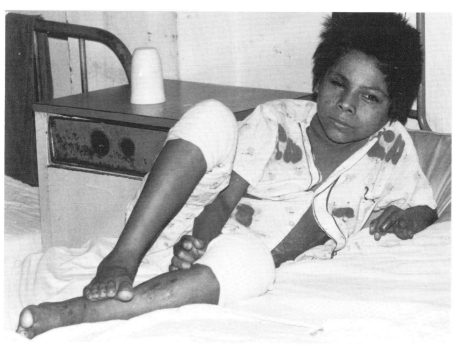

Some of the worst mine injuries have happened on the roads. In one incident, a Contra mine blew up a civilian truck carrying nearly 50 people. Of the 19 who died, five were children under the age of 13.

Children have also been raped and they have been kidnapped. Official statistics record 691 kidnappings of children under 15 up to the end of 1987. Such kidnappings are

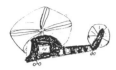

part of general terror tactics but must be regarded as a form of enforced recruitment. The Contras have used the children for carrying supplies. But some have been put into battle, and there are reports of their being used to test paths for live mines.

There have even been reports of children being found dead with their veins cut but no sign of blood on the ground. The assumption is that their blood was used for transfusions to wounded Contras.

The direct involvement of children in the war on the side of the Sandinistas has been to do with the nature of the conflict, in which small communities have had to defend themselves from surprise attacks and children have been singled out for Contra punishment. The introduction of conscription by the government saw a reduction in the numbers of child soldiers. While some boys in their early teens continue to help defend cooperatives, particularly in the absence of men, the practice is not normally encouraged.

Large numbers of people have been forced to abandon their homes and communities. Kitty Madden tells the story of a woman who moved to avoid the danger of her son being kidnapped.

'I think Contras had kidnapped the boy six times. Each time he'd escape only to be taken again. He finally said to his mother, "We need to go and live on a cooperative because I can't do this anymore". Just before I spoke to her the cooperative they'd moved to had been attacked for the fourth time. Her son was the first one killed.'

The psychological scars of the war on children will never be fully assessed. Because of the nature of the war, civilians have been in the front line. Many children have been made to

[81] *Envio*; Instituto Historico Centroamericano, Vol 7 No 80, February 1988.

The machinery of war, drawn by a twelve-year-old at a 'minors at risk' school in Managua

witness the abuse or killing of a parent, a brother, a sister or some other close friend or relative. Abducted children may be forced to fight people they regard as belonging to their side. Anecdotes abound but no detailed research has been undertaken.

The cost of any war to children is to be counted not only in terms of the damage done to life and limb and to the fabric of family and community; it is also to be assessed in terms of the development opportunities lost. This is especially so in the case of Nicaragua. For the first time in many years, following the defeat of the Somoza regime, the country had a government committed to improving the lives of people in general and children in particular. A whole range of health, nutrition and education programmes has been set back as a result of the violence and the economic aspects of the war.

A massive schools construction programme was implemented as part of a commitment to provide all children with primary education. High priority was given to the provision of day-care facilities. In 1979 there were only 1000 children in kindergarten; by 1988 there were 70,000.

However, by the mid-1980s the government had to drop its programme to build two classrooms a day. Those that were built have lost teaching and other staff to the war effort. In many rural areas schools have had to close because of Contra targetting of teachers. It has become too dangerous for some children to go to school. There are chronic shortages of text books and other school supplies.

In 1979, there were only 189 primary health care units in the country. By 1986 there were 606 units, 58 per cent more doctors, 211 per cent more nurses. Infant mortality had dropped from 120 per thousand to 69.[81]

But advances in health provisions have also been disrupted. Health centres have had to close and vaccination campaigns – the cornerstone of preventive care – have not been possible in many areas.

Hospitals are desperately short of essentials. Nurse-midwife Victoria Baker says of the ward she works on that it has only four pairs of scissors and sometimes there are not enough sheets. 'If the washing machines break down we are up the creek, and it happens. We're talking very basic here.'

Medical personnel have been absorbed into the war; some have left to seek better pay overseas, or gone into other jobs in Nicaragua. The effect on the care of babies and children in hospitals is 'severe', says Victoria. She was particularly disturbed about the recent death of a baby. Had the hospital been able to monitor the mother's progress adequately, had the

delivery room not lacked basic equipment, had the orderly not
been totally inexperienced, the infant might have lived.

The need to divert scarce funds into national security has
generally curbed the government's ability to forge ahead with its
development programmes. 'You can't put 50 to 60 per cent of
your national budget into war and defence without that having
an effect in every area,' says Kitty Madden. US economic
sanctions have further helped to cripple the economy. For more
than a century, America had called the tune in its economic
relations with Nicaragua, leaving the country in a state of
dependency. When trade links were severed, the economy went
into a free-fall, helped, some would argue, by the government's
own economic policies.

The war has emptied private as well as public pockets and
had a profoundly demoralising impact on the country. 'People
talk about the inability to feed and dress children adequately,'
says Carrie Parker. 'A pair of shoes for a child can cost up to a
month's salary.' War and drought have combined to reduce
agricultural production. There are indications that malnutrition
is on the increase.

Shortages and prolonged uncertainty threaten community
spirit. 'The Nicaraguan people are by nature very hospitable
and into sharing,' says Kitty Madden. 'But one of the things
that happens when there are fewer resources is that people get
into holding on to what is theirs and not working so
cooperatively.' There has been an increase in petty crime and
in the number of street children. There are also signs of a rise
in alcoholism. 'A lot of people here drink just to pass out and
forget. And that also affects what's happening for children in
their homes,' says Kitty.

The war has resulted in changes in family roles. With fathers
away from home, the women do much of the farm work and
younger children are left more in the care of older siblings. The
loss of many fathers in the war will increase the number of
step-parent households and so, probably, the likelihood of child
rejection or abuse.

Child psychiatrist Anna Maria Solari – an Argentinian
working in Nicaragua – says, 'I think there's been a big effect
indirectly on the families and the grown-ups. The things
mothers and fathers are going through are affecting all the
children. There's a very high level of tension within the family
and a lot of problems – spending problems. And the grown-ups
are not aware of how well or badly the children are reacting or
feeling. Many believe that the children don't feel anything
because they are small. But of course they do.'

At least in Nicaragua, a large proportion of the population

confronted the Contra assault having shared a recent experience of solidarity in the victory over Somoza. In contrast, the Luwero Triangle massacres in Uganda came at the end of demoralising years of political repression, economic anarchy and general violence.

A whole generation of children in Uganda has grown up in an environment of violence. The Tanzanian and Uganda National Liberation Army forces, which drove the murderous Idi Amin from power in 1979, only served to usher in a new era of killing and looting. Three short-lived governments failed to take effective control and the second Presidency of Milton Obote (1980–85) saw indiscriminate bloodshed on a massive scale.

Skulls collected and displayed as a memorial to murdered civilians, Luwero Triangle

The main threat to Obote's regime came from the National Resistance Army (NRA), led by Yoweri Museveni. Ruthless attempts were made to crush the rebel movement, but they failed. As in Nicaragua both sides made use of child soldiers. Faced with mounting defeats, Obote's army stepped up its recruitment of children and, unlike the NRA, sent many into battle. Some people describe seeing child corpses among the army dead piled on trucks.

Child soldiers accounted for about ten per cent of the NRA force and are said to have made an important contribution to the struggle.

'The first and overwhelming impression was the number of children who were bearing arms,' says Cole Dodge – UNICEF's representative at the time – describing a flight he made in 1985 into NRA territory with a consignment of drugs and vaccines.

The NRA prided itself on ensuring its young soldiers were carefully supervised and well-disciplined. They were mainly used in non-combative roles. However, they were better suited to some tasks than adults. There are stories of children being hidden in roadside bundles of wood, from which to launch surprise machinegun and grenade attacks on army vehicles.

Ironically, child participation in the NRA was largely the outcome of a terror campaign waged by the military and the youth wing of Obote's political party against rebel concentrations in the Luwero Triangle. Homes were attacked indiscriminately in a bid to stop people supporting and harbouring rebels. Many children saw their parents butchered and, having no-one to turn to, were taken under the wing of the NRA. Some were just glad of the protection of caring adults, some wanted to fight for the cause, others wanted vengeance.

Kabanda watched Obote's soldiers kill his parents. Now he is a corporal in the NRA. He says he is 14, but looks younger; eleven is nearer the mark. He has not been in battle but has been trained to fight and carries a heavy automatic rifle.

'The men who killed my mother, they make me angry,' says Kabanda. 'Me, I decide to go in the army. I decide to beat them. If I find them, I will kill.'

The people of the Luwero Triangle experienced some of the worst atrocities of modern times. There was an attempt to hush up the carnage. The first major report and condemnation came from the US government in 1984. It estimated that of a regional population of about 750,000, some 100,000 people had died. After Obote's overthrow, estimates rose to as high as 300,000.

To escape the violence, families fled into the bush. In desperation, many women and children sought refuge in camps set up by the government. Their menfolk stayed clear, fearful that their lives would be at even greater risk under government 'protection' than in the open.

Abuse was commonplace in the camps. Children were dragged out of huts and raped, sometimes by several soldiers. Professor Chris Udugwa, head of Paediatrics at Mulago hospital, says he saw 'quite a few children who had been raped, children aged ten, twelve, one or two were eight.' Some mothers had turned a blind eye to the rape of their children, unable to cope.

Amidst the confusion, many children were separated from their families. One nine-year-old boy from Luwero who Professor Chris Udugwa had previously treated for sickle cell anaemia turned up at the hospital in search of him.

'He was in tatters. I looked at him and said, "What happened?" He just cried and cried for about half an hour. We put him in a room and suddenly he asked to see me.

'His parents and all his relatives had been killed. They were sleeping at night and these soldiers came in. They banged the door down. They shot his father. The children could hear the mother crying in the next room. Everyone in the family tried to run. He hid under a sack. The soldiers ransacked the house, and found his older brothers and young sisters, and killed them.

'After what seemed like ages everything quietened down. Everything was in darkness. He went around, he saw his mother in a pool of blood, dead. When he looked in his father's room he saw him dead.

'He crawled out of the house and hid in some bushes. He was there for two days, no food, no water. He couldn't bear to move because he was afraid he'd be seen. When the second night came he moved slowly and, by sheer luck, he encountered his neighbours who were also hiding.'

The boy fled with them but could not keep up and was left again on his own. After joining up with a succession of groups of displaced people, he eventually arrived in Kampala.

Hospital staff arranged for the boy to live with relatives in Kampala. They took him in but said they could not afford to send him to school.

Adults who came across children in the upheaval of the conflict usually offered help – giving them food, allowing them to tag along, trying to trace their relatives, taking them to camps. But others took advantage of their vulnerability. Some of the stronger, healthier children were taken into households for their labour.

Father Pete Hooysehuur ended up sheltering some 70 children at his mission near Kiboga in the Luwero Triangle. He said most of them were very young and could barely walk. Many were sick, particularly with kwashiorkor. 'They were in a miserable state. Some died.'

Professor Udugwa observes of the Luwero conflict: 'Everybody needed some psychiatric help. You can't live in that condition without either going mad or getting some psychiatric problem.' Most of the patients in Ward Seven at the Mulago hospital were children from the Luwero Triangle. Many were suffering from depression or anxiety.

'We interviewed about 150 patients aged between five and fifteen, 65 per cent of them were girls.' Nearly all had experienced violence and losses in the family. Eighty per cent were showing a 'depressive tendency'. Children afflicted by anxiety 'used to cry a lot, they'd sweat and start shivering when

Father Pete's 'orphanage'

you talked about their experiences, sometimes they'd scream. If there was a bang they'd jump.'

Their past also surfaced in other ways. 'Their dreams were often replications of events of intensive anxiety and horror, such as running around, hearing shots, seeing parents or siblings being shot, seeing mutilated bodies or dead bodies. Some were wishful images of being visited by dead relatives.'

At an event in which children staged their own plays, a group from the Luwero Triangle acting as health promoters used machine guns to shoot diseases.

Research into the impact of war and violence on children conducted by a number of experts, including Professor Udugwa, showed that their games reflected their experiences. Strong characters bullying the weak featured in their play. In 'Roadblock', children acting as travellers had to try to outwit a policeman demanding bribes from them.

Results of the research are published in a book: *War Violence and Children in Uganda*. In a chapter on the dilemmas faced by parents, Josephine Harmsworth Andama describes her doubts about what qualities to instil in her children in a situation in which traditional values are challenged on all fronts. Following the murder of her husband, she had to bring up six children

[82] *War, Violence and Children in Uganda* ed. Cole P. Dodge and Magne Raundalen, Norwegian University Press, page 60, 1987.

[83] Kabanda was interviewed by journalist Lindsey Hilsum in the immediate aftermath of the NRA victory.

[84] Father Smeets was also interviewed by Lindsey Hilsum.

[85] *War, Violence and Children in Uganda.*

single-handed on a teacher's salary too small to survive on. 'I tell them that to steal is wrong but when I buy stolen goods I participate in theft. Is it possible to dissimulate? Is it possible to explain? Or do we accept that survival is the primary principle . . . ?'[82]

A great concern of those who care about the future of the country is what the children of the violent years will carry over with them into the peace. In Kabanda's imagination, normal fantasies of childhood keep company with disquietening images of warfare. 'Some days I dream that I fight, other days I dream I am at the village. I dream I am with my mother, we go to the market and buy Coke or sweet potato, and I eat and I come back in the motor car. Then I dream that 'anyanya' (soldiers) beat me and I die. Other days, he beat me, it hurt, I kill him, or I run away and I turn back with my friends and we start to go and beat him.'[83]

A Catholic priest, Father Smeets, says: 'These children can stand anything. These young fellows, they laugh at a dead body. They are so used to it, dead bodies with nails hammered in the head and so on. . . . They are rough and hard. . . . They have a tremendous hurt in their hearts.'[84]

Another perspective is offered by the surprising numbers of children who, surrounded by the most grotesque examples of adult behaviour, choose in war, as they do in peace, to identify with positive role models. Among evacuees from the Luwero Triangle there was a strong wish to help others on the part of children who had been helped themselves. 'They want to be doctors, nurses, teachers and relief workers.'[85]

Of particular concern are the child soldiers. At the time of the interview with Kabanda (January 1986), Museveni had just taken over government after six years of bush war, though remnants of the defeated army were still active in parts of the country.

The participation of the child soldiers in the conflict became a matter of controversy. The NRA defended the role played by children on the grounds that it was a traditional practice in Uganda for them to be taught how to use spears and to learn how to fight. Critics replied that modern warfare creates more dangers and requires more resonsibility than used to be the case.

The debate was further fuelled by the conviction and imprisonment of several child soldiers for murder. 'How could a child immature in mind but trained to kill be held responsible for putting that skill to practice?' some asked.

There was also debate about the future of the young soldiers. A powerful lobby favoured sending them to army schools, arguing that they would not readily settle into the normal education system. An outspoken critic of this proposal was Cole Dodge, who expressed deep reservations about children remaining in a military environment. He advocated their rehabilitation into civilian society.

A year later, fewer children in khaki uniform could be seen on the streets of Kampala, but it was unclear what had happened to them. Some observers said that they were in the north and east of the country, where fighting continued; others thought their reintegration into civilian life had begun.

What has happened to the child soldiers and what their progress will be matters not least because some are likely to move into positions of power in adulthood.

EVERY-DAY WAR

[86] *Modern Wars – The Humanitarian Challenge*; A Report for the Independent Commission on International Humanitarian Issues, Zed Press, London, 1986.
[87] *Refugees, Dynamics of Displacement*; Zed Press, London, 1986.

At the present time, for 362 days out of 365 there is an active conflict going on somewhere in the world.[86]

Modern armed conflict in Third World countries is generally of a kind that places civilians in the line of fire. It often takes place within, rather than between, countries.

'Many of the world's poorer countries are locked into a vicious circle of repression,' says a report by the Independent Commission on International Humanitarian Issues.[87] 'Their governments rule not in the interests of the nation as a whole, but to serve a small ruling elite often drawn from one region, religion or social group. Finding no constitutional means of expressing their opinions, opposition groups turn to terrorism or guerrilla warfare, frequently backed by foreign powers. In response, governments launch repressive campaigns to reassert their authority and to root out the opposition. In doing so the use of state terror, disappearance, torture and indiscriminate killings invites escalating waves of violence and counter violence.

'This pattern of events has been repeated across the globe.'

Outside powers contribute to this state of affairs, both by backing guerrilla groups and bolstering self-serving regimes when it happens to suit their political or economic purposes. In his book, *Mozambique: The Revolution Under Fire*, author Joseph Hanlon describes Renamo as being 'entirely the creation of foreign security services'. He argues that had South Africa not taken over the reigns of support for Renamo from Rhodesia in 1980, the organisation would have disappeared.[88] South Africa's primary objective appears to have been to destabilise its neighbour for its own ends rather than to back a struggle for a viable political alternative.

[88] 'What a child's nightmares tell us about a grim war' by Eddie Kock, *Weekly Mail*, Johannesburg, March 31 to April 6, 1989.

[89] *Mozambique: The Revolution Under Fire* by Joseph Hanlon, Zed Books, London, 1984. For an account of South Africa's role in destabilising its neighbours see *Apartheid's Second Front* by Joseph Hanlon, Penguin.

In wars between governments and insurgents, securing the allegiance of the people and denying it to the enemy is crucial to victory. Where governments or insurgents enjoy popular support their opponents may try to terrorise civilians into submission. According to a document published by UNICEF, half a million children have died as a result of Renamo's incursions and 200,000 boys and girls have seen their parents murdered by the rebels.[89]

Examples of the involvement of children in conflict are common.

Iraq's ruling Ba'athist party has reportedly relied on the widespread arrest of family members of its political opponents as a way of exercising control. Writing in 1986, Dr Oonagh McDonald (Member of Parliament for Thurrock and Chairman of the International Committee for the Release of Detained and 'Disappeared' Women in Iraq) referred to receiving 'reports of the arrest without trial of women and children and their subjection to harsh prison conditions, humiliations, rape and torture in Abu Ghraib and Mosul prison. Latest reports suggest that there are 2000 children in this prison alone, all part of the Government's policy to take wives and children as hostages for war deserters and political opponents of the reigme.'[90]

[90] *News and Views of the JOSEPHINE BUTLER SOCIETY*; November 1986.

In the Lebanon, Israeli Army action in reprisal for Palestinian guerrilla attacks on soldiers and civilians have claimed the lives of thousands of civilians.

Early in 1989, children in the Afghanistan capital, Kabul, faced starvation as a result of the tactical interception of food supplies by the Mujahideen, in an attempt to bring down the government.

South African military bases in Namibia have been sited next to schools as a deterrent to attacks by SWAPO fighters. In 1987 students called a national schools boycott, complaining of alleged mortar attacks directed against schools by the military during engagements with Swapo.

The Observer 31st August 1988

Shell-fodder children

[91] *Children: Rights and Responsibilities*; The Minority Rights Group Report No. 69 by Jo Boyden and Andy Hudson, Minority Rights Group 1985.

According to Amnesty International 500 children and young people were massacred in one evening by the Ethiopian Provisional Military Government during a campaign against counter revolutionaries in April 1979.[91]

The more civilian populations are caught up in war the more likely it is that children will become actively involved in either combat or supportive roles.

Children are valued in war for exactly the same reasons that they are favoured by some employers and criminals in peace time – they are smaller and more agile, easier to control and manipulate and more naive than adults. During the Gulf war, Iranian child soldiers were sent across suspected minefields in advance of adults to test for live explosives. There are authoritative reports of boys recruited into the Renamo forces being given drugs to make them fight more daringly against the Mozambican army.

Children are used as runners and to spy on the enemy, both of which can be extremely dangerous work.

War and civil strife differ greatly from situation to situation. So do children's perception of them. In some cases children are coerced into taking an active part. In others they volunteer, for various reasons, ranging from a taste for excitement to strong personal conviction.

While participation in conflict puts children at risk, non-involvement also has its dangers. Child psychiatrist Robert Coles, writing about the role of children in the negro struggle over desegregation in the United States, observes: 'We can all agree that we oppose mobs and children facing them, but if children must face them, let us find out why, and what will happen to them if they don't. When we find out what happens to them if they don't protest, we will find out about children in daily subjection, who have been asked to forfeit their freedom by the decision that they must endure tyranny rather than face 'danger' or 'trauma', and do so at a time when that endurance hardly seems a necessity. What can be worse psychologically and spiritually for any child? When we find out what happens when these children do protest, there is no neat correlation between external hardship and internal collapse. Dr Martin Luther King has said, "Undeserved suffering is redemptive".'

Coles adds that he has seen 'precious little psychiatric illness' in children who have suffered in this way.[92]

Modern wars and conflicts often strike at children whether they fight or not. Their suffering is not only in terms of exposure to violence. The day-to-day battle for survival is undertaken in an environment in which the very existence of both family and community may be subject to greatest uncertainty. Community support may be weakened or totally destroyed, greatly compounding the stresses of peace time. Whatever state services are normally available can be disrupted, including those crucial to the growth and development of children, such as health and education. Families may be defeated in their attempts to grow and harvest food. In such circumstances, with younger men and sometimes women going off to fight, it falls on mothers to secure the livelihoods of their families as best they can.

[92] *Children of Crisis: a study of courage and fear* by Robert Coles, Publishers Atlantic – Little, Brown, page 326, Boston, 1964.

[93] Professor Jennifer Bryce, a specialist in family and community education and family mental health, worked for three years at the American University of Beirut.

In her research in the Lebanon, Professor Jennifer Bryce found that mothers felt the need of training in how to provide for their children in a war zone and how to deal with the stresses of everyday life. 'They would like information on parenting, they would like information to help them not take out the stresses of war by beating their children.'[93] In a number of countries the disruption of families and communities through conflict has resulted in increases in the numbers of street children.

Children separated from their families may never be reunited with them.

Eleven-year-old Annette looks at a tree which tells her this was once the site of her home. Though an uncle still lives in the area, she learns that her mother has died and her father has gone to live near Kampala.

Nine-year-old Amuli, separated from his family during the fighting three years ago, returns home to find his mother dead but his sister and younger brother still alive. 'We were told Amuli had died,' says his sister. 'Bombs started being shelled by the army. He went one way and his mother went another.'

Fred Kasozi headed SCF's programme trying to trace the families of 'unaccompanied' children at the end of hostilities in the Luwero Triangle. Within the first eight months, he had helped reunite about 100 children with their parents or relatives. But often the time consuming task of piecing together and following up on information gleaned from the children – about their names, home area and clan – ended in disappointment. Intricate tracing trips often led to the discovery that there was little or no hope of reuniting a family. Parents had been killed or had died. The fragmentation of family networks and extreme economic hardship resulted in rejection. Relatives, step-parents and sometimes parents were reluctant to accept responsibility for children. 'At times the parent tells you, "I'm really desperate," and they'll ask you, "Can't you hang on to these children until we're OK."'

Sometimes it was the children who were reluctant to rejoin their families: they would make agile assessments of the life they would have with their family as compared to that at an orphanage, where they might at least be assured of food and schooling.

Children escape no aspects of war, including intimidation and torture. They experience torture both as immediate victims and as witnesses to atrocities against others.

Dr Walter Pereira, who heads a team in Costa Rica treating traumatised refugees from neighbouring countries, believes a wider notion of torture is needed. He says of the patients the team treats: 'They weren't only victims of the specific torture they had gone through, but they were victims of the torture in the group or the village they were coming from.' In treatment their whole experience, including their dislocation from their community and country has to be taken into account.

Refugee children from El Salvador. Among them is a victim of torture who is receiving help from Dr Pereira's programme

Dr Pereira tells of a six-year-old boy among his patients who had fled from El Salvador. He had lived with two grandparents, his mother, an aunt and four other children. The military had gone to his house and said they would return the following day – a common form of intimidation.

'Next day, the grandmother went out, leaving the rest of the family at home. The military came to the house and ordered them to open the door. The grandfather resisted and they killed him with an automatic. They also killed three of the children and attacked their mother. The other daughter heard what was going on and ran into another room with her baby and the boy who became my patient, and hid under the bed. She breast-fed the baby so it wouldn't cry. The soldiers raped and killed her sister, as she and her children lay under the bed, and blood sprinkled down on to them.'

When the grandmother returned and found what had happened, she and the surviving daughter and two children fled. They walked for one to two months and finally sought refuge in neighbouring Costa Rica. 'There are many cases like this,' says Dr Pereira.

Torture is banned under international law, yet it is reported to be practised in one third of the world's countries. Among the countries most noted for allegations of torture of children are Turkey, Iraq, South Africa, Chile and El Salvador.

In the 'dirty war' in Argentina, the families of individuals identified by the military as subversives were systematically tortured. Children were made to watch the suffering of their parents and parents the torture of their children. The brutality of these sessions knew no bounds.

Exploring the motives of this example of the gross 'abuse of children by the state', Marcelo M. Suarez-Orozco argues that the torture of children had a functional and an expressive role. It was enacted in the context of paranoid fantasies of the military that they were confronting a total onslaught by godless left-wing subversives against the Western Christian world. The epicentre of this onslaught was Argentina and their crusade was to rid the country of its threat. The process required both a cleansing and a reorganisation of society.[94] In such circumstances all measures were justified.

At one level, family torture sessions were just an effective means of extracting information about the enemy and persuading victims to sign confessions. But torture was also seen as a way of cleansing society of corrupting influences; it was referred to by a term that means 'to cleanse' while torture chambers were described as 'operating rooms'. Torture was often directed against the reproductiveness of political opponents ensuring a 'cleansing' not only in the present but in the future; it was directed at the genitalia of men and women prisoners, embryos in the womb and children. Children of parents who were seen as subversive were often made available for adoption by 'security' force and upper class families who would assure them of a christian upbringing. Family torture sessions which preceded such adoptions served as a 'rite of separation' through which all bonds between the child and the tainted parents were severed.

In South Africa, school children have taken a prominent role in demonstrating against the injustices of the apartheid system. In the five months after the government called a nation-wide state of emergency, in 1986, more than 8000 children were detained, according to the Detainees' Parents Support

[94] *Child Survival* ed. Nancy Scheper-Hughes, ch. 'The Treatment of Children in the "Dirty War": Ideology, state terrorism and the abuse of children in Argentina' by Marcelo M. Suarez-Orozco, Reidel, B.V. Uitguery, 1987.

Committee. Most were never charged. In February 1987, the Minister of Law and Order justified the detention of children as necessary 'for the combatting of revolutionary inspired crime'. In April 1987 the number of children between the ages of 12 and 18 being held under the emergency laws was officially put at 1424. The authorities deny that children have been tortured, despite extensive testimonies to the contrary. Towards the end of 1988, reports from non-government sources put the number of children still in detention at about 100.

The violent separation from parents at the hands of the military or security police is in itself a form of torture, whether it is the child or the parents who are removed.

'It doesn't take much imagination to think about the scene that ensues when there's a violent banging on the door in the middle of the night. The door is knocked down, soldiers or police rush into the house, seize the parents, who are carried away screaming, leaving the children screaming behind,' says Helen Bamber, Director of the Medical Foundation for the Care of Victims of Torture (UK).[95]

Referring to the abuse of children by the state in South Africa, the Rev. Frank Chikane, now general secretary of the South African Council of Churches, observed: 'The African child in the townships is being faced with state repressive machinery instead of being shielded from it. One would have expected the state to have given the protection of children top priority, but the opposite is the case ... the experiences and exposure of township children to violence will undoubtedly result in the maiming of children in every sphere of their development.'[96]

Helen Bamber believes the response of children to torture is different to that of adults. 'We all know that if children are damaged in their formative years, they are likely to be affected permanently. Therefore we are looking at something rather different in children than we are in adults. Whereas an adult may have known a happy childhood and may have things to fall back on – love, affection, comradeship, a good working life, studies that may serve them well in the future – a child has none of these resources, it has only its mother, its father and its grandparents and extended family, this is its life. And if a child sees this destroyed, it is the whole world that he or she depends on that is destroyed.'

She describes torture victims as being prisoners in their own bodies, 'they're locked in, if you like, with their memories and in some way with their bodily experience, they're constantly reminded of the tragedy of torture. I would fear for children

[95] The Medical Foundation for the Care of Victims of Torture is a voluntary organisation offering a service that combines medicine, social work and psychotherapy to exiles living in England.

[96] *Growing Up In A Divided Society: The contexts of childhood in South Africa* ed. Sandra Burman and Pamela Reynolds, pages 336–337, Ravan Press.

who have not had the opportunity to have some sort of help in bearing the horror of what they experience. If it remains locked inside of them it's inevitable that they will suffer at some time in their later life.'

One of the most damaging and tragic consequences of the upsurge of conflict in the Third World has been the exoduses of people displaced from their community or country.

A report on the causes and plight of refugees from both war and natural disaster argues that there is no immediate prospect for a reversal of this process. 'The combination of population growth, economic stagnation and ecological deterioration is almost certain to lead to increased poverty and social tension. Add to this the burgeoning arms trade, increased militarism and intolerance, and the stage is set for a series of massive movements of populations.'[97]

Between 12 and 14 million people are thought to be living in exile from their homelands, mostly the victims of conflict but also of ecological and natural disaster. More than half of them

[97] *Refugees: Dynamics of Displacement*; Zed Press, London 1986, page 9.

Guatemalan refugee in Mexico.
UNICEF/
DIDIER BREGNARD

are children. These figures give no account of the additional millions displaced within their own countries.

Few refugees get absorbed into the industrialised nations. The majority 'live in states which cannot even guarantee the well-being of their own citizens'.[98]

[98] *Refugees: Dynamics of Displacement*, page 23.

Most of the world's refugees do not live in organised camps and do not benefit from international aid. Because they are uprooted in times of crisis they may have little choice of destination and face hostility from communities that do not want them. Camps usually provide the basics for survival but, despite the best efforts of host nations and the international community, are generally desolate places for children to grow up in.

'In the relative safety of a refuge camp food can be found, medicine can cure the diseases or soothe the sores; but what can heal a child who has lost family, a home and a childhood?' writes Jan Williamson, who worked as a volunteer with Kampuchean refugees on the Thai border.[99]

[99] *Memories of a small lifetime*; World Health, Jan/Feb, 1984.

Refugees by definition are fugitives from harrowing and devastating experiences. No more so than Kampucheans who sought refuge in camps on the Thailand border. The first great wave fled the fighting in the overthrow of Pol Pot in 1979 by Vietnamese forces. His deposal ended four years of one of the most destructive regimes of all time. Pol Pot's Khmer Rouge had imposed a radical plan of reform in an attempt to turn back the clock to the rural economy of an idealised past. In the process, a million people are believed to have died of disease, overwork, lack of medical care, hunger, murder and torture. Families were arbitrarily broken up and members sent to different parts of the country. Children were made to spy and inform on their parents and so 'became part of the process of repression', according to Tony Jackson, of OXFAM, an expert on Kampuchea.

The camps are supplied by the international community but largely controlled by different groups opposed to the Vietnamese-backed government, the most powerful of which is Pol Pot's Khmer Rouge. Outsiders have no access to some of the camps and in the others conditions vary widely. Researcher Josephine Reynell writes of overcrowding, high levels of intestinal diseases and other symptoms of poor living conditions, 'in many ways similar to those found in urban slums'. The combination of these living conditions and the stress of war 'exacerbates social conflict and domestic violence.'

Anxieties suffered by parents have inevitable repercussions on the children. 'In the camps social workers reported that child battering is becoming increasingly common. To take a

[100] *Political Pawns, Refugees on the Thai-Kampuchean Border* by Josephine Reynell, pub. Refugees Studies Programme, Queen Elizabeth House, University of Oxford, 1989.

simple but common example: children reject their monotonous diet and, unable to fulfill the child's wishes, mothers beat them in frustration.'[100]

There is very little provision for the development needs of children. Most have access to primary schooling but there is almost no secondary education. They are being socialised for camp life not for a life beyond. 'They see the misery of their mothers queuing up all day for their weekly rations,' says Tony Jackson. 'A child of peasant farmers grows up thinking that rice grows in a plastic bag on his mum's head with UN markings on it. There's no concept of what real life and work is like.'

Conditions in some camps are very dangerous. 'There is virtually no rule of law, anything goes. Rape, robbery with violence are quite common and virtually nothing is done to stop them unless you happen to be bigger than the person doing the damage.

'Many of the kids are out of control. They don't know how to be children. There are very many cases now of gangsterism among kids from twelve upwards. What else are they going to do all day?'

In 1989 there are still 150,000 children in the camps, about half of them born there. Because of their location in a war zone, the camps are in constant danger of coming under fire and there is evidence of older boys in Khmer Rouge camps being recruited into the military effort to regain power in Kampuchea. Tony Jackson remarks: 'The refugees themselves say they feel like chickens in a cage.'

The director of the United Nations Border Relief Operation, Mr Y.Y. Kim was quoted in the *Bangkok Post* as saying there was a real danger that 'a generation of misfit children is in the making right in front of our eyes'.[101]

[101] *Bangkok Post*, July 16, 1988.

Western politicians frequently boast about having presided over 40 years of unbroken peace. War is curiously romanticised – there is even some nostalgia in Britain for the good old days of 1939 to 1945 when the population was united and really pulled together. Armed conflict has become prime material for entertainment, in which it is often glamorised as a battle between good and evil.

With some exceptions, real wars are played out very much in the wings of western consciousness and seen as unfathomable struggles of peoples in distant places. The closest most of us get to them is as brief news items on television which rarely locate what is seen on the screen in an international political and economic framework that might make them more comprehensible.

Since the Second World War there have been some 150

[102]*Brassey's War Annual 2 – A guide to contemporary wars and conflicts* by John Laffin, Brassey's Defence Publishers, UK, 1987.

military conflicts. Almost all have been in the Third World. Many have been fanned into major or more protracted conflagrations as a result of the superpowers or regional powers using Third World countries as arenas for their political struggles.

In an age in which millions of people die for want of the most basic means of survival, the arms trade has become 'by far the world's most lucrative business'.[102] A million pounds sterling a minute goes on military spending, to the delight of the arms suppliers, but the defeat of development options. The tragedy is that many armed conflicts are born of the injustice of poverty – of large numbers of people being denied a most basic share in the world's resources.

For millions of children, the only world they know is one where gunfire and explosions, death, injury, separation are commonplace. In 40 of the wars in the past ten years children have taken an active part.

Close up there is nothing romantic about warfare.

During the years of Obote's rule in Uganda, there were frequent clashes between the army and the Karamojong in the remote and neglected north-east of the country. Karamojong warriors were well armed after a raid on an abandoned government armoury following the overthrow of Idi Amin.

Mike Wilson, who was helping with drought relief, tells of arriving at a village shortly after some civilians had been shot at by soldiers.

'We stopped for a woman who'd been shot in the foot and thigh. My colleague was fumbling at his door which I thought a bit odd. I was in a hurry to get the woman to hospital and said, "What the hell's keeping you." And he just picked this kid up and held him up.

'The child had the lower half of his jaw blown away – half his neck, throat, just blown away. He'd sort of staggered out of the bush. But he was walking! I just leaned out and vomited. It had happened minutes before and you could still smell the cordite from the bullets. We could see the army going off down the road.

'We asked the woman what had happened. Apparently the kid was in a crowd of children who were running away. One of the soldiers just let loose with a rocket. The kid, who was about eight, got caught by a big chunk of shrapnel.

'We took him to the hospital and doctors didn't know whether to actually give him an overdose of morphine, or what. They decided he wouldn't live anyway. So they just cleaned him up, thinking that was all they could do.

'But the kid wouldn't die! We went round to see him every day, and three or four days later he was beginning to heal up. The doctors had put him on a drip to keep him hydrated. At first he was just fed milk and fluids, then they started giving him solids. Someone would chew up food and blow it down into his oesophagus.

'Then about a week later we looked around for a relative and found a little girl who was a 'sister' – probably a cousin in fact. He went everywhere with her and she fed him, chewing up the food and blowing it down as she'd been shown. And soon the wound had healed over.

'We tried to find other relatives but the 'sister' and people in the village said they'd all been wiped out.

'When I saw him a year later he looked fine. Apart from the

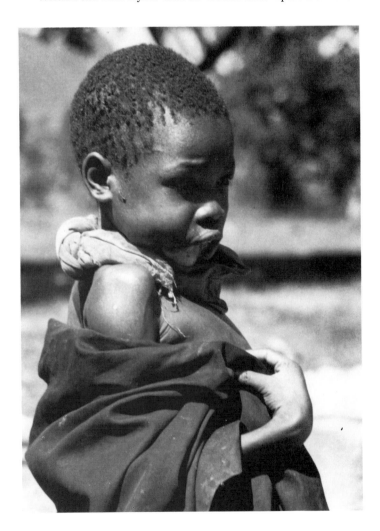

MIKE WILSON

wound he was otherwise healthy and really quite self-sufficient. He was at school, a cheerful soul. It was amazing. He kept smiling – you could tell his smile from his eyes. Other kids would take care of him and help him, like translate for him because he couldn't make sounds. He was a sort of special one.

'But we've heard since that he's dead. I don't know the details. Maybe it was because of an infection or a problem made worse by the injury. And I can't imagine he was getting good nutrition. Perhaps his system was just worn out by the wound and the battle to live.'

Emmanuel, a child ice-lolly seller with Father Ramiro's project

Friends in need

I would change everything. I would make a leisure street for children to play in – one without cars. I would have a football and a basketball area – a sports ground. I would have proper health care.

Brazilian slum child

I believe they are our children in a communal way. This is my neighbourhood earth and I don't think there are sluts and whores. They are children and they're ours and I do feel a sense of responsibility.

Trudee Able-Peterson

... the children of indifference
they are forgotten by the world
Society rejects them
knowing they are the fruit
of its own bad ways
from a song by 'The Guadalupano', Nicaraguan composer and singer

TO THE RESCUE

The problem of unwanted and abandoned children is easily
solved, a senior police officer told a conference of community
workers in Bangalore. 'We should build more remand homes
and put them in there.'

'Your brains are in your boots,' came a withering cry from
the audience, as he paused complacently for applause.

He was speaking of street children. Sadly, he was expressing
an attitude that is broadly shared by authorities and public alike
that society's abandoned children are a nuisance best put away
out of sight. Either intern them or disperse them into the side
streets of the nation's conscience.

But abandoned and neglected children do not invariably
meet with indifference or exploitation in the community.

There are helpers.

Many individuals respond in a kindly and supportive way to
particular cases of hardship they encounter. Such people can
become important touchstones in the lives of disadvantaged
children. A child labourer in Brazil said he was giving up a
regular but very poorly paid job to return to collecting rubbish.
'That way I can visit a woman in the city who gives me a daily
meal and I can get left-over vegetables for my family at the end
of the day from the market stall keepers.'

There is also a huge number and variety of more formalised
helpers. Extensive government programmes have developed
around the neediness of children. The governments of India
and Brazil in particular have in recent years launched more
concerted programmes to reduce the hazards and increase the
development opportunities of some of their working children.

There is an array of non-government organisations many of
which receive support from national or international agencies,
like UNICEF and OXFAM or from the churches.

Benposta is a residential community for severely
disadvantaged children in Colombia. It is organised in such a
way as to place the running of its day-to-day affairs largely in
the hands of the children themselves. It has an 'assembly',
presided over by an elected council and mayor.

Perched high in the Andean mountains, it overlooks the
capital, Bogota – notorious for its many street children.

A visitor's car horn is rewarded by the sight of bright young
eyes darting a shrewd glance through the bars that surmount
solid sheet-metal gates. The gatekeeper – a girl of about eleven
years – opens up and inquires the purpose of the visit. Satisfied,
she shouts into the clear air, 'Angelina'.

Angelina is 16 and leader of one of Benposta's 'districts', as its small residential houses are known. Her serious expression breaks into a welcoming smile. 'I have been here three years two months and sixteen days,' she says, paying tribute to days free of the concerns of poverty.

Her family home is in a poor part of the city. The youngest of six children, she came to the community after her father was murdered and her mother was left struggling to support the family on low earnings as a cleaning supervisor. 'She would come home late and very tired. We only really saw her on Sunday. I didn't feel like anybody was taking care of me.'

Most of the Benposta children are from violent or financially

Angelina

disabled homes in parts of the city where they were in danger of being drawn into drug taking and street life. 'Many of the boys were beaten by their fathers,' says Angelina. Some of the girls had been at risk of being sexually abused.

Children are referred to Benposta in a variety of ways – some by other children or their own families, others by different welfare agencies.

Alfonso and **Carlos** are both 14 and have been at Benposta for several years. Alfonso was brought from a violent home by a former 'mayor'. Carlos is one of the few children to have come to the community from street life. 'I was about eight when I escaped from home,' he says. His mother's boyfriend used to get drunk and beat her and him and his three brothers. 'I jumped the fence of the house and went out to live on the street.' Three years later some community workers talked him into going along to Benposta.

All applications to join the community are put up for approval to the full assembly of children. The main reason for rejection is lack of vacancies, the turnover being low. But there is also a reluctance to admit hardened street boys and girls who might threaten the smooth running of the community.

Carlos and Alfonso

Newcomers are assigned to a district. 'They're presented to all the children in their district and then they make a presentation to the assembly: they give their name, explain why they're here, their home problems and say what they want to study,' explains Angelina. There is a three month probationary period to see if a child will fit into the community.

Benposta was set up in the 1970s by a Spanish priest and is named after a community in Spain which trained children for circus acts. The underlying concept is that of a self-contained children's community. It is easy to get the impression that there are no adults there. In fact there are usually several at hand and a few do live in the grounds. Their role is to guide and teach, not govern. It is part of the philosophy of Benposta to encourage children to take control of their own lives. This extends to child officers having considerable responsibility for allocating and handling finances.

Overseeing the administration is a legal representative who deals with official affairs and is responsible for the children. A child wishing to leave must discuss the reasons with him. 'He will talk to the kid and say, "You have problems with your family, the chances are you'll end up out on the street, there are such and such dangers". If the child still wants to go they are free to go,' says Angelina.

The community is a paradise of resources and opportunities compared to those available to slum children. A high quality education is assured in a country where not all children get to school. There are 15 teachers to 135 pupils. Informal counselling and group therapy are available. A guaranteed secondary education would have been enough to attract Angelina but she has found many other opportunities.

She has taken great pleasure in learning to dance. The community has a group which is acclaimed for its public performances.

Her first responsibility within the community was for drawing up its food shopping list. Now as the elected leader of her district – House of the Young Girls – she sits on the ruling council.

Life at Benposta is structured, but not strict. Some of the districts have mixed ages and mixed sexes. 'The kids in each district decide what time they get up and go to bed and they plan a programme of activities for the year. They elect a leader who makes sure decisions are acted on.'

As Angelina talks of the community, younger boys and girls come up to her to ask a question or seek advice. She responds warmly and attentively.

Despite the lack of adult control, the children appear to go about their tasks cheerfully and conscientiously. A group engaged in an afternoon reading session under the supervision of a child scarcely looks up when there is a knock at the door of their room. In the community kitchen, boys and girls prepare the evening meal.

Chores and studies apart, the children work on various self-sufficiency and income-generation schemes, which also give them some occupational skills. Among other undertakings, they rear pigs and bake bread. These schemes save and earn money for Benposta and give those who do the work a small income. Payment is in the community's own currency, the 'corona', which can be used at the Benposta shop.

Though it is a self-contained community, contact with the outside world is encouraged. Where possible, broken relationships between children and their families are re-established and there are visits home. Angelina, Carlos and Alfonso all believe relationships with their families have improved. 'Everything has been changed,' says Angelina. 'I feel happy. My mother feels happy.'

Children wait for a weekly session of the Pavement Club in Bombay. Held in a church hall, it provides food, games and washing facilities to deprived and street children

Programmes designed to help abandoned and endangered children vary enormously – from the simplest of service organisations, which regularly hand out food or clothing or advice, to comprehensive residential environments like Benposta, which aim at rehabilitation. Covenant House sees itself as a 'MASH' unit patching up 'kids coming off the battlefield' of US city streets. 'We treat any superficial wounds

and hopefully refer kids to hospitals and other agencies that can help them,' says Elizabeth Burnell.

There are highly paternalistic programmes, which simply impose a set of values and a daily regime. Others set out to actively learn from the children how best to help them. Helpers differ in what they are trying to do for children and in their own motivation. They differ in their social impact – some confine their activities to helping particular youngsters, others also try to tackle the causes of child abandonment.

Abused and abandoned children themselves often have a healthy cynicism about the motives of people offering them help. Why in a world that daily demonstrates violence, greed, injustice and unconcern for them, their families and whole communities should anyone want to help, without an ulterior motive?

Child counsellor Lorraine Fox, talking of the wariness that child sex abuse victims have of all adults who invite their trust (including therapist-counsellors), says they have learned to mistrust trusting. They don't wonder if adults will abuse them, 'they wonder who and when'.

In India grass roots organisations trying to build trust with street children are chary about acting as intermediaries between them and such outsiders as potential donors or journalists. They fear the children's quick suspicion that they are being exploited in some way they do not understand – perhaps to collect funds from which they will not benefit.

Unfortunately some helpers do have hidden agendas – they are seeking their own job security, self-satisfaction, social status or the advancement of their religion or cause and even, in some cases, sexual opportunities. But paradoxically in a world that has been so slow to tackle the structural causes of child neglect and abandonment, there are many people genuinely concerned for the best interest not just of their own but of all children.

A useful distinction would seem to be between programmes that try primarily to improve the prospects of individual children and those which aim to secure the child's place and participation in a broader advancement of the deprived communities to which they belong.

The former might be described as 'rescue' or 'rehabilitation' programmes. They try to save children from families or social environments in which they are perceived to be at risk. They may either remove them physically or equip individual children to escape by giving them advantages of education and training usually available to more privileged groups. The latter might be called 'integrative' – they attempt to help children who risk abandonment to become valued members of their families and communities. They see deprived communities as having far richer moral and social resources than their impoverishment always allows them to express. They try to liberate those resources by supporting grass roots initiatives that promise to strengthen community solidarity.

There are problems associated with both types of programme. While some children are so damaged or endangered in a particular situation that they can only be helped by being removed from it, 'rescue' programmes can easily underestimate both the child's and the community's resources for dealing with danger. The very assumption of the role of rescuer defines those to be rescued as powerless, their community as a lost cause and the rescuer as potent, whereas sometimes quite simple investments can release potential in the child, family and community to handle their own problems.

An experiment in the UK, the Newcastle Prevention Programme, found that the introduction of Rogerian dynamic play sessions into the schooling of children showing signs of maladjustment triggered a progressive improvement. The sessions were held for only a term. The increasing gains made by the children are attributed to the sessions having changed their experience of relating socially. Members of a group of similar children who were not included in the sessions continued to experience psychological and behavioural problems.[103]

[103] *Help Starts Here – The Maladjusted School Child and the Ordinary School*; Colvin, I. et al., Tavistock, London and New York, 1971 and 1985.

In conditions of great deprivation, it is common for mothers to beg any institution ready to accept responsibility for children to take their children off their hands. A majority of the children in state institutions in Brazil are there at their parents' request. In many cases a simple support programme for the mother, such as child rearing advice given in the home by an outreach worker, can tip the balance between her feeling she can cope and feeling she cannot. If there were more community crèches and effective schooling and health provisions, fewer mothers would feel compelled to neglect children or try to place them in institutions.

In the West, the reaction to child sexual abuse has seen the 'rescue the child, punish the offending parent' response predominate over that of trying to understand and tackle the causes of the problem. One unintended byproduct of the much-publicised removals of children from their families will have been to heighten the awareness of unidentified victims of the disastrousness of 'telling' – reinforcing their prison of silence. If there were more stories to be told of the successful reintegration of such families, more child victims might be willing to seek outside help. Despite the accumulated skills of the welfare state, the sexual abuse of children remains one of very few crimes where society effectively punishes the victim in the act of trying to help her or him. 'Children don't always want to be removed from their families, or their families to be broken up. They want the offending to stop,' says Ray Wyre, who is pioneering the treatment of offenders and their families in the UK.

Rescue programmes often tragically fail to create an effective alternative world for children to grow up in. State care residential arrangements in wealthy nations like Britain and America have, in a considerable number of cases, failed to ameliorate the damage experienced by children. At times they have proved as damaging as the situations they sought to replace. Some abused children have found themselves abused again in care both in residential and foster placements.[104]

In an essay about young killers, Joan D. Ruhnke, an expert on state provision for children in the US, points out that many have state care in common as well as murder. They are 'the products of disastrous, deprived and terminally damaging childhoods – childhoods purchased with public dollars. Public care does not obviate, and in many instances ignores, what it is designed to remedy: physical and sexual abuse, neglect, rejection, lack of love, emotional and behavioural problems of magnitude'.[105]

Many of the Third World's street children and industrialised world's runaways have fled not from their own homes but from institutions that were supposed to be places of refuge from dangerous circumstances. About 37 per cent of young people who turn up at the safe house run by the Children's Society in London are runaways from local authority care.

Under-resourced, understaffed, badly run institutions for children are to be found in both developed and underdeveloped countries.

During the years of military rule in Brazil (1964–85) large state institutions were set up to contain abandoned, neglected and delinquent children. The programme, thought ideal at its inception, proved a failure with the institutions degenerating into little better than schools of crime, graft and prostitution. In one state-funded institution, four to twelve-year-olds were not referred to by their names but by numbers, according to psychologist Ricardo Viera Alves de Castro, formerly a member of a team trying to reform the institution's educational programme. The professional staff 'saw the children as definitely disabled and condemned to lead a marginal life, without any possibility of being transformed or improved'. Attempts are being made to improve state institutions but they

[104] See *Children's Homes* by David Berridge and *Foster Home Breakdown* by David Berridge and Hedy Cleaver. Basil Blackwell, Oxford 1985 and 1987.

[105] *The Children's Guardian*; Vol 2, No 1, 'The Voice of DCI-USA'.

are still severely underfunded and under-resourced and
subject, with political change, to shifts of policy and staffing.

MAIS, in São Paulo, specialises in identifying and helping
very young children suffering from acute emotional neglect in
privately and government run institutions and crèches.

'These children seem autistic – they don't relate, don't look
at anything,' says Lygia Bove, head of training in MAIS. The
first thing we do is to establish a relationship. We look the child
in the eyes and say, "I love you, I trust you, I care for you." We
tell ourselves that the first time the children look us in the eyes,
they are saved. We work with children that doctors say will die
if we don't establish a relationship with them.'

MAIS has turned to training the supervisors of such
children, who are themselves a neglected and untrained group.
'They know very little, not even that it is important to look
children in the eyes. We tell them they are important. We tell
them it is very easy to save a child like this.' At the end of such
training, supervisors will often cry at having found a way to act
creatively in a situation that amounts to institutionalised
neglect. 'Most available funding goes to institutions that are
deposits of children – most are badly run, they don't have the
staff. There is no training, pay levels are very poor. The
children have a roof and food and that's it. There is no
stimulation,' says Lygia Bove.

Even well-equipped and imaginatively run rescue
programmes risk cutting the children they help off from their
social and family roots, without providing them with a viable
way forward. They can create dependency instead of
independence.

In Calcutta, a residential institution for girls tries to take the
pressure off struggling slum mothers by assuming responsibility
for the upbringing of one or more girls per family. It is a
humane, spacious, caring establishment and the girls it rears
vividly demonstrate that the children of the poor are not lacking
in talent; it is simply that they are systematically deprived of
opportunities to grow and flourish in certain ways.

Musical, artistic, well educated and socially skilled, the girls
would grace any private boarding school. Some speak fluent
English. They express themselves confidently. They also have
vocational training – typing, tailoring, needlework and catering.
They sing and dance and make batiks. And they clearly love the
director and staff who make all this possible.

It is the institution's pride, says the director, that her girls
eagerly return to their homes for the short periods allocated
and welcome weekend visits by their parents. Asked what
returning home is like, they tell of warm welcomes and the

admiration of parents and siblings at their knowledge and the way they speak and conduct themselves. But some go on to talk of the lack of space, the irksome lack of light at night by which to read. Amina, a 16-year-old, is sad that she can find less and less to talk about with her mother, to whom she had been close.

Describing Benposta as a 'little Utopia', UNICEF consultant Bill Myers goes on to say: 'I imagine that the kids must have a shock on adjusting (to the outside world) not in economic terms, but in terms of the quality of relationships and the sense of community.'

Whether the gains made by the children in the better rescue programmes equip them to negotiate such adjustments successfully is largely a matter for speculation. Very few projects follow up the individuals they help in the long-term. At worst, rescue programmes are inept fumblings in the lives of others. At their best they are attempts by individuals and organisations with limited power to create life nurturing zones of benevolence within an economic environment that is not at all benevolent.

Of ten former street children who had been given good vocational training in a first-rate residential programme in Bombay only one had found work. The reason – in the real world of unequal opportunities, whether it be India, Colombia or elsewhere, one needs more than skills to find employment, one needs the patronage of influential people, something not available to former street children.

One of the group, Srinivas, says: 'In the home we were safe. We learned skills. But we didn't learn how to survive in the world or how things work. I am exactly where I was on the day I left the streets.' In fact, at that point of his life, he seemed to have acquired a skill and aspirations he couldn't live on and lost the opportunistic sharpness necessary to the street survivor.

Workers in rescue and rehabilitation programmes are often acutely aware of the limitations within which they work and of the economic and political causes that help make families and communities dangerous to or neglectful of children. But few make a priority of informing the public of the insights they gain or campaign actively against the causes of child suffering. In government institutions, fear of losing jobs tends to keep mouths sealed. In the voluntary sector, dependency on raising funds introduces the marketing constraint of telling the customer what he or she wants to hear. Many people and organisations that give to charity in the West want assurance that gifts of money can successfully transform the lives of poor people without any changes to the structure of society.

Rescue programmes which actively promote this idea risk

Working children from a deprived area of Calcutta

presenting endangered children, not as victims of a system that punishes, rejects or exploits the weak and the poor, but as innocent victims of degenerate families, or of circumstance, and as being dependent upon the 'generosity' of the system's beneficiaries. By defining the status quo as benevolent, they help to obscure public understanding of the real causes and therefore of real solutions. By promoting their programmes as successful they feed the illusion that there are adequate social mechanisms for responding to the needy. A dangerous consequence of this illusion is the judgement that children who fail to respond favourably are ungrateful for the opportunities given them and so must be held to blame for their predicament. This is most evident in the case of state and public reaction to children who drift into criminality. Somewhere along the continuum of that drift, the child defined as disadvantaged or abused becomes redefined as delinquent and deserving of punishment, and loss of freedom.

'Removal from a dangerous home is supposed to offer more to a child: increased opportunities to grow and thrive, to know

love and security, to become a productive adult,' writes Joan
Ruhnke. 'Too often these opportunities are warped by their
progress through filters of changing caseworkers, laws and
placements. The only certainty for the child becomes the one
that nothing is sure or lasting. Not all children in public care
become murderers. When one does, however, the failure of the
state as parent is as real as that of a natural one. The state that
imposes the death penalty in such a case must realise that it is
killing its child.'

In March 1989, the *New York Times Magazine* carried a
report about 27 people on death row for crimes committed
while they were juveniles.

Even in a world committed to eradicating deprivation, there
would probably still be a small minority of children in need of
being rescued from dangerous environments. Meanwhile the
problems associated with attempts at rescuing children have
inspired new approaches. In particular, some of the
programmes working with street children have learned that, to
succeed, help must be based on respect for the children's
ability to interpret their own lives and to make their own
choices.

HELP ON THE STREET

We must remember, we are dealing with courage
Gerry Pinto, UNICEF, India

Each day **Kumar** sits on the stone floor in a shaft of light that
beams down from a small shoulder-high window. The room is
otherwise dark and bare; it would be cell-like were the door not
wide open. Only the boy's eyes move, hungrily scanning the
pages of the schoolbook on his lap. For him, each page is a step
away from life on the streets.

'All street children should learn like me,' he says, confident
of his intelligence.

The room in which Kumar studies is part of Bosco Yuva
Kendra (Bangalore Street People's Service) – a programme run
from an eight-room house, which reaches out to some of
Bangalore's 25,000 street children. During part of the day it
becomes a classroom or a place where vocational instruction
takes place. At night, together with other rooms in the building,
it gives shelter to as many as 70 street children, who come in
and unroll sleeping mats on the floor.

Children on the rooftop
at Bosco Yuva Kendra
KEN HARRIS

Soon after Kumar joined the city's fraternity of ragpickers, other street children told him about Father George Kollashani. 'They said he ran a place where you could sleep safely at night and you could also get some lessons.' Then Kumar met George and noticed that other street children spoke in an open and friendly way with him. He told him how his schoolteacher father had died, his mother had later been murdered and how he had run away. In the city he was no longer afraid but was worried that he was not getting any schooling.

George said he could stay at the night shelter and have the use of school books. There were some short courses that would not interfere with his work as a ragpicker, if he was willing to pay for them.

Kumar began to use the centre regularly and paid a few rupees to take a course in silk-screen printing. He finally told George he wanted to leave street life and get back to full-time education. He was told: 'OK, this is your home now.'

Bangalore Street People's Service is designed to provide opportunities to street children without undermining their independence. It begins to work with the child 'as he is, where he is' on the streets. It attends to boys, over the age of ten, who are living independently of their families. Children below ten 'need more motherly attention than we can offer'. Younger children and the few girls it encounters are taken back to their homes or referred to other organisations.

George, a Salesian of Don Bosco, who has worked with street children for more than 13 years, does not look like a priest. The easiest way for a stranger to find him is to ask his whereabouts of a street child at the main station. An alert, active, slightly built man, he spends six hours a day on the streets, going regularly to 25 points in the city where children know he is to be found. His visits and those by members of his team ensure that each point is attended several times a week. The programme, one of five now established in different Indian cities, keeps regular contact with more than 1000 boys in Bangalore.

In establishing initial acceptance by street children, George and his fellow workers had to overcome deep-seated suspicions. 'They thought we were child lifters or police inspectors. There were many conjectures,' says George. 'We took along first aid kits to dress their sores and injuries. We would get them to a hospital where necessary, if they would agree to come. We took groups of them on trips into the country. It took four months to establish contact with a hundred boys. Once the basic suspicion had been broken it was easy to go ahead.' Now most children are put in touch with George and members of his team by other children.

The programme's first priority is to see whether children can go back to their families. Finding out can be a painstaking process and involve bus journeys to distant places.

'Every child must have a home,' says George. 'If he can't go home, then we say home is where you grow best.'

The programme's roots are in the street level contact. It establishes a reliable adult presence in the children's lives and offers friendship, advice and help in emergencies, such as a child's disappearance, arrest, injury or illness. Each new contact launches a process of building up a detailed picture of the individual child, his needs, capacities and predicament. Back at the centre, case cards are kept on some 1200 children.

'We make a point of giving nothing on the streets,' says George, confounding conventional charitable approaches. 'The children are accustomed to earning their living and expect to pay their way. If a child is very desperate and needs food we will ensure some other child shares his food with him. We may, as an exception, buy food and give it ourselves. We would never give money.'

Ideally, street contact with the children would be backed up by a totally informal drop-in centre in the heart of town, where they could sleep and wash themselves and their clothes. Due to lack of resources, this facility is combined with the programme's secondary stage. The latter is a slightly formalised centre that allows for the transition of children into regular employment, or back into full-time education or on to some other institution.

The freedom enjoyed by street children makes them ill-suited to the disciplines of any kind of regulated environment – whether it be for work or education. The secondary stage offers informal schooling and vocational training in a way that leaves the boys free to pursue their street occupations. They may come and go as they wish but must pay for their courses and so have an investment in completing them. Those who do so are offered some semi-formal but paid work opportunities at the centre – printing christmas cards and motifs on stationary sold to outlets in the city. The aim is to introduce them to organised study and work and help them begin to systematise their lives.

Children may progress to a regular job. Others continue to make the centre a base while studying or undergoing further vocational training. The latter are provided with food and take it in turns to cook their evening meal. They also have some paid work, helping with younger boys coming into the programme.

Kumar has made this transition. Within a few months of basing himself at the centre he had caught up on almost a year of lost schooling and passed the appropriate end-of-year exam. He now lives at the centre, studies and helps out in various ways, including teaching younger children. Like others before him, he is likely to gain his school leaving certificate and may go further. One former street child is taking a law degree and plans to return to join the programme's staff. Another is hoping to go to university.

The programme is not only about the progress of individuals, it builds on the frail support street children give each other. **Kishore** – who fled to the city after being beaten by villagers for allegedly stealing a smaller child's gold ring – was brought to George's notice by other street children when they found him badly injured in the main bus shelter. He too came to be based at the centre and would cry out fearfully in his sleep at night. Later, when he had to go to hospital for an appendix operation, Kumar sat reading in the corridor outside his ward, in case he should need anything.

'When I first came to the centre,' says Kumar, 'I wanted to become a detective to catch my mother's killer.'

And now?

'I would like to be a doctor, to be able to help the other street children.'

Kumar's experiences have made him critical of the Indian

caste system, which allocates social status on a more rigid basis
than the English class system and defines some people as
'untouchable'. 'I now believe there are only two castes – the
good and the bad. Oh, and there are also men and women
castes. The woman is lower because she doesn't have equal
rights.'

What about the children?

'They are like women.'

The programme pioneered by George demands a high level
of concern for and awareness of each child, his strengths, needs
and problems. Progress is rarely straight-forward. Kumar tested
George's reliability in a number of ways. He accused him
indirectly of exploiting the children in the production of
Christmas cards. Twice he left the centre to return to the
streets, only to come back, once badly beaten up. When a
visitor presented him with a photograph of himself he pressed
his own face out with his thumb. 'He had a lot of suppressed
anger to work through,' says George.

Children do not have to come to the centre to receive help
from Bosco Yuva Kendra. If a child chooses to remain on the
streets, 'we will help him on the street. If he wants to try for a
job we will help him to get it, for instance'.

'We try to get the child to make a stand,' says George.

Work has yet to start on a third stage of the programme, a
small residential home for severely damaged children. At

present those needing special provision are referred to other institutions in the city.

The biggest problem of this and other programmes like it is getting the right quality of staff. 'Former street children themselves are best – they can go deep quickly without having to use many words, but it takes us a long time to train them.'

George is aware that his programme is a hospital built at the bottom of the cliff – 'I and some fellow students at theological college took a decision to work with street children because we saw them as being the most abandoned and in the greatest difficulty. Dealing with particular cases is important but in itself will not solve the problem.

'Perhaps someone working in the villages preventing the causes of children coming to the city would be doing something of greater value. But it is not individuals who will solve the problem. At the micro level, the thrust is not on creating awareness but on what, here and now, is best for the individual child and how it can be done at his own individual pace – that becomes the absolute priority. If you are trying to change the situation it has to be done by the creating of consciousness and awareness – seeing the problem at a national perspective. It is very important.'

Programmes which offer street children an element of choices are to be found in many parts of the world and differ in design and effectiveness. What is possible in one country may not work in another.

New York's Streetwork Project, which helped **Angel,** is also based on direct contact with children and young people on the streets. Trudee Able-Peterson says the project's workers make themselves a familiar presence in Times Square and 42nd Street. After a number of approaches the children begin to respond. 'They'll come up to you and say, "I haven't eaten today, can you buy me some food." "Have you got a quarter, I need to get on the subway and I'm short." Or you'll just sit down and talk in fast food restaurants or on park benches.'

They may then start going to the project centre to have a wash, eat a snack or chat with a counsellor. Trudee would like children to choose to move out of the life, but 'if they're not ready to leave, you can't do anything'.

Her worst fears are of 'failing to create any kind of a relationship or that a child is so self-destructive that the relationship won't help'.

'You have to be very committed and you have to stay with that child through this process you've started.

'I could say, "Holy God, where do I go with this kid? There's so much negative. The kid has been abused, is on drugs, is sick all the time and is on the street." But I can look at that kid and say, "Bobby, you survived out here for two years, you're a strong kid, let's take that and work with that" – look for what is there. Don't say, "You can't read and write." I don't have those expectations. If I can get a few kids off the streets I'm damn happy.

'You make the appointment again and again and when they don't keep it you make another appointment and you keep trying. You take them to hospital when they're sick and you share their birthday when they're alone. Through a relationship with the child, they begin to say, "Maybe I'm worth something more."'

Angel's new life, Trudee says, is an example of a 'big success'. 'She's been off the streets for over a year. Living with her child in a home for mothers and babies, doing very well. Drug free, trick free.'

For her part, Angel says Trudee was like a mother to her. 'I started getting used to her and to see that she was serious with me. So I started paying a lot of attention to her, saw that she was right, that I was messing up my life. If it wasn't for her I'd still be on the street.'

Angel revisits her old haunts

Angel, now aged 20, dotes on her 15-month-old daughter. Her other two surviving children are with foster parents but she visits them occasionally and enjoys seeing them. The child who was battered is still backward but is 'getting better'. There is some reconciliation with her family.

Since leaving the street, she has taken a business course, and did well. But her plans for further studies have been dashed. 'I'm pregnant again and we're having problems: the baby's small and lying low and I'm weak.' Her weakness and a medical condition that has recently been detected may be related to her life on the street and prostitution.

When **Kamia** decided to leave the dangerous life of a street child in Nairobi he went to 'Undugu', a Kwi Swahili word meaning brotherhood. Started by a Roman Catholic priest, Father Arnold Grol, the Undugu Society operates a small reception centre for street children. Boys hear of it by word of mouth and just turn up. Jones Muchendu, one of two housefathers, informally asks newcomers a bit about themselves and what they expect of Undugu. 'Most say, "Nataka kusoma" – I want education – then somewhere to sleep and food. Clothing comes later. Usually they're small for their age and not very healthy. Some have big stomachs from hunger or worms, others have skin diseases.'

*Undugu housefather,
Jones Muchendu*

The boys help run the centre, partly to give them a sense of responsibility and confidence. They are offered some lessons and creative activities – drawing, model making and other crafts. Conditions are very simple. After the evening meal, the boys sit around a fire chatting and telling stories.

The housefathers assess each boy's situation. 'A boy may find it very hard to talk about his experience,' says Jones. 'Most of the time he's being very tough. Then he weakens. He cries a bit and it all comes out.

'I asked one boy, "Have you smoked bhangi?" He started crying. I was shocked, I just kept quiet. Later I asked him, "Why did you cry?" He said he remembered something his father said before he died about not taking such things.'

Where possible, the society helps children return home. Where not, visits home are encouraged. Assessment may recommend that a child move to one of Undugu's three small community homes and either attend a government school, or one of its own schools which provide basic education and occupational training for children in the slums.

'Some succeed very well,' says Father Grol. 'Others don't make it. One was a very good boxer and he became a driver in the army. At the other extreme, of course, are boys who cannot be rehabilitated and most of these finally go to prison.

'One of our children once said to me, "I'm a two shilling child". He meant that his mother was a prostitute and got two shillings for her services. One day that poor boy was found stabbed to death.'

Kamia drumming at Undugu

Kamia stayed at the centre for more than a year before he went back to street life, encouraged by his slum friends. He was picked up by the police and taken to a remand home. A court then put him into the custody of Undugu.

Increasingly Undugu is moving away from the 'hospital at the bottom of the cliff' approach towards 'preventive' work in the form of slum development. They hope to demonstrate that, with improved living conditions, there will be less stress in the lives of slum dwellers and fewer children will take to the streets. Undugu is trying to stimulate better housing, local production of furniture and other items, local employment and marketing of goods.

While helping children has largely been conceived of internationally in terms of welfare, there is a new emphasis on responding to their needs by locating them in an overall process of community development. Bill Myers (UNICEF consultant) sees work with children as a fundamental part of achieving development objectives. 'I would argue very strongly that investing in human resources, starting with children – physical and mental and psychological development – is in fact right at the very heart of development.'

TOP OF THE CLIFF WORK

In Brazil today an array of programmes centres attention on work at the top of the cliff. They operate in solidarity with grass roots initiatives likely to foster community spirit and unity of purpose in deprived areas. Brazil is one of the few countries where there has been some mobilisation of deprived children in taking up their cause and publicly demonstrating against the injustices they suffer.

For example, with the help of some nuns, a small group of child sugar cane and crab factory workers of a village near the town of Rio Tinto, formed a union – The United Children of Marcação.[106] In one action they occupied the town's mayoral offices and by so doing won the concession of transport to get them from Marcação after work to evening school in the town. They campaigned successfully for the dropping of a levy charged on each container filled at the village water pump. They have also staged a four day conference of 80 working children from four states about the problems and needs of child workers.

In May 1986, more than 400 delegates of street children's organisations in different parts of the country briefly directed world attention to the injustices they experience by staging a conference in the capital, Brasilia.

Within a given favela several organisations may be working in different ways as part of what is perceived to be a broad popular movement for political and economic change. Some focus on education, some on the cultural development of children; some work to improve mother and child health, others with disabled or crimininalised children. 'There is room for everyone, the problem of deprived children is so great,' says one community worker.

The Luis Freire Centre, based in Olinda, near Recife, in its support work for human rights and community programmes has found that concern for children will stir a community to action more readily than any other issue.

'We have moved from land issues (the struggles of the poor for land rights) and started working on violence in the communities,' says Valdemar de Oliveira Neto ('Maneto'), the centre's director. 'We find that if we talk about police violence in the communities, the people will listen but say nothing – it is easy for us to talk and go and sleep in our houses. We are not the ones at risk. But when you start to talk about violence in the community and children – they really open up and you can mobilise every group; the theatre group, the church, the neighbours' association – everybody is concerned.

[106] For an account of these children see *Marcação 80 – The long walk of the children of Marcação* by Reginaldo Veloso, I.M.A.C./ M.I.D.A.D.E., Paris, 1982.

'We have been going every week to one community for a year and a half and now they have created a commission of 30 people – one from each street. They have done some training about how to understand violence, how it happens, what they can do. It is done in a very participative way. We had one all-day meeting at the centre – people talking about their lives.

'We just asked about how they were educated and what they expected to do with their children. It was a very emotional meeting – a lot of people cried, remembering their relationships with their fathers, what they have suffered in their lives and what they want for their children. It was a really fantastic day.'

Despite the disruptive and demoralising influences on life in deprived areas, many people struggle to improve their lives and educate their children, says Maneto. 'The morality of poor people is very strong. They are far less cynical than the middle class for instance, for all the difficulties they face.'

Particularly impressive in the work that receives some support from the Luis Freire Centre has been the establishment of schools by 60 poor communities.

The schools have found immediate and strong parental interest. 'A large number of children is eliminated from access to government education,' says Maneto. He believes this exclusion to have been a deliberate policy to ensure the existence of a large exploitable labour pool.

Children at a community school with their teacher, Jocelini

Community schools pick up on children who have been turned down by the state system, perhaps because their parents did not apply for them to start at the right age, or who have dropped out having failed to pass grades.

Illiterate or semi-literate parents with low expectations of their children are not always motivated to send them to school. The community schools get the children to the appropriate standard for their age, so they can again claim an education from the state.

In the kind of area where one might expect high truancy rates, Jocelini finds her pupils come to call her out of her house if she is a few moments late. 'Are there no lessons today?' they demand to know.

Her school is located in Vila de Prata (Silvertown), a favela built on partly reclaimed swamp land. The area is very poor with few employment opportunities. People survive by doing odd jobs. The building is a single classroom with a tiny office/storeroom at the back and there is a small area of levelled ground, jutting into the swamp. It has 100 pupils aged 7 to 20. They come in three shifts between seven in the morning and ten at night. Jocelini teaches the morning shift of under twelves. In the later shifts older children come to do literacy classes.

Children of the neighbourhood helped to build the school – carrying bricks and mortar. 'Now when I stop them tearing the place apart,' says Jocelini, 'they will say. "but I carried the

cement". I have to explain that helping to build doesn't give them the right to tear down.'

Because the school is located in the favela, it is easier to involve and gain the confidence of the parents as well as give the children much more individual support than is normally the case. 'They have more trust in us than in a state school,' says Jocelini, who is from Silvertown herself.

In such communities, parents are too poor and have little time or motivation to take their children anywhere. There is nothing for them except for the dusty streets. The violence of the area is mirrored in their behaviour even within the school. Minor disputes rapidly escalate. 'They threaten to kill each other and hit each other. They poke and pinch. They are pretty rough,' says Jocelini.

'These kids don't obey their parents and don't know how to behave in a classroom. So we teach them that, as well as reading and writing. We go very gently here. We'll say: "Hey, don't do that!" We give them lots of love and understanding. They don't have that at home. They like it. We had one child here the other day who didn't even know his real name. He said he was "Gas Cylinder".

'We give the kids plenty of outings. I am taking them to the zoo this weekend if I can arrange a bus. We give them art and music and dancing.' The school helped the children form a dance group to take part in Olinda's famous carnival parade.

'I read to them. We have games. And, of course, there is the daily snack. We have little parties when one of them has a birthday. They want to participate in everything. In the state school they don't have any of that. They are very serious and it's all homework and obligation.'

Not surprisingly many children press their parents to be allowed to go to the community school. (Often one or two slightly older ones come along as well just 'to help out'). Most parents are only too glad that they should have such opportunities and be off the streets. The parents are encouraged to participate in monthly meetings and are invited to criticise the school and the teachers and help in various ways. In an environment that offers few opportunities for communal activity, the school provides an important focus bringing people together and giving them hope in the progress of their children.

'I believe all the kids are intelligent and able to do what I teach them,' says Jocelini, 'though some have even greater powers of laziness than intelligence.' Most of the pupils attend the community school for a year before going on to a state school. 'We make sure they get in – we all go along, teachers, parents, director. We sign bits of paper. We do everything necessary. We really press for that.'

Children from the community schools often stand out when they get to state schools. They have been encouraged to question and challenge what they don't understand. 'They sometimes suffer a lot from teasing. Other kids say to them – "Oh, you've only been to a rubbishy school" or, "You're from that community over there". When we hear of that happening we will go along and speak to the teachers. Usually it stops."

The teachers at the community schools are from the local neighbourhood and are rarely professionally trained, though they receive some training from the project. Jocelini, who is 20, is studying to retake her own school finals exam. The work is essentially voluntary – Jocelini earns the equivalent of less than £5 a week. She can live on it because she lives with her parents. But she is highly committed to her work. She says she loves the children and feels she is making a useful contribution to them and to her community.

'The school is the only chance they have,' she says. 'It is the best way to hold them in the community. If our school wasn't here they would be off maltreating animals, or other children or old people or vandalising people's houses. Even though they only spend a few hours here and then are free, they go out with teacher's words in their heads, "Don't maltreat animals. Don't do this and don't do that." It is something.'

Through the community schools poor people are enabled to challenge the state to provide their children with an education that is rightfully theirs. They also inject into the government system boys and girls with an educational experience likely to make them question the authoritarianism of formal education.

Further down the line of child abandonment in Brazil are 'street educators'. They work mainly with children who have been expelled from, dropped out of, or never gone to school. These youngsters do what odd jobs are available, or earn money from begging or thieving and robbing – some do all three. Most are still living with their families and contribute part of their 'earnings' to them.

With the educators' help they organise themselves into local associations and elect their own office bearers. The associations are properly constituted and affiliated to the National Movement of Street Boys and Girls. Their executives hold regular meetings at which problems are identified and courses of action resolved upon.

João de Deus, of the Community Association of Street Boys and Girls, has worked in a dormitory area of São Paulo for 13 years. 'We work at the beginning of the street children's lives. It is in areas like this that they learn to assault and steal.'

Street educator João de Deus

Unlike alternative-to-custody rehabilitation programmes in the West, which operate within a definition of the child as offender, street educators see children as in danger of being criminalised as a consequence of their abandonment by the economy, the state, the community and sometimes their own parents. Those who turn to crime are reacting to the theft of their own childhood – their denial of an education and any other creative opportunities for their development as individuals.

Work, when it is available, is almost invariably of a kind and on conditions that reflects their powerlessness.

Asked whether they would rather work or steal, most children say they would like to work but in properly paid jobs that lead them somewhere. Those who take the criminal path move into an increasingly dangerous no-man's land where they may be killed by either law enforcers or gangs. They run the risk of becoming isolated from what little protection their neighbourhood might offer them.

'Once you are in a gang you must stay there until you die. If you try to leave they will kill you,' says a child that João works with. 'The gangs invite us to sniff glue or smoke dope. But thank god I was never in any gang.'

'My brother was in a gang. He was killed a few weeks ago,' pipes up another small child.

Inspired by the pioneering work of alternative educationalist Paulo Freire, the educators live in or near the neighbourhood where they work. Like Father George in India, they establish themselves as a reliable adult presence in the lives of the children and will intervene at times of danger, approaching feared gangs and police stations, where necessary, to try to get children out of serious trouble. They will ensure a child gets emergency medical treatment. One educator has developed a dialogue with a gang and is able to dissuade it from taking young children along on 'jobs'.

The educators believe that children who experience society's rejection have a valuable insight into the way society works. If they can be encouraged to learn from what happens to them, instead of reacting to it, and discover their ability to influence events, they will have an important contribution to make to social change. For this reason the educators see themselves as learning from the children they teach. In the words of João de Deus: 'The street child listens to us, leads us, trusts us. We trust him. It is he or she talking to the educators. They know some things and we know other things. They talk about their

João's wife, Gildete, who works in the community with her husband. The child immediately in front of her had a narrow escape, with his brother, when their father set fire to the family shack

impressions and we talk about our impressions. We dialogue. We walk together. The world is the mediation of our love, the place where we have respect. It's a dialogue between educators and children.'

For many of the children there is no hope of rejoining the state school system and there is little motivation to do so. João believes the system is both elitist and divisive – designed to inculcate the very values that allow millions of people to be abandoned in slums.

'These children have resisted it, which is something we, their teachers, didn't do,' says João. 'What we offer is an alternative education that happens in the child's own environment.'

'You would never get these children going into a classroom. If you want to teach them it would be best to start by going with them to a beach,' says Joe MacCarthy, who works in poor areas near Olinda. The process is very informal and gradual. It is a matter of taking an interest in the children – being with them and talking with them, playing games, taking them on outings, encouraging them in non-directive ways to explore their environment critically instead of disdaining it and to take responsibility for each other.

The neighbourhood, the children's experiences in it, the history of its development, their cultural identity become the material of their education. Changes in the children's view of themselves promotes a change in the community's view of them. When Joe or his wife, Jackie, who works with women and young children, walk through favelas where they are known they are greeted naturally by children, teenagers and adults alike. Youngsters tag along with them for a bit and exchange news. Just by valuing and respecting the children they help reverse a life process that at most turns stamps them as 'worthless' and 'unwanted'.

Joe, a former priest, does not see himself as creating a project. 'Probably too many projects are designed from the top down,' he says. 'We believe that if worthwhile change is to take place it will have to come from the ones who suffer most and who really need the change – from the children. Change brought by people who aren't really suffering may be something they care about a lot but society doesn't change, the structures don't change.

'We still don't have a plan. We take it step by step and see what emerges.'

The boys and girls he works with have tried recycling paper in a more organised way. They came up against the market system that earns very little for the collectors, a living for some smaller middlemen and big money for the man at the top, who can afford to buy in and transport what others have collected.

When they tried to open their own scrapyards in the slums, older and tougher kids moved in and begun to use the yards for their own purposes, attracting police attention. They were forced to close down. Now they have taken up some small self-employment opportunities – baking, silk-screen work and broom making – sponsored by the local council. The main value of these projects is the opportunities they provide for the children to organise themselves, work together and identify with each other.

Cleide (centre) and friends

Cleide and her friends are involved in a broom making project, which operates in a small house in their own street. Previously, she had worked as a domestic.

She says, 'We like to be together here at the centre. I prefer it though I don't earn as much money. As a domestic worker you work hard and are treated badly sometimes.' Her friend Betania, who is still attending school, described the area as good because it was near the beach, had a school nearby and there was even a place to dance. It was bad because it was violent. 'There are many robbers and many drug addicts. There are a lot of killings, gun fights.'

Joe believes there should be small centres – perhaps one in each street but like the other houses in the neighbourhood – where children can get together and undertake simple projects likely to give them a sense of achievement.

He is also trying to reach some of the more violent youngsters in the community because they are the more endangered and working with them might help reduce the general level of violence.

In São Paulo, the members of the association João works with have identified crime as self-defeating and damaging to others. 'There's no future in it,' says one child. 'You rob today. Tomorrow you might have no money. You might be shot at any moment,' says another. To make money, some have started a vegetable growing cooperative, cultivating empty plots on the fringe of the city and selling their produce at the local market. One group works for tips carrying shoppers' bags.

They earn no more than they would working for different employers but most job opportunities both isolate and exploit children. Work undertaken by them in groups gives them a sense of unity and provides a learning opportunity while they look for new ways forward. The same children have successfully raised a small sum locally for a camping trip, winning community support instead of rejection, and they have staged demonstrations in the city centre against police inertia over 'justice' committee killings.

Street educators are not trying to rehabilitate children in the sense of making them conform to society. 'We want to give them back to society but with a critical grasp of what has been imposed on them and a knowledge that they can use their experience to bring about change,' says João de Deus. 'It is not a quick thing. Even the child does not see how he or she is changing. It is being together, caring and discovering things in the area. It is life itself.'

Most impressive is the quality of the trust the educators establish with the children and their long-term commitment to them.

Asked how it would be if there were no Associations of Street Boys and Girls, some children reply: 'We would be either arrested or stealing everywhere', 'We would be in bad shape', 'We would be talking with you here and already ripping everything off we could see.'

CHILDREN OF THE STATE

Governments like to boast publicly of their achievements and have exceptional opportunity to do so through the media and their own publicity departments. They rarely focus on their omissions. This book sets out to present the perspective of children who are not adequately provided for and who have no voice – by definition it is about omissions.

Because children have had no political clout, governments feel no great compulsion to respond to their needs. As UNICEF consultant Boris Yopo says of deprived children: 'They are not organised. They cannot make a strike. They cannot walk into the President's house and say, "Where are our rights?".'

Children have nevertheless become a political problem, as a result of the negligence of governments and their reluctance to acknowledge the failure of their social policies and controls, says Jo Boyden, of the Oxford-based research organisation, Children In Development. 'Hence a desire to hide street children away or pretend they don't exist.' Some Third World governments that have shown determination to improve the lot of deprived children have been unable to put their programmes into practice for want of funds and/or because they have been plunged into conflict.

In both industrialised and Third Worlds, state concern for disadvantaged children tends to be aroused only after the damage is done. In the absence of programmes to tackle the causes of severe abuse, neglect and deprivation, it often falls to the police to deal with the consequences. Time after time, children on the streets answer the question of what they fear most by replying, 'The police'.

Asked what he would change in his community if he had power, a Brazilian boy worker said: 'I would change everything. I would make a leisure street for children to play in – one without cars. I would have a football and a basketball area – a sports ground. I would have proper health care.

What else? A police station?

'No!'

But didn't the police protect him.

'They take care of us – they beat us up.'

Children fear the beatings they may receive at the hands of the police and the loss of liberty. Represented by its officials and institutions, the state can appear as a neglectful and abusive parent whose main role seems to be to disrupt the attempts of its abandoned offspring to make whatever sense they can of their lives.

'I was holding the underground train door open to let in a little air,' said the child who wanted the leisure street, 'so the policeman came and beat us on the head and back, so hard I was crying. Then he arrested us and I said, "I'll pay you and then you let us leave". He beat us again! The only reason I offered the money is that the last time I was caught the police asked me to pay a "fine" to be free again.'

'They will grab the box where we keep the ice-cream or candy we sell,' said a companion. 'Apart from losing all the ice-cream we still have to pay a fine to get the box back. But this amount has no receipt, it's for their pockets.'

In some countries, youngsters rounded up by the police have been held 'protectively' in adult prisons, for want of other places to send them.

It was reported in 1988 that children picked up by the Turkish police for offences ranging from murder to stealing oranges were kept together in isolated wings of adult prisons. Reports described a gruesome world in which there were dehumanising initiation rites and the strongest and most brutal dominated. The children were unsupervised and received no clothes or eating implements – 'the situation is very bad'.[107]

In a BBC Radio programme, based largely on the evidence of an adult ex-prisoner, it was said that child prisoners did not exist officially. The law forbade the imprisonment of under-18-year-olds. Among the detained children were street 'urchins' held for the duration of the tourist season, so as not to offend foreign visitors.[108] There is some indication that a ten-year-old campaign in Turkey to establish alternatives to the incarceration of children in adult prisons is beginning to take effect. Commentators have emphasised that the problem needs to be seen in the context of a lack of resources rather than as a deliberate disregard for children's rights.

The recourse in some poorer countries to punishment as a substitute for more expensive care programmes was reflected in the remarks of a Zambian Ministry of Social Development official. He said that corporal punishment of young offenders would continue to be necessary until the country could afford to extend its probation services.

The police, like the staff of institutions, are often a neglected group themselves. Underpaid and poorly trained, they are expected with inadequate resources to deal with the fall-out of major social and economic problems. Their job is to protect property, keep the peace, and exercise control. The more out of control the situation, the more they are likely to take on the aspect of a battering parent and rely upon the discredited short, sharp, shock approach. Their action takes place in a wider context of neglect in which the claims of abandoned children weigh least.

Nevertheless, there are helpers within police and other state departments as well as some authorities who understand that the least influential of their citizens have needs and that it is important that these should be met.

[107] Minutes of the Annual General Meeting of DCI-UK held in December 1987.

[108] 'Face the Facts', Radio 4, May 1988.

A change to a progressive state government in Pernambuco, north-eastern Brazil, has been reflected in some key personnel changes in departments dealing with children. Among them a woman social worker has been appointed as chief of the Children's Police Department. Her brief is to introduce a non-repressive approach to police work with children.

A vase of bright flowers on her desk signals her opposition to authoritarianism and to the sombre paintwork of the offices she inherited. With a background in community work and the church-backed street children's movement, she has a strong commitment to children's rights. As a social worker with no police training, she met determined opposition to her appointment. She had to contend with death threats, false allegations on the local radio that she was a drunkard and various other tests of her authority, including the beating of children by police officers to see what she would do.

At the core of her reforms is the introduction of a team of experts – psychologists and social workers, specialised in working with children, as well as police officers trained in these disciplines. All children referred to her department are now seen by the team.

Most offences are minor; theft- or drugs-related. But the law stipulates that children must not be left in unsuitable environments and, for their protection, may be apprehended and taken to the Children's Police Department by 'anyone, for anything'. Hundreds are brought in for the most trivial offences, from 'stealing fruit, or throwing a stone, to just being on the street'. They are indiscriminately arrested by the police or members of the public, or brought along by parents wanting their children disciplined. In the latter case, 'it's generally poor mothers. A mother may bring a daughter in because she is worried about a boyfriend keeping her out at night. It is the fear of parents who have no control over any aspect of their lives that makes them turn to the police. The team will see the mother and try to convince her that police stations are just not the right places to bring children – the responsibility is her own. We will warn parents, "If your child stays here he is just going to learn more about crime".'

Anna Maria Lira has tried with partial success to persuade the major police forces, which operate independently in the community but also bring children to her offices, to reduce indiscriminate arrests. Her new team investigates the children's family backgrounds and, where possible, returns them to their homes. Constrained by limited resources, they do their best to monitor the children's progress and they inform families about community support organisations.

Within eight months of introducing this approach, the department sent more than 900 children back home. Only 15 of these were brought in again for new offences. By contrast, children who have gone before the courts have escaped from custody to come back as many as three times in a week – 'it's a case of the street, the police, Febem (the state institution for child offenders) and back to the street again'.

The new police chief moved in diverse ways to stem police violence towards children. 'We are aware that the police staff were trained in a very repressive way. They were taught by the civil police how to find and catch people, how to shoot. There is nothing about public relations, or what is a child, what are children's rights.

'In planning our own training programmes, we asked our officers what their main worries were and told them ours. They were very confused and insecure; when should they beat children, when shouldn't they beat them? How could they make children confess without hitting them?

'We try in our training to depict the social problems that cause children to be on the streets – the economic problems, lack of a father, the migration to the cities. We do a critical appraisal of the child laws.' The course emphasises the police role as a public service and provides training on what resources are available in the community to struggling families. It stresses that the atmosphere in Children's Police stations should be one that is respectful of children.

The course is 'not a thousand wonders' but there are signs of a new attitude developing, particularly among younger policemen who are beginning to use the new team of experts as a resource.

Under this new regime, all complaints of violence against any police officer, whether from her own police or the other forces, are made official. Officers who seem resistant to the new values are warned that the beating of children can result in their suspension, sacking or prosecution.

Children arrested by members of the other police forces are commonly held overnight in cells occupied by adults. They face the twin dangers of 'being treated violently by the police and sexually abused by the prisoners'. Ana Maria Lira has increased the number of Children's Police stations in the city from three to five and made arrangements in rural areas of the state for children to be held without having to be incarcerated with adults. She has also managed to get a little money to do up the 'dreadful cells' in which children were held in her police stations and has tried to put a stop to any child being held for more than 24 hours before a decision on his or her case is made.

The department's records reveal the futility of the past policy of arresting children and having them sent to state institutions. 'We find we had kids who were first arrested in 1982 at the age of twelve for loitering, for instance, and by the age of 18 they are in for armed assault. One child has 140 entries here and at Febem, which shows how flawed the whole system is.'

The Children's Police now participate in regular meetings with representatives of the major police forces and those of justice, education and other relevant departments. The aim is to establish an integrated approach, deal with problems and define new and more creative policies.

In New York, officers of the Runaway Unit, who have received special training in dealing with children and youngsters, have a good grasp of the social causes of their plight and show real concern for them.

Also in America, some youngsters with criminal records are lucky enough to end up at Glen Mills instead of a conventional reformatory. When Sam Ferrainola took over as head of the privately run institution in the mid 1970s, he changed the emphasis from control of the youngsters to helping them discover their strengths and abilities. He disposed of the guards, the bars, the locks and the social workers. The money saved by these cuts is spent on first class facilities. Among other

*A seven-year-old
'gamin' placed in the
care of the Colombian
police in Bogota by Red
Cross workers after he
told them he wanted to
leave street life.*
DR ALMA BACCINO-
ASTRADA/LEAGUE OF
RED CROSS SOCIETIES

things the school boasts an all-seasons swimming pool and an
expensively equipped photographic department. It also earns
money by imaginative use of its vocational training facilities –
like the optical lab – to serve the local community.

Sam Ferrainola believes that children who have problems
should have the best, not the worst, and that the authorities
should expect a return on the vast sums they pay to keep
children in detention. 'When the court adjudicates a young man
they take the authority for what happens to him away from the
parents. But do they accept the responsibility?

'The authorities are sending these kids to schools which are
not being held accountable for their education and are not
protecting them. Kids are being locked up for days, weeks and

months; they're going to bed hungry; they're not getting the right medical care; they're not properly clothed; they're being beat up and raped. Now, would you spend 20, 30, 40 even 50 thousand dollars a year to send your own son to a place like that?'

At Glen Mills the teachers and administrative staff keep order and provide counselling. The boys are encouraged to express their views and there is an elected student council which has a participative role in management and the formulation of policy. Control is exercised through 'norms'.

Bill, a giant teenager, who has spent 18 months in jail for illegal arms dealing, explains: 'Norms is not rules. It's expected behaviour.' The norms tend to be the reverse of those the boys have grown up with. Says Sam: 'In the street you increase your status by beating people up, here you lose it.' Though many of the boys came to Glen Mills having been labelled as 'thugs' and 'vandals' there has been no vandalism in the school for years and very little violence.

Sam Ferrainola believes the labelling of children who have problems as 'unruly', 'losers' and 'bad' is self-fulfilling. 'If you believe they're bad, you'll continue with the same system that hasn't worked and isn't working and is never going to work. These kids aren't bad, they've done bad things. They have great potential. In the right environment they're fine young men, and you don't need locks and bars and punishment.'

Bill is now a member of the basketball team and is on the student council. 'It's a lot of challenges, I get to speak a lot, I like to speak up. I finally get to say something about how I feel about things.' He is working hard at his studies and hopes to go on to college.

Fifteen-year-old **Jose**, formerly caught up in drugs dealing, now wants to be a lawyer. 'I'm going to try,' he says. 'Before I wanted to do things that were right but I did them bad. Now I'm doing them right and I want to stay like that. I used to feel a failure – now I feel I'm going back up.'

In Brazil there is an attempt at a broad shift away from established policies of arresting and institutionalising abandoned children to one of investing in them.

Teresa Duere of the Brazilian Legion of Assistance (LBA), within the Ministry of Social Welfare, sees her department as having set out on a new path of social development. Its responsibilities range from deprived children in their pre-school years to elderly people living on or below the breadline. 'LBA used to offer paternalistic assistance which only helped to maintain poverty,' says Teresa Duere. Pamphlets outlining its

Boy at Glen Mills.
Former crack dealer
Jose

new approach acknowledge the millions who 'suffer intensely the weight of social injustice'.

The Legion now sees itself as 'listening' to people in deprived communities and then entering into a partnership with them to help them get their initiatives off the ground. 'What we want to do is to create development opportunities, not give assistance. . . . People who survive on the breadline are tough. All they need is the means. Government departments have to be resources for them to use.'

LBA works with other government departments and with residents' associations and community-based organisations and gives support to many community ventures. For instance, it provides some food to the Recife community schools programme.

One of its major initiatives is its day-care centre programme. In 1987, it assisted more than two million children in such centres and in 1988 more than twice that figure. Jocelini Rocha, who works within LBA's family and citizen support department, says that improvement is being vigorously pursued in both the quantity and quality of day-care provision. 'It is the right not of the parent but of the child. We don't see the child as a problem of the mother that LBA has to solve. We see the child as a person with his or her own rights. Children have the same basic rights as adults – proper food, proper sleep, clothing, housing and respect, but they also need more care.'

Day-care centres provide opportunities to reach parents and increase their awareness of children's needs. Where care is given for eight hours a day, the children get four meals. They receive stimulation, recreation and some medical and dental attention. Nearly half of Brazil's needy children who start an education fail in the first two years of school. The average for children who have been regularly to day-care centres before entering school is 20 per cent.

Teresa Duere believes there are people really committed to change both in LBA and other government departments. But it is a slow process. 'We do not change others, we are changing with them. We are interacting.'

Only ten per cent of the centres in LBA's programme are its own. The rest are established by private, community and other public bodies and it supports them on a project-agreement basis. In this respect its programme is in keeping with an 'Alternative Services for Street Children Project' launched by the authorities in close collaboration with UNICEF.

The project has tried to spearhead a policy swing away from arresting and institutionalising abandoned children towards encouraging and supporting alternative non-government community development programmes. A recent evaluation expresses a number of concerns, including the fear that the government might welcome a policy of funding alternative programmes as a substitute for extending its own responsibilities, for instance, in the field of education.[109]

Because there aren't enough volunteers of the right calibre and community programmes are unevenly distributed, such a development would continue the system of different qualities of service for rich and poor. A Ministry of Education official is quoted as saying that, to prevent this happening, the government will have to elaborate 'a serious public alternative to the alternatives'.

In a country with 20 years of military rule in its recent past, a crippled economy and a huge disparity in the distribution of wealth, people seeking a new deal for the nation's children face enormous obstacles. Old guard appointees in government departments, the country's bureaucratic, economic, political and social structures, entrenched attitudes of dependency within deprived communities, corruption and mistrust of government are among those frequently mentioned.

A new Indian government programme to improve the conditions of child workers issues from the passing of the Child Labour (Prohibition and Regulations) Act in 1986. The act replaced a total ban on child labour which was going unobserved. It prohibits the employment of children below the

[109] *The Brazilian Approach* by William Myers, Part 2 of *Combatting Child Labour*, an ILO study of attempts by governments to tackle the problems of working children. Eds Jo Boyden and Assefa Bequele, 1988.

Boy on metal polishing machine

age of 14 in industries identified as hazardous and establishes a basis for the development of government programmes that regulate child labour.

There has since been the formulation of a National Policy on Child Labour. Under this policy the extensive provision of non-formal education for child workers is planned and the target of providing free and compulsory education up to age of 14 by 1995 has been set. In addition ten pilot projects are scheduled to be undertaken in areas known to have high concentrations of child workers. They are to serve as a basis for the formulation of a national plan of action.

The project in Sivakasi, Tamil Nadu, one of two already underway, aims at the elimination of child labour in the match and fireworks industry in the area. It is represented as a multifaceted assault on the problem, involving various state and central government departments and non-government organisations. It includes the introduction of income and employment generating schemes, aimed at reducing the need of poor families to send their children to work. Extensive improvements in full and part-time education and in the monitoring and attendance to the health of child workers are planned.

Improvements are to be made in the working environment and employment conditions – including working hours and pay and changes to the piece-rate method of payment. Child workers are to receive at least one substantial meal a working day, initially through the extension of the school meal to students attending non-formal education centres.

And finally there is to be enforcement of the labour laws governing the employment of children below the age of 14 in the match and firework industry and in dangerous processes, 'like wax dipping and the handling of chemicals'.

Ambitious though they sound, these pilot projects will reach a tiny proportion of the country's child labour force. The programme has met with other criticism, not least that it seeks to regulate the work of children in industries in which their employment is banned.

Nicaragua stands out as a country trying to orientate its policies to the needs of people, though the war and the economic blockade have disrupted the progress of the revolution. One of its achievements has been in combatting illiteracy. A legacy of the Somoza regime was that only 20 per cent of Nicaraguans were literate; now, ten years later, there is 70 per cent literacy.

Rosa at school

An example of the variety of welfare and education facilities the government has tried to provide is the 'minors at Risk' schools. These schools, of which there are nine in Managua, are for severely disturbed and disadvantaged children. **Rosa**, who is 14, has been a pupil at one of them for four years and now hopes to be a secretary. She had no previous education and used to lead a gang of pickpockets, who operated on buses.

She and four of her brothers were referred to the school after complaints by neighbours and the police. A teacher at the school said of her and children like her: 'It's not a social problem. It's a political problem – these children have been abandoned not only by their families but by society.'

KILLING INDIFFERENCE

At an international level there is an attempt to improve the experiences of endangered children by strengthening the concept of childrens' rights. The flagship has been the Declaration of the Rights of the Child adopted by the United Nations in 1959 which established ten principles for the protection of children.

During the International Year of the Child in 1979, the United Nations took up a proposal by Poland that there should be a Convention on the Rights of the Child. Though not legally enforceable, the convention will be binding on its signatories, and so is seen as a major step forward by those who have fought for it.

The details have been thrashed out over ten years at annual meetings of a working party, lobbied by non-government organisations, most notably Defence for Children International. A final document was agreed in late 1988, with the intention that the convention would be adopted by the United Nations General Assembly during its 1989 autumn session. Ratification by countries agreeing to abide by its terms is expected to start in 1990.

The principles, set out in 41 articles, define rights relating to a broad range of issues, from health provision and education through to protection from exploitation. Apart from rights intended to protect children, the convention – unlike the declaration – acknowledges some 'enabling' rights, including freedom of expression, association and of peaceful assembly.

Because of the widely differing resources and cultural values of different countries, reaching agreement has been tough going. There have been accusations of Western bias. Disagreement has arisen, for instance, because of differing cultural views on the role and value of child work. Inevitably, the attempt to be comprehensive has produced vague and cautious wording, leaving great room for interpretation.

How many countries will sign the convention and how many will seriously attempt to act in the spirit of it remains to be seen. A lot of good international and national law which promises to protect children goes unheeded. According to Mike Jupp (Defense for Children International – USA), 'In terms of the protection of kids from a whole host of issues including warfare, child labour, sexual exploitation, physical abuse, it is seldom the lack of legislation that stops us protecting kids; it's lack of political will to put in the necessary resources to bring about the enforcement, the social work, the education – the basic social policy input that is needed to correct it.'

Observers hope that the convention may at least help to give pressure groups more standing and leverage in seeking a better deal for children. 'It's caused people to examine their attitudes towards some kids,' says Mike Jupp. 'It will give something that child advocates can use and it may even in the end produce something that's of benefit to kids. So on balance I think it's worth it.'

Among the helpers of disadvantaged children, both inside and outside government, is an unco-ordinated company of courageous and imaginative people who can see unfolding before us the tragedy of lives full of promise going to waste. They act like gardeners, trying to encourage growth in the world's wastelands. In the zones of neglect, they attempt to establish concern of human beings for one another as a working principle in society. Without them many more of the Kumars,

Children at play in Mathare Valley slum

the Kishores and Angelinas of this world go to the wall. But though hope lies in the orientation of the best of the helpers there are simply too few of them to bring about a general reversal.

Their efforts to improve the prospects of children are curbed by a set of predominating attitudes that underpins the lack of political will to prevent zones of neglect developing or to do much about them once they are in place.

Prime among these attitudes is that it is adequate and even appropriate for people and nations to pursue their individual welfares with little or no concern about how the fortunes of others are affected. Closely associated with this view is the belief that poverty is inevitable. The poor are largely to blame for their condition, or are someone else's responsibility and even that they are there to be exploited.

Attitudes that clinch the fate of children destined to be abused and neglected in both rich and poor worlds include the assumption that adults do not need to consult children, they know what is best for them; that children are safe in the care of parents who are themselves subjected to great insecurity, need and stress; that if children become anti-social it is because their parents failed or because they are bad children; that society has no responsibility for children until things go wrong.

Sam Ferrainola traces the problems of boys, whose prospects are so often dramatically reversed at Glen Mills, partly to the discrediting process in schools which defines children as either failures or successes. 'When they fail, the school denies them any opportunity of gaining status with their peers. Because they fail, they're not considered for a school team or allowed to join a club. My type of kids sub-group with similar kids. How do they get status? – by rejecting the school's codes of behaviour. The school says you should respect teachers, they get status by giving teachers a hard time.' Professor Howard Polsky (Columbia University, New York) describes the process as one of 'rejecting the rejectors'.

Allied to the notion that children are safely left to the care of their parents is the assumption that there are adequate state and private mechanisms for helping damaged and disadvantaged children. In the West, failures in the response to child abuse demonstrate how flawed this assumption is. So does the number of youngsters living on the streets and the rise in violent crime and problems of hooliganism.

In the Third World, in addition to the millions of children who die from diseases which are easily and cheaply prevented, many more millions survive to lead impoverished lives, despite the combined efforts of the helpers.

The struggles of poor people take place in the context of an international and unequal scramble for power and resources that frequently erupts into violence and warfare. It pits individuals against each other in their attempts to survive in conditions of want, or to escape the pit of poverty, or to avoid being dragged into it. The most disadvantaged in this struggle are children.

Father Ramiro Amigo, who runs the Cooperative de Picolé (Ice-lolly Cooperative), a project for street children in Jaboatão near Recife, is known internationally for his work with street children. The project tries to foster their self-respect and acclimatise them to work. It provides good quality occupational training in the hope of saving them from turning to crime. But Father Ramiro has few illusions that, in the given economic climate, such training will free them from miserable lives on minimum salaries.

Above all and 'most difficult', he wishes to give the children the sense of awareness that they are not isolated failures but members of an oppressed class. He hopes they will gain some experience of the value of standing by each other and getting organised as a way to liberate their class. Blame for the situation goes beyond national policies, he says. 'We get a lot of visitors to this centre. We ask only one thing. The cause of all this misery here lies in the first world, so you need to help there as well as here. We live in slavery to the first world. Please help us to combat this injustice.'

A young boy cuddles his brother at a project for orphaned and abandoned children in Calcutta

If you ask abandoned children what they want of life, their first reaction is likely to be surprise. It is not something their experience encourages them to think about. 'They have lost the capacity to dream,' says Father Ramiro. But having given the question some thought, they can express just what they want. They want to be well fed and well dressed. They want time to play and space to play in. They want schooling and the chance to develop skills that will give them a useful role in society. They want decent housing and a decent environment. Above all they want to feel they are cared for and respected.

In their relationships with each other deprived and abandoned children often express the very sense of fellowship that they have been denied – readiness to share resources and give each other affection and support. The denial to them of such loving affirmation reflects a chilling adult world which has seen a widening rift between the world's rich and poor.

During the 1970s poor countries were eagerly encouraged by Western governments and banks to borrow massive sums of money. High interest rates and the world recession multiplied the burden of repayment. In the past decade, the real prices paid by the rich world for the poor world's main commodities – such as rubber, jute, minerals and tea – fell by 30 per cent. Debt repayments swallow up a quarter of the poor world's export earnings. Average incomes in many African and Latin American countries have fallen dramatically. In nearly 50 countries the proportion of children enrolled at primary school is now falling. Spending on health and education has also dropped – by as much as 50 and 25 per cent respectively in the poorest nations.[110] In 1988, rich countries gained 43 billion dollars from their dealings with poor nations.

[110] *The State of the World's Children* 1989, UNICEF, Oxford University Press, Oxford.

Adjustment loans by the International Monetary Fund to countries in economic crisis are made on condition that certain goals are met and cuts in national expenditure made. It is not suggested that a country cut its expenditure on arms (brought from the industrialised nations) or on state security provisions (used to contain the dissatisfactions of the poor). The cuts are often made to welfare and social services on which the poor, and ultimately children, most depend.

Britain's major development aid agency, OXFAM, is finding increasingly that conflict, environmental degradation and Third World debt are impeding long-term development efforts. As a result of debt adjustment policies for instance, non-government development programmes are having to find ways to compensate for cuts in government services. In its emergency relief work Oxfam is increasingly having to respond more to man-made rather than natural disasters.

Following the imposition of IMF conditions on Zambia, a new roadside stone-chipping industry has sprung up near to a major building materials supplier. Small groups of women and children chip stone for concrete and syphon off some of the supplier's customers by undercutting the market rate. 'We hit ourselves and sometimes splinters of stone fly into our eyes,' says one woman. 'But what else can we do?'

Writing of his research on child abuse in Zambia, Robert Mushota observes: 'We identified the present economic situation in the country as a major force in the increasing cases of child labour and child neglect. The low family income, common to most urban families, coupled with the harsh realities of IMF conditionality ... have compelled many parents to seek additional sources of family income, and child labour and child sexual abuse (prostitution) are among the cheapest sources of extra income.'

It is against the background of such remorseless economic processes that UNICEF has broken with its tradition of diplomatic restraint in its pronouncements, to lay some of the Third World deaths of children forthrightly at the door of international economic relations. In its 1989 State of the World's Children Report, the agency says that in its daily work, in over a hundred developing nations, it is 'brought up against a face of today's economic problems which is not seen in the corridors of financial power, not seated at the conference tables of debt renegotiation. It is the face of the young child'.

Of the poor world's £600 billion debt to the industrial world, the report observes: 'The fact that so much of today's staggering debt was irresponsibly lent and irresponsibly borrowed would matter less if the consequences of such folly were falling on its perpetrators. Yet now when the party is over and the bills are coming in, it is the poor who are being asked to pay.'

The report concludes: 'Allowing world economic problems to be taken out on the minds and bodies of young children is the antithesis of all civilised behaviour. Nothing can justify it. It shames and diminishes us all.'

For this process to stop requires nothing short of a new public consciousness and motivation, of a kind that has placed women's issues on the political agenda and is emerging belatedly in concern for the environment. The pursuit by people and nations of their short-term individual welfares, irrespective of the consequences to others, must give ground to a recognition that personal welfare is inseparable in the long term from that of the local and international community. Without such a shift, the weaker members of society will continue to pay the price for the successes of the stronger. And the promise that each child's life represents will continue to be broken in millions of cases, both in terms of lives lost and of lives saved only to be stunted and damaged in their preparation for tomorrow's world.